City Zoning:
The Once and Future Frontier

City Zoning:
The Once and Future Frontier

1144

Clifford L. Weaver
and
Richard F. Babcock

Planners Press
American Planning Association
Chicago, Illinois   Washington, D.C.

To Donna
and
To Betty

Table of Contents

Authors' Preface
and
Acknowledgments

The reader may be aided by a few pages devoted to an explanation of the book's organization and a preliminary glimpse at a few of the principal thoughts developed in what follows. We wish also to acknowledge the debt we owe to the many people who have helped us in this effort.

Part I of this book covers some of our preconceptions, assumptions, and attitudes—those biases that invariably shape and color both the collection and the analysis of data in any work such as this. As in the federal regulation of securities transactions, full disclosure is no guarantee of value, but at least it gives the consumer a fighting chance at making a fair assessment of the inherent worth of the offering.

Part II identifies those features of current urban land use problems, practices, policies, and developments that appear to us to be significant because they demonstrate vitality and the emergence of new ideas. Among them:

The persistence and, in some cities, the emergence of the urban neighborhood as a potent force in land use policy is an event that disputes the assumption that despair is the principal motive and attempts to escape the principal goal of inner-city residents. The growing evidence that city planning is turning away from Year 2000 plans and focusing more on the community or neighborhood as the basis for planning suggests that professional planners are engaged in a major and—we believe—healthy reappraisal of the limits of the possible.

We also note the importance of the unprofound in urban land use policy—those issues that agitate more city residents more continuously than the survival of a Grand Central Station or the location of a new metro airport. These annoying land use issues, with which most people must struggle, we call "bothersome uses" in the hope of applying as neutral a term as possible. They range from adult movies and fast-food outlets to halfway houses. The suburban vigor with which urban residents debate and dispute these intruders is testimony to the commitment residents have to their neighborhoods.

We have tried to assess the role of zoning in the central business districts, and we find that here there is the greatest need for a complete overhaul of traditional zoning rules. If, as we conclude, zoning is alive and well in many of our urban neighborhoods, it is moribund downtown and new techniques of public policy need to be invented. In some places such is being done. We also have tried to seek out attempts to deal with that most depressing land use phenomenon, the obsolescent commercial strip area.

Perhaps the most striking departure from traditional zoning practice is the emergence of special districts, an attempt, in effect and implementation not unlike the suburban planned unit development, to create a separate zoning ordinance for a portion of the city. Building on the use of the device for historic (and economically significant) areas, special districts are now sprouting in urban areas about as historically significant as Levittown is aesthetically pleasing. The special district deserves attention; it may be a useful tool, or it may be a Band-Aid to cover a black mole.

We also examine the impact of supramunicipal agencies and policies—regional, state, and federal—upon urban land use policy. Recent attempts to rearrange the focus of decisionmaking have received more attention when they were directed toward the peripheral areas in our metropolitan areas: the use of sewer policy to control new growth; the allocation of housing in our suburbs; the control over shopping centers through environmental laws; and the direct control of a variety of land use and zoning matters by regional, state, and federal agencies. The impact of these new policies and new forums upon the central city has received less attention than it deserves, and there may be a need to rethink some conventional wisdom in this area.

The suburban misuse of zoning as a tool to prevent certain people from locating in certain areas and, secondarily, as a means to promote other parochial interests is, to a significant extent, responsible for the increasing demand for some nonlocal role in the area. Whether the medicine being proposed for suburban ills might do for the more complex, and now more fragile, city patient is a question that must be carefully considered.

Finally, Part II deals with the zoning process in the city, the method of decisionmaking, the relationships between staff and elected officials and lay policymakers, and the frequently irrational and chaotic administrative system within which they function.

In Part III we turn to considering proposals and ideas for change. We begin with a look at a number of currently popular proposals and find them plagued by a common malady: they are so radical and fly so in the face of many of the basic assumptions upon which our current system of land use regulation operates that there is little realistic hope for their widespread acceptance and adoption. Our suggestion, dull though it be, is to put aside grand schemes in favor of devoting more attention to analyzing and correcting the specific, known problems of the system we already have.

Next we consider the question of where control of city land use policy and decisionmaking ought to lie. Despite our continuing belief that federal and state intervention may be the only solution to many of the problems and abuses that have come to characterize land use and land use regulation in nonurban settings, we are forced to conclude that urban land use problems neither require nor are amenable to deus ex machina solutions concocted and administered by federal and state legislatures and bureaucrats. We suspect that the remedy of less local control is just the opposite of what is needed in the cities.

We are not, however, prepared to accept business as usual at the local store as a solution to urban land use problems. If land use in the cities is to be trusted to the discretion of local officials, we believe that such discretion must be controlled. We devote a separate chapter to some preliminary thoughts on how that might be done.

In the final chapters of the book, we turn to the substantive problem of regulating urban land use in the two most important areas of any major city, its residential neighborhoods and its central business district. Our prescriptions for the two areas are, as might be expected, radically different. In residential areas, we see a need to create a system that will permit and encourage the gradual redevelopment of city neighborhoods without aggravating the problems that originally created the need for redevelopment. The necessary regulatory tool must be capable of encouraging, permitting, and dealing with small-scale developments; it must be as free of costly red tape and uncertainty as possible; and it must result in new development that is consistent and compatible with an existing neighborhood. In the central business district, the system should encourage and be adaptable to excellence and innovation, even when those concepts cannot be defined in advance. It should be a system that addresses not merely the development of individual high-rise monuments but also the total relationship of those individual structures to the urban environment in which they exist and to the human needs for which they exist.

If there is anything that should now be self-evident about the regulation of land use, it is that the political, social, economic, and physical realities of each community are so different from those to be found in any other community that there will never be such a thing as a useful model zoning ordinance or a significant how-to-do-it manual in this area. For that reason, we are, in this book, not terribly concerned with offering or advocating specific solutions. Our interest lies in convincing our audience that a variety of fresh approaches to urban zoning are possible, that some of them offer reasonable hope for improving the quality of life in our cities, and that pursuing them can be not only challenging and rewarding but even a bit of fun.

One of the joys of working in this area is the generosity with which others in the field freely devote their time and counsel to efforts such as this. No list of acknowledgments can ever be complete, and, in any event, inclusion is small thanks for the effort expended. We wish, nevertheless, to single out a few people for special note.

We begin with all those elected officials, professionals, property owners, developers, and citizen participants in the urban zoning system who gave generously of their time for interviews and discussions with us in cities across the country. They are too numerous to mention individually, but references to many of them appear in the pages of the book. We thank also those officials, staffs, and citizens of cities across the country who have been our clients and have paid us for the privilege of learning with them much of what we report here.

We must also extend special thanks to Judy Heyman, now a member of the planning staff in Lake County, Illinois, who, as part of her graduate work at the University of Illinois, helped us substantially with the preliminary analysis of the land use regulations of the cities we visited. Several members of the profession and friends were good enough to read some or all of the manuscript, and we both thank them and apologize for not always heeding their advice. Among them are Frank Bangs, Jr., John Costonis, Allen Fonoroff, Paul Gapp, Claude Gruen, Ada Louise Huxtable, Norman Marcus, Remick McDowell, Jack Noble, Don Priest, Arden Rathkopf, Frank So, and Is Stollman.

Anyone who has ever been through this knows that it puts extraordinary demands on those responsible for typing and retyping transcripts and manuscripts. We thank Virginia Bertz, Marie Franciscus, and Susan Jenner.

Finally, a special note of thanks goes to Bill Matuszeski and the Council on Environmental Quality for their early support of this project and the Council's financing of much of the preliminary research. We must add that the Council has exercised no editorial control whatever and accepts no responsibility for content.

The old king felt refreshed,
clear-headed, almost ready to begin
again. There would be a day—there
must be a day—when he would come
back to Gramarye. . . .

T. H. White, *The Once And*
Future King

Part I

Introduction

Chapter 1
City Zoning: Of What Importance to Whom?

In the last decade of the reign of Elizabeth I the population of London reached 120,000. So serious was this thought to be that Parliament passed an Act in 1593 entitled "An Act against New Buildings." The Act made it an offence to erect any dwellinghouse within the cities of London or Westminster or within three miles of the gates of those cities. To do so was punishable by a fine of 5 pounds. Such was the effect of this enactment that when it was repealed, in 1888, London's population had grown to 4 million.

—M. B. Layfield

For the last few decades, zoning has been a suburban toy, not a city tool. But is that state of affairs permanent?

As attorneys and consultants who spend much of our time dealing in the often-related areas of land use policy and regulation and municipal government and affairs, we have observed two significant and recently accelerating trends that bear on the issue. First, there has been an outstanding surge of interest in the general field of land use regulation. Concern over the degradation of the natural environment, on the one hand, and the inadequacy of the supply of housing that is both within the means and reasonably accessible to the jobs of a growing number of families, on the other, have propelled the topic of public regulation of private land from a matter of limited interest to an issue of hot debate in both state and national government. Second, there is a growing fear that the nation's cities, particularly those that are older, may be hopelessly and helplessly doomed to slow—or not so slow—decay. Such fears have grown to paranoid proportions in some quarters.

We find neither of these developments surprising: decades of neglect and abuse in both areas were bound to come home to roost sooner or later. What *is* surprising is the scant attention that has been paid to the relationship between these two issues. The use of the police power—the government's right to regulate the use of private property without paying compensation for the privilege—has been seized upon with enthusiasm and employed with notable success this past decade to control development in outlying areas. We are finding it both legally and politically acceptable to protect our estuaries, swamps, and hillsides from being savaged.[1] With somewhat more hesitation, we are accepting the idea that, in the booming suburbs, zoning should become a positive tool of social change.[2]

The prospect of using regulatory tools to revive our urban cores, however, has seemed far less promising to most commentators, who seem long ago to have quit thinking about zoning as an innovative device in an urban setting. In modern times in the U.S., developers, it is said, get what they want by way of zoning changes in Seattle, Chicago, Boston or Indianapolis, either because the city is starved for development or because venality is a way of life or because there is no community of public interests to stand against the private interest of developers. With that conventional wisdom in mind, we asked scores of people in dozens of cities whether zoning had any importance or relevance in the context of a major city. The responses from some quarters tended to support the accusations. In those city areas where development does not impact upon residential neighborhoods (*e.g.*, in most cities, the central business district), the conventional wisdom about the irrelevancy of city zoning has been, and has been perceived to be, pretty accurate. Atlanta provides perhaps the clearest example of the phenomenon.

At least until recently, there was so much pressure for new development in downtown Atlanta that the city could have, had it so desired, been more choosy than many cities can afford to be; as it was, the city exercised practically no regulatory control. It is not much of an over-simplification to say that the central business district zoning under which most of Atlanta's downtown development occurred consisted of two regulations: to control permitted uses, the ordinance adopted by reference the same use list as available in Atlanta's light manufacturing district; to control bulk, the city "imposed" an astronomically high floor area ratio (FAR) of 25. To the extent that Atlanta's downtown is well-developed, it is a result of private initiative, not public regulation. One member of Atlanta's downtown establishment with whom we spoke admitted that the supposed "controls" contained in the Atlanta ordinance were "entirely unrealistic" and concluded:

> The thing that has governed the quality of development in downtown Atlanta has been more peer pressure... and influence of the market by people like Portman. ...

But even with the near-total lack of public control, another Atlantan was confident that if a developer wanted more he could get it:

> I think I can say accurately that even to the extent that the CBD Zoning Ordinance provisions would inhibit somebody from doing something, he could always get that waived anyway. If Tom Portman came in and said I'm going to build a 70-story hotel, why if there's any silly rule in the way, they'll take care of that.

By and large, that same assessment was repeated by elected officials and private developers across the country. With rare exceptions, zoning has been neither a guiding, a controlling, nor an inhibiting factor in the development of the business and commercial centers of our major cities. In those areas, as one elected official put it, "we're sometimes willing to waive some of the niceties of land use or zoning... to get some development going."

But that is far from the whole story of city zoning. While many people don't believe urban zoning is important, the people who don't also don't live in urban neighborhoods. In cities, as everywhere else, the importance of zoning is most clearly recognized by those citizens who view it as an understandable, workable, and controllable device for protecting their homes and neighborhoods from whatever they define as a deteriorating influence. While businesspeople, developers, and planning professionals express widely varying views about the importance of zoning in cities, it is clear to us that, for the people who live in cities, zoning is becoming more, not less, important. It came as no surprise to us to find a significant band of urban residents, from an assortment of political, social, and economic backgrounds, who believe that zoning and land use issues are, in fact, among the most important of current urban issues.

People who once fled from neighborhoods are now zoning them. People to whom neighborhoods were once abandoned are now rezoning them to undo the effects of the rezoning process that invariably accompanied their arrival. Anyone who believes that businesspeople or developers can get, by either fair means or foul, any zoning they want in most cities hasn't visited the city neighborhoods where that simply is not true. No one who has talked to the people who live there, or to the city officials whom they elect, can accept either the theory that zoning is an impotent and meaningless tool in the cities or the notion that all hope for preserving our major cities is lost. No better illustration can be found than in Chicago.

Until February 27, 1979, the fateful day on which the Chicago political machine got stuck in a snow bank, a "minority" alderman was a rare gem. The term did not mean he was black or brown; it simply told all in Chicago who understood that he was one of those unusual beasts—an alderman who did not genuflect to the commands of Mayor Daley and his successor, Mayor Bilandic. Alderman Martin Oberman of the 43rd ward was a minority alderman. This is the scene of a petition to rezone a parcel of property in the 43rd Ward from M1-2 (Manufacturing—Light) to R5 (General Residence) in order to prevent its development as a McDonald's restaurant. Present before Chairman Edward Vrdolyak and the members of the zoning committee of the Chicago city council are Alderman Oberman, Democratic Committeeman, Edward O'Brien of the 43rd Ward (who is also a member of the state legislature), and a teaming mob of 43rd Ward objectors. Vrdolyak, his committee, and O'Brien are all "regular" Democrats. "Regular" is the opposite of "minority," and the two are honor-bound by their respective creeds to give no comfort to the other. Cut sharply, the scenario goes as follows:

Alderman Oberman: When the concern arose in the community that a fast food restaurant was going to go in this site, there was a great community concern that that not be allowed to detract from the growing and improving residential character of the neighborhood.

Chairman Vrdolyak: Is it safe to say that we are all here because of the fact that you don't want a Burger King or a McDonald's there?

Alderman Oberman: I think that is essentially the reason why people are interested today but I think that the record should show that the Wrightwood Neighbor's Association, in whose territory this property is located, adopted for themselves a long range land use program two years ago after meetings and so forth and specifically part of that plan was to prevent, in general, fast food restaurant development. . . .

Chairman Vrdolyak: I would be remiss if I didn't state that we all know that this is a political year and campaigns are coming up soon for all of us; you, me, all of us. . . .

Mr. O'Brien: We want to see to it that our alderman stays on his toes and represents the community adequately. . . .

I find myself in an unusual position of being against McDonald's. . . .

I would like to say to the people present that McDonald Corporation is an excellent corporation and the Lincoln Park Community and the 43rd Ward, Ray Kroc, who is a friend of mine, and was one of the major contributors to development of the new wing at Children's Memorial Hospital and in addition, located in Park West, the McDonald Corporation bought an old rooming house and made it the Ronald McDonald facility so that parents could stay near the hospital while their children were being treated in Children's Memorial Hospital rather than having to live in a hotel or motel.

Quite frankly, I am in favor of some sort of zoning change that would prohibit McDonald's from going in that location. . . .

Chairman Vrdolyak: Just for the record would everybody who is in favor of this application please stand up?

(The people stood)

Thank you very much.

Alderman Oberman: I don't usually get that kind of a vote in this chamber.

(Laughter)

Chairman Vrdolyak: Well, you haven't had Danny O'Brien with you before. . . .

(Laughter and applause)

Mr. O'Brien: Well, Mr. Chairman and members of the Committee:

Whatever the Council—whatever the action the Council takes today, there is no doubt in my mind, in Marty's [Oberman's] mind or anybody else's mind that there probably will be a lawsuit filed and that the Council's action will be enjoined in that lawsuit. . . .

Chairman Vrdolyak: I would like to say this:

I have pretty much made up my mind, without having to hear all of these people, by the very fact that I see all of these people here. . . .

Mr. O'Brien: Mr. Chairman and Members of the Committee:

I think everybody understands the problem and the issue.

What we have got is a community which is 100 percent against it, and I would just ask the members of the Committee to take a vote to deny the McDonald's and let's get on with the business. . . .

Alderman Pucinski: Mr. Chairman. . . . We have heard the statement made by Mr. O'Brien in support of this, also the statement made by the Alderman in support of this and I would move that this recommendation—that this ordinance be recommended to the City Council as a do pass ordinance.

Chairman Vrdolyak: You have all heard the motion of Alderman Pucinski which is do pass.

All in favor signify by saying aye.

(Chorus of ayes)

Opposed?

(No response)

The matter passes. . . .

(Applause)

Can anyone doubt the power of a local group armed with a zoning ordinance?

What was somewhat surprising to us was the frequency with which some professionals in the process failed to appreciate what was happening around them. Typical of that group was a staffer in a large northeastern city who told us:

Zoning is a tool of the sophisticated. The average Joe six-pack guy doesn't understand zoning, and I really don't think in a typical urban area it makes much difference.

Several other professionals concurred in this view of a midwestern real estate man:

The people in the neighborhoods think it's important. They think it's a whole lot more important than it really is. It doesn't make a hell of a lot of difference.

The voice from the neighborhoods, however, revealed both substantial interest in, and ample understanding of, the land use process. This comment came from a resident of a reviving white middle-class neighborhood:

Land use and zoning is the number one concern. It's the one thing that we can all hang together on. . . . Time and again, there have been either rezoning, special use permit or variance requests, and we've gotten the system set up where we can get the people to the hearings. For the last two years, probably three years, we've been successful in opposing every rezoning request.

The councilman of a black middle-class district stated:

Without question, the number one concern of my constituents . . . is zoning and land use. There are a number of active community organizations elected by the people living in the various communities. Their number one concern by and large is zoning and land use. . . .

A councilman in another city representing a low-income neighborhood put it this way:

[The people] felt that they should at least protect themselves against the kind of businesses that come in when a neighborhood is in decline. . . . Zoning will at least protect the neighborhood from some of these more offensive kinds of businesses. You must have zoning because you must protect the weak against the strong.

And, finally, a plan commission member told us:

Zoning is probably the most relevant thing to the activism of communities that there is. . . . These communities can beat City Hall ten ways against the middle, and if they can't do it with their own resources, they know damn well where to hire it and get it, and many of them do. And they can get it for nothing in many cases. . . . And they know by this time zoning shapes their communities, that what zoning is is what their community is.

Despite the reverence for zoning that we found in the neighborhoods, it should not be supposed that anyone views it as a panacea. The devotion to zoning is not attributable to overly optimistic or mistaken notions about its effectiveness as a salve for all of the problems of urban America. The importance of land use problems, and of zoning as a tool to deal with them, is directly attributable to the fact that, in a world where the causes, effects, and cures of most problems are quite beyond the understanding of most of us, land use and zoning stand out as areas where most people believe they can, and actually do, have a direct and immediate impact on perceived problems by the use of a relatively uncomplicated tool.

So, at least for city neighborhoods, while zoning may not solve all of the problems, it does visibly contribute to the solution of many problems that directly affect the quality of peoples' lives. This summed up the response of most city residents to the idea of abolishing zoning because it's irrelevant in cities:

> Zoning isn't the biggest thing in this city—the schools are probably bigger—but zoning makes the difference. Houston is atrocious. I was frightened to death in Houston. You walk down the street and there are curb cuts all over; there are cars always crossing the sidewalk. I went to a nightclub there and there were private homes on both sides. Atrocious! Those really affect property values. You get a bunch of drunks going down the street at 1:00 every morning; it's got to affect property.

What we have seen and what we report here convinces us that zoning has a role to play in the future of our cities. The present and potential scope of that role is what this book is about. Even after hearing our arguments, some readers may conclude that zoning will never be more than it has always been, a negative tool to retard the forces of inevitable change. Especially in a fully developed city, however, that may not be as damning an indictment as it sometimes is made to sound. This response from one planner could not have been better:

> I'm ready to go so far as to say that zoning is not a positive tool to implement plans. But, hell, if it's nothing more than *the imposition of process on change,* if it simply retards change a little bit and makes people think about whether a change is good or bad, if it imposes some kind of order on the question of how land gets used and reused, that's not bad! Maybe that is not fulfilling its full destiny, but just because of that, I can't go to the other extreme and say it's no damn good at all.

But we are convinced there *is* more to it. Our study of the current scene gives us hope that zoning may, in our older cities, be about to advance at least another step or two toward " . . . .fulfilling its full destiny." Zoning in cities shows some hope of becoming a vital tool of positive change. The stale ideas and negative controls that characterize most of suburban zoning practice are clearly insufficient to deal with the land use problems of our cities. As city zoners thrash about for new ways to skin a cat, it seems a good bet that they will move quickly to the forefront of land use theory. In the next 10 years, if there are to be bright new ideas in this field, it seems likely that they will emerge, like much of Western civilization, out of the need to cope with the diversity, conflicts, and challenges that result from the massing of people, things, and power in our great cities.

This is, on balance, an optimistic book, which may be a refreshing change in an account of any activity in our older cities.

FOOTNOTES

1. *Just* v. *Marinette County,* 56 Wis.2d 7, 201 N.W.2d 761 (1972); *Sibson* v. *State,* 336 A.2d 239 (N.H. 1975).

2. *Metropolitan Housing Development Corporation* v. *Village of Arlington Heights,* 558 F.2d 1283 (7th Cir. 1977); *Southern Burlington County NAACP* v. *Township of Mount Laurel,* 336 A.2d 713 (N.J. 1975); *Berenson* v. *Town of Newcastle,* 38 N.Y.2d 102, 378 N.Y.S.2d 672, 341 N.E.2d 236 (1975).

Chapter 2
The City and Zoning: A Perspective After 50 Years of Suburban Pre-eminence

*"You are old," said the youth, "and
your jaws are too weak
For anything tougher than suet;
Yet you finished the goose, with the
bones and the beak—
Pray, how did you manage to do it?"*
*"In my youth," said his father, "I took
to the law,
And argued each case with my wife;
And the muscular strength, which it
gave to my jaw,
Has lasted the rest of my life."*

—Lewis Carroll, *Alice's
Adventures In Wonderland*

In 1926, 10 years after the birth of American zoning as a regulatory tool to deal with the urban problems of New York City, the United States Supreme Court decided its first zoning case, *Euclid* v. *Ambler Realty.*[1] It is noteworthy that, in choosing the case in which they would announce their landmark ruling on zoning's validity, the justices selected a case challenging a zoning ordinance adopted in a quiet suburb of Cleveland rather than one adopted in a city. By the end of zoning's first decade, it was obvious to everyone, even to the comparatively insulated justices of our highest court, that the real zoning issues for decades to come would be suburban issues.

And so it has been. The history of zoning this past half-century has been largely written in the suburbs. While zoning swept through the

13

villages of this nation, the attention paid to it in cities was comparatively minor. Of the more than 10,000 zoning cases that have been decided by federal and state appellate courts in the last half-century, the overwhelming majority have involved suburbs, not cities.[2] The major ideas and major issues that have occupied scholars, practitioners, and judges alike, from planned developments and flexible zoning to exclusionary devices and fiscal zoning, have been suburban issues. For the most part, regulation of land use in our central cities has been shrugged off as a silly exercise: at best, futile; at worst, counter-productive.

It is, nevertheless, the thesis of this book that zoning can, in the coming decades, become as significant in the reshaping of urban America as it has been in the creation of suburban America. Perhaps our conclusion is explained by the fact that we, unlike some critics of urban land use policy, do not view the often misguided, sometimes irrational, frequently futile efforts of cities to control their land use destinies as either pathetic or pathological. When by most accounts the city should belly over and accept rigor mortis as, so to speak, a way of life, we regard those efforts as evidence that the urban organism is still exploring, testing, and venturing in land use techniques.

For those who say that the problems of any major city are beyond the capacity of zoning or any other regulatory device to solve, we admit the allegation—with the hope of then putting it behind us. There is no question that many urban problems—even urban land use problems—cannot be solved by the mere application of a new set of land use regulations. Reform of major federal programs, reform of local property tax laws, significant public expenditures on both social and physical infrastructures, fundamental redirection of transportation concepts, and entirely new approaches to the relationship between the public and private sectors would be extraordinarily helpful and could do much more toward solving the problems of our cities than anything we discuss in this book. But all of that is no reason for ignoring the potential inherent in such a traditional, well-understood, and universally accepted regulatory device as zoning. For purposes of this effort, we are content to let others continue to struggle with grandiose "total system" approaches to urban problems. We wish them well but can hold but little hope for any immediate success from their efforts. Carter & Co. came to Washington with the grandest of ideas and best of intentions; they labored long and hard but after a year of intense effort came up with mostly the same old pablum and platitudes parading under yet another new name—this time "The New Partnership." Jerry Brown's "Urban Development Strategy for California" identifies 13 policies, most of them excellent, and nearly 50 specific program actions, most of them sensible, aimed at renewing and maintaining urban areas; but not much has happened since the report's release, nor is much likely to happen given the combination of Proposition 13 and California politics.

Certainly money can solve problems, if you can get it and get anyone to agree on how it should be spent; we simply suggest that many problems can be addressed, without the expenditure of scarce public funds, through the implementation of thoughtful, innovative regulatory measures. That lesson has not been missed by those concerned with land use problems in non-urban settings. Marinette County, Wisconsin, probably could have afforded to condemn a lot of wetlands in order to save it from destructive development; instead it passed a zoning ordinance prohibiting virtually every economic use of such lands. When it got sued, it argued that its new law was a "reasonable regulation" and not an unconstitutional taking. To the delight of environmentalists, the dismay of property owners, and the shock of skeptics, the court agreed and sustained the zoning.[3] While extreme, the result is not atypical of the willingness courts have recently shown to allow expansions of the police power in the name of protecting environmental values. There is no reason to expect that courts cannot, if properly educated, be persuaded to a similar course in the name of preserving our great cities. Chief Justice Breitel has already begun to clear the way in his extraordinary opinion in *Penn Central Trans. Co.* v. *City of New York*,[4] in which the court sustained the application of New York City's landmarks ordinance to Grand Central Terminal:

> In times of easy affluence, preservation of historic landmarks through the use of the eminent domain power might be desirable, or even required. But when a less expensive alternative is available, especially when a city is in financial distress, it should not be forced to choose between witnessing the demolition of its glorious past and mortgaging its hopes for the future.[5]

If that is not good enough to encourage new faith in the potency of the police power, remember what the U.S. Supreme Court said in its original validation of the concept of zoning:

> Until recent years, urban life was comparatively simple, but, with the great increase and concentration of population, problems have developed, and

constantly are developing, which require, and will continue to require, additional restrictions in respect of the use and occupation of private lands in urban communities. Regulations, the wisdom, necessity, and validity of which, as applied to existing conditions, are so apparent that they are now uniformly sustained, a century ago, or even half a century ago, probably would have been rejected as arbitrary and oppressive. . . . While the meaning of constitutional guaranties never varies, the scope of their application must expand or contract to meet the new and different conditions which are constantly coming within the field of their operation. In a changing world it is impossible that it should be otherwise.[6]

So, we simply suggest that the admitted need for other programs and reforms should not dissuade urban leaders, advisors, and citizens from also giving careful consideration to zoning as a potentially valid and vital tool for dealing with many urban problems.

If zoning is again to become such a tool in an urban setting, many of the assumptions and principles that 50 years of suburban zoning experience have burned into our hearts and minds, and into our planning texts and law books, will require significant rethinking. The process of redefinition and redirection may be as gradual as, but can be no less dramatic than, the process by which the architects of suburban zoning transformed the rigidity of Euclidian zoning ordinances created to protect already developed and stable urban neighborhoods into discretionary, flexible devices to direct and control the development of major new suburban centers.

In thinking about what urban zoning may become in the future, one must start by paying some attention to what cities are now. In Part II of this book, we address in some detail the existing physical, political, and social realities of major U.S. cities. For the present, it is sufficient to establish a perspective by noting two overriding facts about cities, both of which are so self-evident that one can hardly avoid being dumbstruck by the frequency with which they are overlooked by would-be reformers of urban zoning.

CITIES ARE NEITHER SUBURBAN NOR VIRGIN

In neither their physical nor their political and social makeup do cities have much in common with the suburban and virgin territories in which most recent zoning theory and law have sprouted. The ideas and principles developed in the last half-century to direct the suburban boom, as well as those developed in the last decade to stop the rape of the hinterland, must be carefully and critically analyzed and thoughtfully adapted before being grafted like some misfit appendage onto the urban zoning organism.

The physical differences are as plain as they are dramatic. Cities exist. What is, more than what is planned, will determine what will be. For the most part, cities are not only already built; they are old. It is folly to think that a zoning device created to control the development of a cornfield can, without serious rethinking, be used to foster the redevelopment of an urban neighborhood. By and large, it is also a fact that many cities are no longer growing. Their populations are declining, their commercial and industrial bases are shrinking, and they are confined to their existing corporate limits by a circle of independent suburban municipalities. In such a context, devices created to control the post-war population boom and to permit snobbish selection of the cream of humanity and the most ratable of ratables are both immoral and nonsensical.

Out of these physical facts comes the realization that, unless what exists in our major cities is preserved or redeveloped, it is bound to decay and the development that takes its place will be somewhere across the artificial line that divides city from suburb. This seems almost too intuitively obvious to say, but in a society that has a 350-year history of using up land and then moving on, the realization of a need to re-use *anything* comes most slowly. In a country where we will still take extraordinary pride in ourselves for recycling tin cans, one should not assume that the need for redeveloping cities is self-evident.

Once we admit that the challenge in cities encompasses a continuous, gradual process of re-use and redevelopment in response to the unpredictable evolution of an existing physical situation, it is hard to avoid the conclusion that planning for cities must be something very different than planning has been until now. (We treat that subject in Chapter 18.)

In considering how a system of land use regulation might be restructured in light of the physical facts that distinguish most cities, it becomes important also to consider the political and social differences between city and suburb. The need for physical planning to control and direct both development and development regulations in many suburban communities is, we believe, a direct result of the absence of social and political mechanisms capable of performing the task. Perhaps the greatest single difference between urban and suburban society is the presence of economic, social, and political diversity in most cities and the absence of any significant diversity whatever in most suburbs. That urban diversity should (as we discuss in Chapters 18 through 20) be a principal determinant of the structure of both the procedure and substance of urban zoning. However, having said that cities are characterized by diversity uncommon in suburbs, we must add that cities are also characterized by a unity that is atypical of post-war suburbia. While we believe that individual city neighborhoods should have a say in planning their own destinies, any scheme for providing that voice must recognize that city neighborhoods are not, in fact, independent villages.

FAMILIARITY BREEDS ACCEPTANCE

The second fundamental notion that seems, surprisingly, to escape many who ponder the future course of land use regulation, in whatever context, is that legislators and citizens alike can be expected, perverse as it may seem in this arena, to cling to the familiar. As will be seen later, so far as the procedural aspects of land use regulations are concerned, no one is willing, despite the incessant grumbling, to jump headlong into an entirely new system or to eliminate wholly any of the current participants in the existing system. While a wealth of procedural reform is certainly necessary to ensure fairness and rationality in land use regulation, we are convinced that reform, not revolution, offers the most hope for success. Substantively, resistance to reinventing the wheel is inevitable. Later (in Chapters 16 and 17) we discuss many of the system-shattering suggestions that have gained much popularity in the literature. Here again, however, it is our conviction that more progress can be expected from the thoughtful refinement of familiar techniques than from the attempted introduction of alien ideas.

As for those who are too discouraged or too bored with the existing system to be willing to work within its general confines, we offer the following bits of advice:

> The problem is not to create new transcendent technologies but to discover why we are not using the humbler technologies we already know—or even why we use so rarely the most prosaic and useful tech-

nology of all, which is common sense. Otherwise we will simply add to the frustrating backlog of technique we fail to apply....[7]

'Tis hard to venture where our betters fail
Or lend fresh-interest to a twice-told tale
And yet, perchance, 'tis wiser to prefer
A hackney'd plot, than choose a new, and err....[8]

Zoning? My personal preference is just to get rid of it. However, a lot of people attach almost primary significance to zoning. If they're going to do that, that means it has social and political value. They would more likely support constructive changes in the name of zoning, even though it really isn't zoning, than they would the creation of a whole new law.[9]

FOOTNOTES

1. *Village of Euclid* v. *Ambler Realty Co.,* 272 U.S. 365 (1926).

2. Norman Williams, Jr., *American Land Planning Law: Land Use and the Police Power* (Chicago: Callaghan & Co., 1974), vol. 1, §3.01.

3. *Just* v. *Marinette County,* 56 Wis.2d 7, 201 N.W. 2d 761 (1972).

4. *Penn Central Transportation Co.* v. *City of New York,* 42 N.Y.2d 324, 397 N.Y.S.2d 914, 366 N.E.2d 1271 (1977) *aff'd,* 437 U.S., 98 S. Ct. 2646 (1978).

5. *Id.* at 397 N.Y.S.2d 914, 922.

6. *Village of Euclid* v. *Ambler Realty Co.,* 272 U.S. 365, 386-87 (1926).

7. Richard Cornuelle, *Demanaging America: The Final Revolution* (New York City: Vintage Books, 1976), p. 63.

8. Lord Byron, *Hints from Horace.*

9. Personal interview with William Smith, director of development, Department of Community and Economic Development, Detroit.

Chapter 3
Methodology:
Observations from the
Growing Edge

*We forgive the poet his absurdities for
the sake of his occasional great stroke.
The scholar's work is [judged] no
better than his single worst error. [T]o
err is human, to forgive,
unscholarly.... [T]he scholar cannot
be concerned with the world, for the
world is something only partly and
opaquely known to us—and a scholar
must be able to give an absolutely
correct answer.*

—James Redfield

*Were it not for a fortuitous set of
circumstances, I might have become a
lawyer....*

—Studs Terkel

Before proceeding further, we should briefly describe our method-
ology. It was, we freely admit, neither scholarly nor lawyerly. In our
practice and in this book, we are concerned with understanding urban
zoning; such an understanding is not to be had from a scholarly analysis
of the subject. It must come, if at all, from participation and observation.
We have been more than willing to risk the human errors of which
Redfield warns as the price for this concern with a subject that can, at
best, be "only partly and opaquely known..." to any of us.

In the course of our professional assignments for public clients we
have participated and observed matters of land use practice and policy

in a number of large and medium-sized cities, including Atlantic City; Baltimore; Buffalo and Rochester, New York; Chicago; Cincinnati; Columbus and Toledo, Ohio; Dallas and San Antonio, Texas; Denver; Memphis; Portland, Maine; Sioux City; and Washington, D.C. For this project we elected to observe 11 additional cities:

Atlanta	Jacksonville
Boston	Minneapolis/St. Paul
Detroit	New York City
Honolulu	San Diego
Indianapolis	Seattle

We believe this group offered a wide spectrum of demograhic, geographic, and political conditions; it also offered a good mix of those older cities that everyone knows are in trouble and those newer cities that, despite their generally better press, are beginning to offer evidence of slipping.[1]

In the January 1975 issue of *Harper's*, in an article entitled "The Worst American City," Seattle and Minneapolis were heralded as cities with a comparatively benign way of life (and each has experienced the impact of state or regional policy upon its land development). The view of Detroit and New York, on the other hand, is often accompanied by cries of anguish. San Diego, a young city, is struggling to control its growth and, it turns out, may have a less hopeful prospect before it than an old center such as Boston. Jacksonville, Florida, and Indianapolis provided insights on the impact of the expanded city, consolidated with the county, upon land use policy. Honolulu offered the opportunity to observe the consequences of both the state's presence upon urban policy and also the city planner's dream: absolutely no place to go to escape city land use control. Atlanta, the alleged boom city where growth is not a four-letter word, is all the more interesting because the bloom is now at least temporarily off the boom. (Another look at Houston, everyone's nonzoning archetype, was more than we could bear even to satisfy those few zoning critics who think it is relevant. We don't. In Chapter 16, we give a few of the reasons why anyone interested in urban zoning really has nothing to learn in Houston.)

We have, of course, examined the zoning ordinances of all of these cities, and we have assembled and studied drawers of written materials on the process and policy of land use regulation in each. These written materials, particularly the ordinances themselves, must be read with caution. Often the written word does not reveal what is really happening in this turbulent field. To read the Chicago zoning ordinance, for example, is not to grasp how the zoning process really works in that highly political city. If one were to read the UNIGOV legislation as it appears in the Indiana statutes, it would be fair to assume that the City of Indianapolis was divided into legally mandated subdistricts, each with its own elected community council. The Indianapolis city council, however, continues to ignore the state legislature's command.

We have relied heavily upon interviews in each city, and in each place we tried to cover a broad spectrum of those involved in land use policy. Usually this group included elected officials, professional staff, consultants and critics, representatives of neighborhood groups and of the building interests, lawyers, and architects.

We focused on these interviews in part because our experience has taught us that, at least in this field, what Dean Charles E. Oxnard of the University of Chicago calls "the unclear, uncertain, foggy view that one sees by standing at the growing edge" is seldom seen from behind a pile of "definitive" books on an office desk.[2] (Nor, for that matter, is today's reality easily seen from that vantage.) There is, however, another reason for this emphasis upon conversations with knowledgeable participants. It is our hope that our audience will be mainly among those of the kind we interviewed, those persons who are actively engaged in the land use regulatory process in our cities. We believe, for the most part, a book full of charts, statistics, and surveys would not be read by those people—and few else.

Professor Jonathan Barnett describes the problem in his provocative book *Urban Design as Public Policy*.[3] In it he constructs an imaginary conversation between Mayor Lindsay and his planning advisors:

Suppose the issue of the Astor Plaza building had gone to the Mayor; but instead of putting forward a course of action that the Mayor could back, the dialogue had gone something like this:

"*Mayor:* Well, what do you suggest?

"*Ourselves:* We're not prepared to make a recommendation yet. First, it will be necessary to make a comprehensive survey of the theater district.

"*Mayor:* Oh? How long will that take?

"*Ourselves:* With luck, Mr. Mayor, about four months.

> "*Mayor:* Four months is a long time. . . .
>
> "*Ourselves:* Then, of course, we shall need to construct and evaluate alternative policy hypotheses about the future of the theater industry. For this purpose we propose to construct a mathematical model. Now assuming that our computer program works the first time, we shall then . . .
>
> "*Mayor:* (standing up) Well, the questions you raise are certainly interesting ones. Why don't you put all this in a memo to me and we'll take a look at it."

Barnett then adds:

> Obviously we would not have gotten very far with the Mayor if we had approached him in such a theoretically oriented manner. In order to produce an answer within the same time-frame as the problem, we had to be "low church" in our methodology. We talked to informed people in the theater world, and in the hotel and restaurant business. . .instead of taking surveys.[4]

This, then, is a book about and for persons who, as C. P. Snow has described the administrators of public policies, have "to think of a great many things, widely, in their interconnections, for a short time." [5]

One additional word of caution. Some of our conclusions are based upon conjecture, albeit conjecture grounded upon many years of exposure to, and participation in, the arena of land use practice in big and small cities, suburbs, courthouses, and legislative halls. We accept Professor Edward Banfield's dictum on that "flaw":

> What most distresses my critics is not that I have (as they suppose) made conjectures that are not in accord with the facts. Rather it is. . .that I have asserted (and everyone who reflects knows it to be true) that conjectures unsupported, or slightly supported, by facts are the stuff of which social policies must always mainly be made.[6]

FOOTNOTES

1. See "Young Cities Sliding into Old Patterns of Blight," *Atlantic City Press,* November 2, 1977, p. 26.

2. Charles E. Oxnard, "Our College Today: Toward Liberal Education," Occasional Papers from the College No. 2 (Chicago: University of Chicago, 1976).

3. Jonathan Barnett, *Urban Design as Public Policy* (New York City: Architectural Record Books, 1974), pp. 22-23.

4. *Id.*

5. C.P. Snow, *Science and Government* (Cambridge, Mass.: Harvard University Press, 1961), p. 72.

6. Edward Banfield, *The Unheavenly City Revisited* (Boston: Little, Brown & Co., 1974), p. ix.

Part II

A Report on What Is

Chapter 4
The Residential Areas:
House and Hope

"Fight on, my men," Sir Andrew sayes,
"A little Ime hurt, but yett not slaine;
Ile but lye down and bleede awhile,
And then Ile rise and fight againe."

— "Sir Andrew Barton" in Bishop
Thomas Percy, *Reliques of*
Ancient English Poetry

The resurgence of zoning as an issue in the residential neighborhoods of every city we studied is one of the most hopeful signs that cities are, like Sir Andrew, having lain down to bleed awhile, now prepared to fight again.

Nevertheless, one of the great paradoxes of zoning everywhere, including zoning in the cities, is that in the very residential neighborhoods where zoning is most revered and most powerful it has also been the least innovative and, therefore, frequently the least able to cope with threats to viable residential living. Most of the attempted innovations in zoning have been in the context of regulating large-scale new developments. Precious little time and attention have been paid to innovation in what everyone assumes is easy—preventing change. Prevention of change may well be easy in a suburban community where most of the development is new and nearly all of it is monolithic. Neither of those factors is present in the average city neighborhood. Furthermore, there is no such thing as the "average" city neighborhood.

The increasing power that neighborhood groups exercise in the zoning process is the subject of Chapter 14. However, to understand the motivations of those groups and the resurgence of zoning in city neighborhoods and to begin to formulate programs that can successfully respond to the challenge of preserving and rehabilitating city neighborhoods, it is necessary first to gain some understanding of the physical and social fabric of those neighborhoods and of the threats to that fabric. It is to that task that we turn in this chapter.

THE NEW DEMAND FOR CITY HOUSING

The increasing demand for middle-income housing in central cities is explainable on several grounds. A recent Urban Land Institute research report[1] points out the cost advantage that central city housing is beginning to enjoy over suburban housing:

> More stringent controls on new development and sewer moratoria [in suburban areas] have tended to limit the supply of developable land and force up land prices. Inflation in construction costs have further added to the price of new suburban housing. In addition, many suburban communities now assess heavy development fees on new projects to offset the public costs required to service new development. The combination of these cost increases has resulted in a large segment of the middle-income market being priced out of the suburban market and appears to have made new housing less attractive on a space-cost basis than much of the older housing in the central city. These conditions should also make new construction in the central city more competitive because of a decrease in land cost differentials and the absence of heavy development fees.[2]

Of course, much of the increase in costs of suburban housing can be attributed, directly or indirectly, to a long history of exlusionary practices in suburban areas. While a few state courts have begun to condemn those practices, it will be some time before the rhetoric of those decisions has any noticeable effect on the availability of reasonably priced housing in the suburbs. And, so long as the United States Supreme Court continues to write opinions like *Belle Terre,*[3] *East Lake,*[4] and *Arlington Heights,*[5] even the moral commitment to housing for all in the suburbs is not likely to gain widespread acceptance.

All of that is not much different than it has always been. What is different is that, as the cost of suburban housing and the cost of commuting to suburban housing from central city office jobs continue to increase, the class of the excluded includes higher and higher socioeconomic levels. The white middle class is slowly but surely joining the ranks of the excluded. What is also different is that increasing numbers of people have, for a variety of reasons, become disenchanted with suburban attitudes and life-styles and are voluntarily turning away from the suburb as the ultimate residential goal.

Minorities that have traditionally been shunned by the suburbs are not likely, as they continue their steady climb up the economic ladder, to flee to the suburbs with the same fervor that characterized the flight of the white middle class after World War II. The reaction of the influential black civil rights organization Operation PUSH to the United States Supreme Court's decision in *Hill* v. *Gautreaux*[6] was predictable and typical. In *Gautreaux,* the Court held that an order directing placement of housing for Chicago's poor in its suburbs was not, as a matter of law, an impermissible form of relief in a case where the Department of Housing and Urban Development was shown to have discriminated in the location of subsidized housing. PUSH saw the decision as a threat to the political and economic power base that blacks are trying to establish in Chicago.[7] The 1970s have, in fact, seen a growing movement among influential black leaders in support of black power in cities and in opposition to dispersal of the black middle class into the suburbs.[8] PUSH's outraged response two years later to the Court's *Bakke*[9] decision provided an instructive contrast. The exclusion from education and jobs that *Bakke* threatened was cause again for war with the white community; the exclusion from suburban housing involved in *Gautreaux* was not. The new black leadership seems clearly to have decided what is important to ultimate equality, and it is not a home in the suburbs.

It is also clear that life-styles and attitudes toward the traditional family are changing in ways that increase the number of households demanding adult-oriented dwellings and communities. Thirty-eight percent of all U.S. families consist of two persons, and another 15.5 million people, including 1.3 million under the age of 25, live alone. The fertility rate of U.S. women has plunged to 1.8, the lowest in U.S. history. Approximately six out of every 10 households consist of adults only.

Census figures released in February 1977 indicate a surge in the number of households composed of "unrelated adults," which is bureaucrateze for a variety of "unconventional" housing arrangements. The economic and educational levels of these adults-only families is, along with their demand for convenient cultural and entertainment facilities and activities, on the rise. More and more of them are working in white-collar positions located in the heart of our central cities, which have in recent years enjoyed a spectacular boom in downtown office construction.

Whatever the reason or explanation for the surge in formation of unconventional households, it seems plain that there is no room for them in the suburbs. It must certainly be some sort of comment on the closed-mindedness of many suburban communities that the first zoning case to be accepted by the United States Supreme Court in 47 years, *Belle Terre* v. *Boraas*,[10] involved an issue of such earth-shaking importance as whether or not some college kids could share a house in a small bedroom suburb on Long Island. The suburban city of Evanston, Illinois, has been wringing its municipal hands for nearly half a decade trying to decide whether or not to amend its zoning ordinance definition of "family" enough to allow for the continued existence of a nationally heralded religious community that has succeeded in stabilizing and upgrading one of the suburb's declining neighborhoods. The problem is that the group believes in communal living arrangements in which an "extended" household might include one or more traditional families and several unrelated adults and children. In Grosse Pointe Park, Michigan, just outside Detroit, concerned neighbors succeeded in driving out two single men who had rented a four-bedroom home, complete with a "wide yard" for the kids of one of them.[11]

As long as suburbs continue their aversion to anything different, our rapidly changing society can be counted upon to produce an increasing number of middle-income individuals and families in search of a more accommodating, more interesting place to live. Those who shun, or are shunned by, the traditional suburban life-style will find the cities an attractive alternative.

It is difficult to predict the future of this new demand, but its potential for expansion should not be lightly dismissed. At the moment, the new demand seems largely dependent upon individuals, childless young couples, and nonconventional households, but those groups form a growing percentage of the total population. Perhaps more important, the new urban residents share two important characteristics with a much broader segment of U.S. society, affluence and mobility. Both make city living both more enjoyable and less frightening:

. . . with relatively high earning power, they can find ways to "live around" such urban difficulties as poor public education; and if they cannot, they have the means to leave them behind rather quickly.

That passage is from one of the best, though one of the least scientific, studies of the new demand for city housing we have seen, *Young Professionals in City Neighborhoods,* by Boston's Parkman Center for Urban Affairs.[12] It offers as much by way of prognostication on the future of this trend as we think is possible:

> While middle class resettlement in cities may or may not become a significant force in the urban equation, it is in theory quite possible that a middle class taste for city living could become an appetite that grows by what it feeds on. The more popular such a movement, the broader its potential base; the broader the base, the more likelihood of changed conditions (reduced crime, improved public education, enhanced civic amenity) which would further tend to enlarge the migrant pool. . . . Pioneers, trend setters are followed by colonists, by consumers who have been educated through the example of others about what is desirable. If a settlement "takes," it will invariably be because of the presence of "followers" who make up the bulk of the demand for any commodity or fashion, whether it happens to be Victorian mini-mansions or flared trousers or whatever else.[13]

In the meantime, cities can take at least some comfort from the knowledge that the small, young, affluent households that are the current mainstay of the new demand for city housing are, from a municipal cost-benefit point of view, the creme de la creme of U.S. households. If cities can capture an increased number of those households, they can quit worrying about their loss of total population. While the replacement of a middle-income family of six with a childless couple of two affluent young professionals is a minus on the roles of the census taker, it is a plus on the books of the city treasurer.

THE "REDISCOVERED" CITY: SIGNS OF LIFE IN CITY NEIGHBORHOODS

While urban problems, principally bad schools and fear of crime, continue for the moment to limit the number of families with children who would choose to live in cities, the increasing demand for city housing from "nontraditional" households has already had marked effect in a number of cities. The impact of that demand is most evident in the growing number of "rediscovered" or "regentrified" city neighborhoods. In 1975 the Department of Housing and Urban Development was able to find 600 separate programs across the country dedicated to neighborhood preservation.[14] A 1975 survey by the Urban Land Institute found that 75 percent of all cities with populations over 500,000 were experiencing private market, nonsubsidized housing renovation programs in their older, deteriorated areas.[15]

It is difficult to find any major city in this country that does not have at least one neighborhood where, despite precious little encouragement or cooperation from city government, people have been willing to spend more money to rehabilitate dwelling units than they spent to buy them in the first place: Lincoln Park in Chicago; Inman Park in Atlanta; Riverside-Avondale in Jacksonville, Florida; the Third Ward in Rochester, New York; the South End of Boston; Lowry Hill in Minneapolis; even in Detroit, limited movements toward middle-class rehabilitation of dilapidated housing can be found.

Rediscovered areas vary a good bit from city to city, but one feature they all have in common is uniquely available inside central cities and probably impossible to duplicate anywhere else. That feature is proximity to the diversity of employment opportunities, public and private services, and cultural and recreational facilities typically available in and around the core of any major city.

Another quality that all of these neighborhoods have in common—be they in Chicago, Boston, or Atlanta—is, of course, a stock of well-built housing conducive to rehabilitation. But the great diversity of housing types and quality that fit that definition suggests that it is the attraction of city living and the cost of suburban housing more than the particular type of dwelling unit that is really important. In the oldest and largest cities, rediscovered areas are frequently characterized by solid old brick and masonry walk-up-type buildings. Some, like the brownstones of New York, were originally designed as sumptuous townhouses for the wealthy; others were designed as two-flats or three-flats with sometimes enormous apartments for the working middle-class family. In Boston and Philadelphia, one can find street upon street of so-called "triple-decker" or "trinity" houses, so labelled because the father lived in one apartment, the son in another, and the "holy ghost," the tenant who helped to pay the mortage, lived in the third. In other cities, like

Atlanta, Jacksonville, and Indianapolis, beautiful old single-family neighborhoods exist practically within walking distance of the central business district. The housing stock in these neighborhoods varies from the great old mansions of the wealthy, which characterize the Riverside-Avondale area of Jacksonville, to the much less pretentious clapboard houses crowded together on the narrow streets of Atlanta's West End. Whatever the housing style or original construction, if the location is right, it appears that rehabilitation is a possibility.

Another feature that rediscovered areas are thought to have in common may be more fancy than fact. At least in city neighborhoods, historical distinction is most often found more in the eye of the discoverer than in the annals of time. There are approximately 175 officially designated historic residential districts in central cities.[16] There are certainly many more unofficial "historic" areas. Historic has come to mean practically anything that is, in some fashion or another, not run-of-the-mill. Many a street lined with big old houses that would look absolutely typical and ordinary in any wealthy turn-of-the-century suburb has become a special, historic place when located 20 miles closer to the central business district. Historic designation does a lot of things: it may make loans easier to get, and even sometimes cheaper; it's a convenient way of drawing a line around an area and saying that this is somehow different than the squalor across the back alley; it gives nostalgia buffs a warm glow and a reason to invest their money in what would otherwise be just an old house; it provides municipal officials with an excuse for relaxing various codes that would be difficult for the renovators to meet; and, perhaps most important, it says in a very affirmative way that there is something worth preserving and enjoying about the style and character of many inner-city neighborhoods. It is, in short, in many ways a splendid, if somewhat contrived, device.

City zoning policies have, in a perverse sort of way, encouraged the revival of these close-in residential areas. Unfortunately, rehabilitation is always a pride that comes after the fall. The relaxation of zoning standards and enforcement and the withdrawal of city services are frequently significant contributors to the decline and abandonment of a neighborhood to the point where "discovery" becomes attractive. Ironically, the same zoning that permits the original disintegration also permits the economic rehabilitation. As Wade Burns, an architect who has single-handedly rehabilitated an Atlanta neighborhood, commented when asked if he had any zoning problems, "It was already zoned 'slum'! Anything was allowable. . . . You can have up to six rental units in what should have been a single family home."

This, of course, is not the first time that a blundering application of government police power has created social good despite itself:

> Back in 1895, the "Drys" tried to deglamorize the saloon. The general assembly ordained that public drinking spots had to be located in a single ground floor or basement room fronting the street or highway. No music was tolerated, no booths or partitions were allowed and only beer, wine, liquor and tobacco could be sold.
>
> Ironically, by forbidding the sale of food, the free lunch counter came into existence; by forcing the removal of chairs, the comfortable massive bar and brass rail appeared; and by ordaining clear vision from the street only during *closing* hours, the famed swinging doors and ornate curtains came into being to shield the drinkers from public gaze.[17]

It is not surprising that zoning has played such a small and unintentional role in fostering the rediscovery process. No greater role may be possible. Almost by definition, a rediscovered area cannot become such by means of zoning. There is something about explorers that thirsts for the uncharted. If the area is well-known enough to be mapped, it is too well-known to be discovered. In fact, by the time the mapping starts, it's a good bet that the real explorers are either gone or getting very itchy. Dan Ahern's characterization of Boston's South End discoverers provides a fairly accurate picture of the genre:

> [I asked her] why it is that you resent white, middle class people moving into the South End and buying townhouses and fixing them up when you did it yourself ten years ago. Her answer was, "Ten years ago the people that came in here were different; they didn't have much money; they bought these little houses cheaply; they put in sweat equity; they fixed them up with their own hands; they loved the houses, the neighborhood. The people who are coming in now are rich bastards; buying $80,000 houses; they hire contractors; they don't care what's going on; they're indifferent; they're arrogant; they're no good. We don't want them. . . ."

In any event, it is a good bet that any zoning ordinance that attempted to provide an atmosphere conducive to "discovery" would probably end up being meaningless or worse. If the idea was to provide for the "discovery" of a slum, the "discovery" zone would in all probability end up being more restrictive than the existing zoning. Slums don't usually get that way without lax zoning provisions. Like closing the barn door too late, tightening up the zoning in an undiscovered slum not only fails to keep the horses in but could keep them out as well. On the other hand, rezoning an area that has not already bottomed out in the hopes that "discovery" can stop the slide is fraught with danger. Invariably, rezonings in that situation have contemplated more intense uses or a greater mixture of uses. However, as we point out later, it is in just such "gray areas" that such concepts have proved to have the least validity.

For these reasons, the zoning battles in the rediscovered areas have come not at the beginning but at the end of the rehabilitation process. In neighborhood after neighborhood where the rediscovery process has taken hold, the pattern has been the same. Those who arrive first create an environment that is pleasing to themselves and immediately march on city hall to have that pattern of development cast into the permanent stone of the zoning ordinance. In this respect, the rediscoverers of the city are no different than their predecessors, that intrepid band which, two or three decades before, set out to settle the suburbs and to produce a generation that is now flirting with a return to the cities.

The pioneer discoverers who take advantage of lax zoning regulations and enforcement to convert dilapidated structures into economically productive uses soon see those same regulations and policies as a threat to the viability of the environment they and their fellow right-minded adventurers have so painfully created. Like the folks who are still fighting to keep the walls up around their suburb or the Vermont environmentalist who moved from New York last year or the retired Cincinnati stockbroker with the condominium in Palm Beach, the discoverers have implicit faith in their own good motives but are convinced that the public health, safety, and welfare demand a zoning ordinance to control the libidinal tendencies of others to pillage, plunder, and rape "their" turf. It is, perhaps, inherent in the makeup of man that he writes rules of admission in his own image.

As an aside, it should be noted that the tendency for the haves to zone out the have-nots is not limited to either suburban or city residential neighborhoods. In Atlanta, there was general agreement by both government officials and private sector representatives that the major developers of Atlanta's central business district would welcome a downzoning of the area in order to protect the monuments they have built to themselves. In fact, the renowned (perhaps now the word is "notorious") Omni-International development was not even complete before the zoning in the area around it was revised to protect against "incompatible" uses. Central Atlanta Progress, an organization composed largely of major downtown interests, prepared a plan suggesting downzoning (albeit a modest downzoning) of the central business district. The major push for a drastic downzoning of the Waikiki district in Honolulu came from the hotel chains, which had already developed their massive beachfront complexes. A similar reaction appeared in Detroit when gas station operators petitioned to forbid any additional service stations.

This instinct for protection from "newcomers" is not entirely misplaced in the rediscovered residential areas of a central city. The revitalization of an inner-city neighborhood is a process in which success breeds failure and disasters are frequently snatched from the jaws of hope. In city after city, we found neighborhoods that were either healthy or on their way back up threatened by a variety of haphazard assaults by those who sought to reap for themselves the benefits of city neighborhoods that had again become valuable as places to live and work. Whether it is a hamburger stand in Albany's Center Square, one halfway house too many in the East Avenue District of Rochester, New York, a medical clinic in the Riverside-Avondale area of Jacksonville, a bar and restaurant on Boston's Newberry Street, a massive high rise in Lincoln Park in Chicago, or the invariable request to rezone the whole rediscovered single-family neighborhood for apartment buildings, the scenario is much the same. The stability and rising values of the area act as a magnet to more intense residential uses, to commercial uses desirous of locations near stable and relatively affluent residential populations, and to institutional uses requiring the type and size of structure and the proximity to population, services, and transportation that are characteristic of most rediscovered areas.

The problems posed by such "bothersome" uses (addressed in more detail in Chapter 8) have been met by an amazingly uniform response. The weapon is always the same—the zoning ordinance. It is always used in the same way—the way zoning ordinances are used everywhere—as an exclusionary device. "Downzoning" has, in the past ten years, become a familiar term to describe the programs instituted in a variety of suburban and non-urban growth centers to rezone for less intense and less varied uses than were formerly permitted by zoning ordinances drafted during the post-war decades when "growth is good" was the popular mania.[18] Except in such unusual cases as San Diego or the Waikiki district in Honolulu, people are not accustomed to thinking of "downzoning" as a meaningful term in the lexicon of central city zoning. That, however, was the old days.

In the city neighborhoods all over the country, citizens are demanding, and very frequently getting, massive zoning rollbacks in their neighborhoods. In the Back Bay area of Boston, when a mayoral commission voted six to five in favor of allowing high-rise zoning in the area, the neighborhood rose up. A few thousand signatures on a petition was all it took to override the blue-ribbon boys and get the entire area downzoned. In Minneapolis, neighborhoods have demanded and gotten large-scale downzonings to prevent the construction of small walk-up apartment buildings in single-family neighborhoods. In that case, the sort of constitutional problems that have produced consternation over, and treatises about, the "taking issue" in suburban and rural downzonings posed little difficulty for the determined neighborhood groups. As one neighborhood leader put it:

> Once we started talking downzoning, people would say, well, you are taking away my economic advantage; you are making my property less valuable; and we sort of figured, well, how do you combat that? Until suddenly, people said, that is not a valid answer at all to the situation.

So much for the "taking issue." In Atlanta, vast neighborhoods that were zoned for apartment development in 1954 are gradually being zoned back to single-family and duplex. Nor do the neighbors stop at downzoning to a duplex classification. In one middle-class black neighborhood in Atlanta, a citizen's group was demanding, and apparently succeeding in obtaining, rezoning of a 100-acre vacant parcel for open-space use. They claimed, having learned much about the game, that the site had environmental, historical, and archeological significance.

The downzoning phenomenon is by no means limited to neighborhoods in those cities enjoying comparative health. Neighborhood pressure in Detroit has resulted in the downzoning of major industrial and commercial areas to prevent their encroachment into existing residential neighborhoods. In fact, it would appear that one need climb no more than one rung up the social and economic ladder before the benefits of downzoning and exclusionary zoning begin to appear. A Detroit staffer explained the recent surge of downzonings in Detroit as follows:

> [Bothersome uses] have followed racially changing neighborhoods. If the neighborhood is changing, many times the uses that they were running from or that they were moving from tend to follow them. They don't want

them to follow them because those uses were the very reasons why they moved out of their former neighorhood. So they're asking for the tightening of the zoning restrictions to prevent some of the uses—some of these abrasive, more obnoxious uses—from following them.

In fact, the Detroit ordinance requiring spacing of pornographic stores and theaters, which the United States Supreme Court sustained in a landmark decision,[19] had its origin in complaints from Detroit's rising black middle class, which saw such uses beginning to appear in the strip commercial areas bounding neighborhoods into which it was gradually expanding.

While city folk have taken up the downzoning cry with a vengence, their elected leaders do not, for the most part, approach the subject with the same single-minded unanimity and carefree abandon that charaterizes the process in suburban and rural areas. As is frequently the case in cities, the desire for neighborhood protection and preservation is invariably tempered by some competing interest. As one councilman put it:

> You have to balance that situation [neighborhood desire for downzoning] with the reality that the city has become a large metropolitan type environment and that you have growth and growth potential. . . . You have to balance the need for industry, the need for more commercial development, the need for higher density, more effective and efficient land use, with the desires of citizens who are saying, "hold it, wait a minute, we want to protect our neighborhoods and our environment." This is becoming more and more a part of the decision making process.

In Detroit, many officials were strongly opposed to the downzoning of strip commercial areas being pressed by various neighborhood groups. Those officials saw the strips suffering higher and higher vacancy rates and opposed any change that would compound the problem. If a pornography shop would prevent one more storefront from becoming vacant and vandalized in Detroit, they were for it. The result of the competing pressures in that case was that financially strapped Detroit appropriated $50,000 to make a study of the appropriate zoning for these commercial strips. In Rochester, New York, there is a constant tug and pull between the desire of city officials to protect residential neighborhoods and their equally strong desire to encourage the expansion of the industrial concerns that frequently butt right up to those neighborhoods. In Jacksonville, Florida, the cries of some citizens for downzoning were balanced against, of all things, the rights of other citizens to retain zoning upon which they had relied. One member of the city council explained his vote against a controversial request for a downzoning as follows:

> The citizens . . . asked us to take away something the property owner already had. And I think that property rights have to be protected; and my feeling is all law is good law and if you want to come in to change the law you have to make a positive case for a change in the law. . . . That normally works to the benefit of the citizens that are in a uproar, but it sometimes works the other way. . . . If you buy something, the citizens around you shouldn't be able to take it away from you. It's adverse condemnation. And it's wrong—if we're going to operate that way, the city should condemn the man's land and take it and then zone it. . . . I think property rights are awfully important.

While such competing concerns frequently temper the response of city legislators to the demands for neighborhood protection, when push comes to shove, the well-organized middle-class neighborhood usually gets its way. Keeping and attracting a middle-class population is considered the sine qua non of big city survival; that fact assures that the middle class will be protected and nurtured. What this deference to the returning middle class means to those who are being pushed and shoved by their return is the next subject.

"FINDERS, KEEPERS: LOSERS, WEEPERS": WHERE HAVE ALL THE POOR FOLK GONE

By the time the pioneers who rediscover inner-city neighborhoods begin tightening up the zoning regulations to keep out the various sorts of intruders that concern them, they have already forgotten that they too came as intruders. One of the most troublesome aspects attending upon the revitalization of our cities as livable places for the middle class is the problem of the poor people who are frequently driven out. It is no longer uncommon to go into a run-down city neighborhood and see signs such as one in the Capitol Hill section of Washington, D.C. that advised:

RICH WHITE FOLK FROM MD. AND VA.
STAY OFF OUR BLOCK

or the graffito on a building in the predominantly black Third Ward of Rochester, New York, that said:

UP THE WALL TO WHITEY'S HISTORIC DISTRICT

The following quote is an excerpt from a "fact sheet" prepared by a black neighborhood group in opposition to a historic preservation district:

> 1. FIGHT IS *NOT* opposed to preserving property.
>
> 2. FIGHT is opposed to any plan for property conservation that will mean "black folk" removal, no matter whether it is instigated by a Preservation Board or the Urban Renewal Department.
>
> 3. Preservation districts were established in three other places across this country. These places have received national notoriety. They are: Society Hill, Philadelphia; College Hill, Providence, Rhode Island; and Georgetown, Washington, D.C. In all three of these places "black folk" removal has been the result....
>
> 8. FIGHT, as a result, is uncompromisingly calling for a rescinding of the declaration of ... as a preservation district.

The City Council repealed the Historic District classification.

Why are poor people, who used to march more or less meekly out of their neighborhoods with the urban renewal bulldozers close behind, now standing and fighting? Certainly part of the reason is that, having been chased out of their homes once by bulldozers, poor people in the cities are more resistant to being chased out again by a white-middle-class takeover. Another part of the explanation is that poor people, along with everyone else, have learned the value of shouting in defense of their rights as they perceive them. In addition, more and more "poor people" have a meaningful investment in their neighborhoods; there is something about the first upward move, whether it be a move from rural poverty to a city ghetto or from the worst slum to a slightly better one, that gives people a sense of having invested part of themselves in their new situation. That investment makes them less willing to be pushed out. Another part of the explanation, of course, lies in the growth of racial and ethnic identification and pride: what was once disparagingly referred to as a ghetto is now defended as an enclave of ethnic culture and tradition. And, finally, those to whom the cities were abandoned in the heyday of the suburb are now understandably resentful of being pushed out by the returning prodigals. A Boston neighborhood leader captured those sentiments:

> ... I think they are resentful too, as people who made a commitment, either forced or voluntary, but very often a voluntary one, to stay in the City. Now they find people who, in their minds, are associated with those

who left the City behind and moved out and indirectly caused some of the problems. And they say, "What? Are we going to give up again because now they want to come back and build walls around themselves?"

Any program directed at the regeneration of inner-city neighborhoods must face this problem. Whether there is an answer is hard to say:

> I think that when you regenerate a neighborhood, that happens; and it's not fair. But I don't think that there is a decent answer to it, with the possible exception of rent or purchase subsidies. But I don't see enough of those to really make a difference. And, I don't always know whether anyone really chooses to go on living in a neighborhood where he's not able to keep up with the Joneses. . . .

In faint defense of the neighborhood revival movement, at least it can be said that it is more gradual, more effective, less socially and economically disruptive, and less costly of public funds than any of the government programs that have attempted in the past to deal with the same problems. There is also some hope that, if open-housing movements can create broader opportunities for the poor and minority populations being driven from rediscovered neighborhoods, the impacts of, and opposition to, this latest round of displacement may be considerably softened. It is by no means clear that the majority of the inner-city low-income population would have any objection to abandoning their old neighborhoods to the young rich if there were some reasonable alternative housing available to them.

While the charms of an inner-city neighborhood may glitter in the eyes of a refugee from the suburbs, it is a good bet that, despite the attitude of some black leaders toward "dispersal," the grass in newer city and suburban neighborhood areas may look a darn sight greener to many of those poor and minority families who have been in old city neighborhoods by compulsion, not choice. (As Carl Westmoreland, head of the Mt. Orborn Housing Foundation in Cincinnati, said of his group's effort to rehabilitate one of Cincinnati's worst slums by an 80 percent reduction in the number of dwelling units: "You can't put but so many people in this gulley. Black ain't but so beautiful.") According to reports of one study, even given the money and opportunity to renovate, 45 percent of the sample of poor people interviewed would prefer to move anyway.[20] The tendency of the white middle class to assume erroneously that its latest notion of the good life is shared by the whole world was poignantly illustrated by the efforts of some do-gooders to provide an inner-city playground in Hartford, Connecticut.

In a not-uncommon example of doing things just the wrong way, the black neighborhood group hired a highly esteemed white playground architect to design a monkey-bar monument to their virtue. Having great experience with what children from the best sorts of families longed for, the architect created a playground out of old sewer pipes, tires, and other "natural" and "mind-expanding" paraphernalia. The black kids, of course, were crushed. They thought they were going to get shiny swings and slides; instead, they got another vacant lot strewn with an assortment of all-too-familiar junk. Similarly, some black people to whom we spoke in the course of this effort suggested that many black families who have always lived in antiquated dwellings of one sort or another would like nothing better than a single-family house on a quarter-acre lot. The last thing they are interested in, or equipped for, is investing a lot of time and money to live in an old house or apartment in the city.

At the same time rich young singles and couples are being attracted back to the city, poorer families are feeling a stronger pull to the suburbs. The same suburban zoning ordinances that have, during the past two decades, prevented low-income wage earners from moving out of the city have also enticed manufacturing, commercial, and service industries into the suburbs. The design of white-middle-class transportation systems took no account of the need of blue-collar workers to get from their city homes to their suburban factory jobs. The result has been increasing pressure from employees, and increasing support from employers, for the right of wage earners to live close to their suburban jobs. The inevitable effect was foreseen in a 1971 *Ebony* editorial:

> As the Cities grew progressively worse following World War II, the white urbanite found his solution—he created suburbia. . . .
> The black man did not lose terribly much at first as whites fled to the suburbs. In fact in some areas, he gained. . . . The flight of the whites at least gave the blacks in the inner city a little more room to stretch out. But now a more serious migration is taking place. Hundreds of factories both large and small, are moving to industrial parks in the suburbs. . . . Today for many blacks, it is not a case of escaping to the suburbs to get away from the crowding, the poor schools and the crimes; it is a case of finding living quarters near enough to a job to keep home and family together. Blacks who never before would have considered moving among whites in the suburbs, may now find that they are forced to do so. . . .
> The black man must go where the jobs are. He left the South to move to

an alien North because of economics. He may have to learn to live with suburban whites for the same reason.[21]

While the rhetoric of all colors and classes may find satisfaction in praising or decrying all of this as a white takeover of the cities or a "ghetto-ization" of the suburbs, and while we in our own gloomier moments have thought that the forces we see at work may lead to nothing more than a new, but just as clear, pattern of racial segregation,[22] the situation can be viewed in a more hopeful light.

The result of inner-city revival coupled with more open housing in the suburbs may be that the "trickle down" process becomes a process of "push up." Instead of the housing needs of an economically and socially stagnant minority population being met by the gradual deterioration of the housing stock, the next decades may be characterized more by a rising population gradually moving into housing that is newer and better than what they left behind in the city. That has been the middle-class pattern ever since there was a middle class. The difference in the future, however, may be that the rising cost of transportation and new construction, coupled with the shortage of close-in vacant land, will accelerate the trend toward families with more substantial housing budgets "moving up" by undertaking the costly renovation of existing inner-city housing, which, while economically more attractive to them, is still beyond the means of lower- and lower-middle-income budgets.

Cities being what they are, suburbs being what they are, and existing patterns of living being what they are, it is most unlikely that we will ever see a time when all the white folks who have fled to the suburbs move back to the city or all of the black folks who are now trapped in the city move to the suburbs. In that light, we can hope that the emergent patterns of class migration will mean that cities may become less crowded and more healthy with the return of a viable, and probably integrated, middle class, and that suburbs may be enriched by a broader cross-section of humanity. To be sure, some suburban communities that were not much to begin with may degenerate into pockets of poverty; many city neighborhoods will never be havens of middle-class morality, but, over all, our urban areas could become more uniformly livable population centers.

A few preliminary successes offer some hope. Indianapolis probably has a greater percentage of its low-income housing dispersed in the suburbs than does any other major city in the country, and yet there has been no noticeable evidence of the suburbs being "ghetto-ized." Although Minneapolis has a lower minority population that most other large cities in the country, it may still be cited as another example of successful dispersal of low-income housing outside the central city. Through the vehicle of the Metro Council's so-called "Policy 13," all local government applications for state or federal funds for streets or sewers or whatever are ranked according to the community's record in providing low- and moderate-income housing. Those with bad records get negative A-95 reviews from the Council. The results have been literally incredible:

> As a result, we now have, for every dollar we get, 13 suburbs applying for it. Now they're all fighting, trying to get it. . . . Now we've gone the other way; we have set out point systems to qualify. . . . It started to work so well, Minneapolis and St. Paul have been complaining. They aren't getting enough of it anymore. . . . After our housing allocation last year, Minneapolis and St. Paul complained bitterly. We said, sorry, that's all we're allocating to you because we want to disperse these out in other areas. They're complaining that the suburbs are getting too much money. That Minneapolis now wants more of it back. I know it sounds crazy, doesn't it?

Crazy, but effective:

> In 1971, when the council's housing plan was first adopted, 90 percent of all the subsidized housing was located in the center cities. Only 1,800 units were located in the suburbs, and these were primarily for the elderly. Six years later, nearly 11,000 units—35 percent of the subsidized housing units—were located in the suburbs and 58 percent of the suburban units serve families. The number of communities providing subsidized housing has increased in six years from 13 to 90.[23]

The pattern of dispersal in Indianapolis resulted from UNIGOV giving the city the same sort of ability to condition desired approvals upon cooperation in providing dispersed subsidized housing. According to one official, the city followed a conscious policy of demanding that large apartment developers undertake subsidized projects in appropriate areas as a quid pro quo for zoning approval for the luxury projects they were eager to build. The arm-twisting approach is more formalized in the regulations governing the Clinton Special District in New York City. Under those regulations, if a developer wants the maximum FAR for luxury apartments on Eighth Avenue, he must make a commitment to providing a certain number of units in the Clinton neighborhood for low- and moderate-income housing. (Both schemes are discussed in more detail in later chapters.)

Of course, these exceptional records must be contrasted with the rather more typical approach of cities and suburbs to subsidized housing, capsulized in the explanation given by a Boston Housing Court judge for why 40 percent of all the units in one city neighborhood are subsidized:

> Why has it happened? Because there's no resistance to locating such subsidized housing or at least the neighborhood is divided on the issue. There is no united front like there would be in the suburbs. There is some vacant land down there and the development occurs in the City for two reasons. One, the people fight it like hell in the suburbs; and two, the politicans get campaign contributions from the developers. It's as simple as that.

Nevertheless, the emerging trend toward middle-class occupation of the cities and the flickering hope that the displaced poor may find greater opportunities for decent housing, both market rate and subsidized, throughout the city and the region are, for cities, signs of considerable hope. In fact, some have begun to suggest that cities ought to encourage and capitalize upon the forces that are not only gradually reducing their populations but also gradually increasing the percentage of middle-class families and individuals in that population. At hearings conducted by the House Committee on Banking, Currency, and Housing on the future of cities, late in 1976, retired industrialist Paul R. Porter proposed that "decayed and obsolete inner-city districts should be transformed into neighborhoods attractive enough to compete with suburbs, especially for people who work in the central business district and other nearby places...," and that the poor and underemployed population of the central cities "should be assisted to obtain suitable housing and nearby work opportunities outside large cities."[24]

Roger Starr, an editor of the *New York Times* and former administrator of New York City's Housing and Development Administration, stirred up a hornet's nest by proposing that the most deteriorated sections of New York City be subjected to "planned shrinkage" of city services. Simply stated, Starr's position is that cities can no longer go on planning on the assumption of constant growth. But, as Starr has noted, "... even if the city declines in population, it can continue to provide a richly rewarding environment for millions of its people of every class and race...."[25] In his view, the way to capitalize upon the current decline in city population is simply to cut back on services in the worst sections of the city and to encourage their abandonment in favor of other areas capable of affording a higher quality environment.

As Starr sees it, the role of the city planner "...is not to originate the trend of abandonment but to observe and use it so that public investment will be hoarded for those areas where it will sustain life." Thus stated, Starr's theory is far more humane than the actual practice has been for many years. In practically every city, no one planned the withdrawal of city services from areas abandoned by the white middle class; it has just happened as a matter of course. Rather than being a conscious response to already existing deterioration, it has been a cause of it. Rather than being combined with programs to ensure that the area's population would be gradually relocated into a better environment, it has been teamed with policies consciously directed toward preventing the escape of low-income and minority families from these areas.

Whether it be by downzoning rediscovered neighborhoods to be certain they are protected from high rises or by pouring money into middle-class city neighborhoods or by bombarding middle-class suburbanities with commercials on the "Tonight Show" that sing the joys of city living (as Seattle has done), it is plain that cities in the United States are making a growing commitment to the resurrection and preservation of middle-class city neighborhoods. Concern for the displaced poor has been all but lost in the shuffle. The pace of the rediscovery process may be sufficiently slow to allow emerging social and economic forces to work a gradual solution to the problem. On the other hand, it may be that we will go on as a racially and economically segregated society, with the players simply switching sides of the city line. For the present at least, the problem is being addressed, at best, with nothing more than—what was that phrase?—benign neglect.

SLUMS AND GRAY AREAS

The problems created by areas that have been "discovered" are bearable; they are the problems of hope. The problems of stable areas threatened by the intrusion of bothersome uses are bearable; they are problems for which solutions are comparatively easy. But the problems spawned by the slums of our cities and by those gray areas that are neither slum nor stable are the problems of despair and there are no easy solutions. The most glaring failures of urban zoning policy and practice are to be found in these areas.

With rare exceptions, like San Diego (or Watts) where the slum looks like many middle-class neighborhoods in other cities, or Honolulu where land and housing shortages make it very difficult for anything like a slum to get started, every city has areas that have plain bottomed out. No zoning ordinance is going to make much difference in those areas. There are limits to what the police power can do. In most cities, however, instead of helping, or even being neutral, zoning policies seem to compound the problems by pretending that the slum does not exist. Some of the slum may be zoned for apartments or commercial, even though the existing development pattern is single-family or duplex. The hope seems to be that if you pretend it is new apartments and stores, it may become that. What happens, of course, is that the increased density is crowded into structures and infrastructures that were not designed to and cannot handle the load.

Some slums, on the other hand, are subjected to the same "R-2" or "R-3" regulations as the middle-class neighborhoods, which they resemble only in the remnants of nearly obliterated development patterns and densities. The result of treating the R-2 slum as though it were a subdivision of tidy bungalows is that low-income residents who would welcome any convenient shopping are protected from its "intrusion" into their neighborhood; similarly, the same zoning provision that protects the middle-class homeowner against having the doctor next door open an office in his house safeguards the welfare mother against the adverse effects of a free clinic locating in her neighborhood.

The greatest failure of zoning, however, is not its inability to deal with slums once formed but, rather, its role in the creation of those slums in the first place. Atlanta, Georgia, and Jacksonville, Florida, provide prototypes of how a gray area can be turned into a slum by, in one case, scandalous zoning practices and, in the other case, well-intentioned but misguided zoning policies.

What happened to Atlanta neighborhoods two and one-half decades ago as they went through white flight and racial transition is typical of a pattern evident in other cities. As the racial transition of a neighborhood begins, white owners begin selling their property; but, before they do, they get their friends at City Hall to rezone it for commercial or high-intensity residential use to jack up the price. In Atlanta, that meant that vast single-family neighborhoods circling the central business district were zoned for multiple-family use. The zoning ordinance contained no standards to control the conversion of structures and lots from single-family to multiple-family use. The lots were too small to accommodate both apartments and parking, and so little parking was required. Densities of 40 units per acre with parking requirements of three-quarters of a space per unit became the norm. Just as increasing population densities demanded increased levels of public services, those services were withdrawn in favor of what the city considered to be more "viable" areas. If someone were asked to draft regulations for the "R-40 Slum Residential District," it would be difficult to improve on that model.

Jacksonville provides an example of another typical pattern. Like practically every city, it is plagued by the existence of neighborhoods full of large old houses that are simply too big and out-of-date to serve as economic dwellings for most families. In many ways, these neighborhoods are physically like those being "discovered" by people who are turning boarding houses back into single-family homes. But they probably are not as conveniently located or else have not yet declined to the point where gut rehab is warranted or economic. In any event, there are only so many well-heeled young professional couples who think they need nine or ten rooms for a two- or three-person family. So the question becomes what to do with these large old relics.

One answer that has been very popular is to rezone them to a very intense use in the hope that someone will knock them down. A classic example is Jacksonville's Powell Place, a narrow, half-block-long residential street that dead-ends at the St. Johns River.

When Jacksonville was consolidated with Duvall County in 1968, the planners decided that Powell Place was one of those single-family areas destined for decline. Their response was to draft a zone of the type with which many of us have toyed in our more hopeful but less inspired moments. The name of the zone told the whole story: it was dubbed the "Residential-Multiple-Office-Institutional District" (RMOI). The idea was to permit anything that anybody wanted to do in hope that somebody would do something. Having created the district, the planners had to map it; and, not surprisingly, it was decided that only one side of Powell Place should be zoned RMOI. It then became obvious that some "transition" zoning would be required for the other side. The planners could see that once the magical transformation took place, no one who could afford not to would want to live across from what RMOI wrought. So they made lower cost housing economically feasible by zoning the other side of the block "RG-30," which permitted 30 units to the acre on a dead-end street not wide enough for parking on both sides.

The Powell Place rezoning worked about as well as those things ever do. For several years, just about no one knew that there had been any change. All the people living in the big old single-family houses kept living in them. Then, gradually, some of the houses were taken over by absentee owners. As the leaders of the local neighborhood group put it, instead of being maintained, the houses were "carried" as investments by their absentee owners.

The block continued to deteriorate until, seven years after the rezoning, the remaining resident homeowners banded together to request a downzoning back to the single-family designation, which many of them had not realized they lost. At the time, every house on the block was still used for residential purposes.

The move to abolish RMOI was the impetus required to make RMOI work. One of the absentee owners got wind of the community movement and took immediate steps to get a building permit for a medical-office building. As the rezoning battle gained heat, the absentee owner played his trump card. It does not take much of anyone's approval to demolish a house. So he knocked it down. The neighbors did not give up; they continued to press the city to rezone the entire block, including the now-vacant lot. Before it was done, the city's labor unions, the Northeast Florida Builders Association, and a neighboring hospital, which had been buying up lots in the area for its future expansion, all joined the absentee owner in fighting the rezoning. Despite a massive effort by a well-organized neighborhood group and the support of one of the major daily newspapers, the move to downzone Powell Place was defeated. At last report, Powell Place remained zoned RMOI and RG-30, and several houses were for sale. The lot, naturally, remains vacant.

Powell Place does not have to happen too often before you realize that "RMOI" is not the way to go. A number of other ideas are being tried in the gray areas. Each has its own problems. Planners in Atlanta tried rezoning some of the big old houses on larger streets for low-intensity, low-traffic commercial uses. According to the author of the idea, not much was ever made of it. Even if there were a substantial market for that sort of use, most cities would be tempted to funnel it into the abundance of commercially designed space that now stands vacant or underutilized along the old commercial strips. Some cities have attempted to impose regulations on conversions that would permit minor increases in intensity geared to the availablity of lot area and parking and conditioned upon maintenance of the structure's exterior. That sort of regulation probably offers a lot of hope for protecting areas that are basically stable or in some stage of being rediscovered; the demand is strong enough not to be killed by a reasonable level of regulation. Whether or not such regulations can salvage an area in decline is open to more question. In Rochester, New York, the problem was approached, in part, by making limited boarding-house uses a permitted home occupation in some neighborhoods characterized by large old single-family houses; the idea was that a few boarders were okay if they encouraged owner occupancy and maintenance.

To the extent that the 10- and 12-room relics of the past cannot be converted to some economic use, they will gradually deteriorate to the point where they are either boarded up or knocked down. At that point, they join the "passed-over" parcels in the inventory of underutilized and vacant scraps of land to be found scattered throughout our cities. Encouraging the redevelopment or development of these parcels is another of the serious problems to be confronted in any declining neighborhood: after preservation and conversion have failed, "in-fill" is the hope.

Insofar as anyone has thought about how to encourage the in-fill development of these underutilized and vacant parcels, the prescription has usually been for more of the same medicine that killed the patient in the first place. Here, again, the usual approach has been to increase the density in the hope that the land would become valuable enough either to justify redevelopment or to overcome whatever negative factors caused it to be passed over initially. Here again, that approach is almost sure to make things worse, not better. Later, we will discuss the reasons and offer some alternate suggestions (see Chapter 19).

There is, we suppose, nothing surprising about the fact that the new demand for in-city living is moving only half a step ahead of the new interest in urban zoning. Zoning may have started on Fifth Avenue, but businesspeople soon took the idea home with them, and it has, ever since, been considered nearly as essential to comfortable residential living as is indoor plumbing. Sooner or later it was to be expected that urban dwellers would seize on it as the most logical device to protect their concept of the good (or even better-than-nothing) life. How much it can help them remains to be seen.

FOOTNOTES

1. *New Opportunities for Residential Development in Central Cities* (Washington, D.C.: Urban Land Institute, 1976).

2. *Id.* at 9.

3. *Belle Terre* v. *Boraas,* 416 U.S. 1 (1974).

4. *City of East Lake* v. *Forest City Enterprises, Inc.,* 426 U.S. 668 (1976).

5. *Village of Arlington Heights* v. *Metropolitan Housing Development Corporation,* 429 U.S. 252 (1977).

6. *Hill* v. *Gautreaux,* 425 U.S. 284 (1976).

7. *Chicago Tribune,* June 16, 1976.

8. See our "Exclusionary Suburban Zoning: One More Black Rebuff to the Latest Liberal Crusade," in James F. Blumstein and Eddie J. Martin (eds.), *The Urban Scene in the Seventies* (Nashville, Tenn.: Vanderbilt University Press, 1974).

9. *Regents of the University of California* v. *Bakke,* 438 U.S. 265 (1978).

10. *Belle Terre* v. *Boraas, supra,* n. 3.

11. It should be noted that some state courts have taken a dim view of such activities and of the *Belle Terre* decision. See *City of White Plains* v. *Ferraioli,* 357 N.Y.S.2d 449 (1974), and *State* v. *Baker,* 386 A.2d 890 (1978) *aff'd* 405 A.2d 368 (1979).

12. *Young Professionals in City Neighborhoods* (Boston: Parkman Center for Urban Affairs, August 1977).

13. *Id.* at 13.

14. U.S. Department of Housing and Urban Development, *Neighborhood Preservation: A Catalog of Local Programs* (Washington, D.C.: U.S. Government Printing Office, 1975).

15. *Private Market Housing Renovation in Central Cities: A ULI Survey* (Washington, D.C.: Urban Land Institute, November 1975).

16. *New Opportunities for Residential Development in Central Cities* (Washington, D.C.: Urban Land Institute, 1976), pp. 12-13.

17. *Indianapolis Magazine,* February 1976, p. 43.

18. Some call it "up-zoning." See Norman Williams, Jr., *American Land Planning Law: Land Use and the Police Power* (Chicago: Callaghan & Co., 1974), vol. 2, §38.01 and §38.04

19. *Young* v. *American Mini Theatres, Inc.,* 427 U.S. 50 (1976).

20. *Preservation News,* April 1977, p. 4.

21. *Ebony,* July 1971, p. 112.

22. "Five Noted Thinkers Explore the Future," *National Geographic,* July 1976, p. 70.

23. Trudy P. McFall, "Fair Share Housing: The Twin Cities Story," *Planning,* August 1977, pp. 22, 25.

24. *New York Times,* September 28, 1976, p. 20.

25. *Chicago Sun Times,* December 26, 1976, p. 34.

Chapter 5
The Commercial Areas:
Out of the Irrelevant, the
Portentous?

This is about zoning in the commercial areas of our cities, the central business districts and the commercial strips. If zoning is an important tool in the urban residential areas, it is, in its most common and traditional form, irrelevant to the strength, revitalization, or collapse of urban business districts.

THE CENTRAL BUSINESS DISTRICT

Many activities are there just because they are there, in response to linkages which disappeared years ago.

—Edward Ullman

I wish the city had been less generous to me.

—Harry Helmsley

The CBD's of our cities are almost all in trouble. In some, one feels hope; in others, however, it is hard to feel anything. The difference is apparently dependent upon circumstances over which urban policymakers have little control.

If one discerns some reason for hope in the CBD of an Atlanta, a Boston, or a Chicago, that may be because these cities are old. If there is less reason to hope for success in the downtowns of Phoenix and San Diego, that may be because they have emerged from adolescence in the last half of this automobilized century. There is, we surmise, less of a commitment, involuntary or otherwise, by the commercial interests of such *nouveau arrivée* centers, and probably less cohesiveness among the commercial leaders in our younger urban areas. Often it is more difficult just to see downtown in our newer cities. As Gertrude Stein is reported to have said of Oakland, California, "When you get there, there is no there, there." Certainly there is less romance in saving such nondescript downtowns, a fact too often discounted as a motive driving many Establishment Doers and Shakers. Even though the automobile has replaced rail transit as the principal mode of transportation for commuters in old cities and though the jobs are moving outward, there remains the form of a downtown created a century or more ago, and that inspires an effort to rebuild on it, as in Philadelphia, Boston, and Chicago. No such motivation exists in the case of, say, San Diego.

In a perceptive series in November 1976, Charles W. Ross and James J. Mitchell of the *San Diego Union* wrote about downtown San Diego:

> The new high rises—clean, sharp and sparkling on the skyline—would make a lie of the deterioration facts were they not a part of the overall problem themselves. . . .
>
> There is a glut of vacant space in downtown office buildings, with 30 percent of the 11 major structures empty and 21 percent of all downtown buildings vacant, figures deemed extraordinarily high. . . .
>
> The 24-floor San Diego Federal Building, two-years-old, is 48 per cent vacant, and the early morning sun shines completely through the building's empty offices, creating a gap-toothed symbol of a city's festering economic problems.
>
> Other cities measure the decline of their downtown area by the drop in the central business district's share of retail sales in the entire city. Most civic leaders get concerned when it drops to 10 or 15 per cent, and panic at 10.
>
> In San Diego, less than 2 per cent of the [dollar value of] goods sold in the county were sold in the downtown area, according to the latest survey, which is four years old, out of date, and optimistic.

Ross and Mitchell quote an economist: "Every progressive forward-looking community needs a bank with assests over $1 billion." Nineteenth-century cities such as Seattle and St. Louis have four apiece. San Diego, the article points out, has none.

But age alone may not explain the divergence in the prognosis for central business areas; there may be other reasons for the relative states of their health, as we shall observe when we return to San Diego later and consider urban design and its relation to zoning in the CBD. For now, it is enough to caution the reader that generalizing about urban business centers is more difficult and less certain than generalizing about urban neigborhoods. That problem will not, however, stop us from trying.

From Minneapolis to Atlanta, from Seattle to Boston, the refrain was the same: "Zoning is meaningless downtown." "You wouldn't waste your time on zoning." "You could build the Empire State Building under our ordinance." "Our FAR is 25 and that can be waived." The IDS Tower in Minneapolis soars over all other downtown structures, and it did not consume all the FAR permitted in the zoning ordinance. If the bulk controls in the business center *appear* tough, that appearance may be misleading. In Boston there are six separate methods for obtaining additional floor area above the permitted base. An unpublished report by the staff of the Boston Redevelopment Authority states:

> Although the present zoning ordinance nominally limits the FAR to 10 [in the CBD] most of the major buildings constructed in Boston since 1965 exceed this ceiling by at least 40 percent. In effect, the official FAR limit has become inoperative, with permissible density being established on an *ad hoc* project-by-project basis, primarily through appeals for zoning variances.

Oddly enough, New York City was the only place where we observed any serious complaint that *local* regulations, not just state environmental laws, were frustrating developers in commercial areas.

If zoning does not play a significant role in CBD development, there are other issues that do count. Tax abatement for new development is endemic in many cities, but probably nowhere has the practice been elevated to such an art as in Boston, a city with one of the highest percentages of tax-free land and buildings in the country—about 61 percent of all the land in the city. When governmental and institutional development is subtracted from the rolls, and when new commercial development is given a tax break, it is no wonder the Boston newspapers have been trumpeting the tax protests of the owners of homes and old commercial buildings and that the city administration finally decided to sue the state to recover the local revenue lost on the tax exempt property. But not all the tax deals are made at the state level.

One way to make a tax deal for a new commercial building in Boston is under law 121A, passed by the state legislature to accommodate a major development and commonly known as the "Prudential Law." If an area is determined to be "blighted," an assessment on new commercial construction, including apartments, may be limited to 20 to 28 percent of the gross revenues. Blighted? Number One Beacon Street is a 121A building, but the ads say it's the greatest place in Boston. It is located on the corner of Tremont and Beacon Streets, halfway between the State House and City Hall, as lucrative a corner as there is in downtown Boston. "Blight," as State Representative Barney Frank observed, "is in the eye of the beholder." The Boston Redevelopment Authority, the agency that controls planning, holds the hearings to determine if a proposed development should receive 121A treatment. If it is not possible to get 121A treatment, or if a better tax deal is desired, it is common for developers of new buildings in downtown Boston to make informal agreements with city hall on tax abatement. In either case, the tax is at a substantially lower rate than on old buildings. So, as one Boston observer put it, because the mayor "runs the show in Boston" and controls the Boston Redevelopment Authority, he would have effective control over development downtown, even if there were no zoning ordinance.

Tax increment financing, where authorized by state law, has been used in a number of cities, including Minneapolis and Cincinnati. The effect of such arrangements is to make the difference in the real estate taxes before and after redevelopment available to pay off the bonds used to finance the acquisition and clearance, or to earmark the increased taxes for public improvements in the vicinity of the project.

The other major public impact upon private development in the central business district is usually outside the control of city hall. That is through state environmental laws, which we will treat in Chapter 14.

There are, however, some attempts to influence, albeit not control, development in the CBD through zoning techniques. The three most significant of these may be classified as (1) incentive zoning, (2) urban design policy (closely associated with the first), and (3) mixed residential and commercial uses downtown.

Incentive Zoning

This concept was probably first introduced into a major city's zoning ordinance in the 1957 comprehensive revision to the Chicago ordinance. It has been widely copied, though probably nowhere as enthusiastically as in New York City (see Chapter 9 on special districts). It is a way to tell a developer, "We will give you something more than you are permitted as-of-right if you'll give us something in return." It must be trumpeted that the scheme will not work in most cities unless the political climate permits a substantial reduction in what is presently allowed as a matter of right. As one disgruntled planning director put it, "the basic allowable densities were so great that nobody bothered with the bonus."

As the old New York zoning ordinance produced the wedding cake architecture along Fifth Avenue and Park Avenue, so incentive bonuses have sired what has to be the plaza generation in urban architecture, a mixed blessing, we are sure, to thousands of commuters who, six months of the year, would readily trade the frigid wasteland of the civic Center Plaza in Chicago for one adequate underground pedestrian passage from Franklin Street to Michigan Avenue.

The market downtown has been responsive to incentives, exchanging more open space at ground level for more rentable bulk above. In New York City the incentive system led to at least a temporary glut of vacant office space. One researcher, Jerold S. Kayden, concludes that New York's plaza bonus produced 7,940,792 square feet of floor area between 1963 and 1975 and contributed to high vacancy rates and deterioration in rental prices in the New York City office market.[1] No wonder Mr. Helmsley, one of Manhattan's larger developers, is reported to have said he regretted the city's generosity in granting him a whopping 312,000 square feet of bonus floor area in his One Penn Plaza building.

Of course, as might have been predicted, the glut of office space in 1976 has been replaced by a tight market in 1978. More than 30 major commercial and residential structures are under way. AT&T, IBM, and Philip Morris are building world headquarters. Now the concern is the over-concentration in the spine of Manhattan, but the incentives remain. As Paul Goldberger noted in the *New York Times,* "shoehorning" is becoming popular, particularly by private clubs that have felt a serious financial pinch. Squeezing in towers over low-rise buildings by purchase of air rights is occurring at the Racquet Club on Park Avenue; the landmark Villard Houses are saved but incorporated as part of the Palace Hotel on Madison Avenue. The prospect is terrifying to some. One developer observed, "You can't have a system in which nothing but monsters can survive unless you want to create nothing but monsters." And the *New York Times,* on December 2, 1978, gave in to a cry of anguish:

As practiced by astute real estate lawyers and batteries of experts, zoning-busting has become a high art. And the discretionary powers of the city's zoners have been exploited by the builders.[2]

Two months later, the *Times* returned to the theme:

> The builders have converged on the midtown East Side, where property is almost unobtainable, in pursuit of the best addresses and prices. To see them all scrambling to build on top of or around something else is bad enough; to see such construction encouraged at the city's expense where it is least needed is worse. The West Side continues to deteriorate for lack of new building, and Third Avenue is treated as the edge of Outer Mongolia.[3]

Besides producing massive office buildings, the plaza bonus has also produced probably more barren, uninviting plazas than anyone wanted. New York's plazas have become, in the words of one critic, "pompous and sterile." "Unfortunately," the *New York Times* editorialized, "what the city has often received in the guise of a plaza in residential construction is a decorated driveway or a bleak northern corner in permanent shadow. The 'public' space has been closed off by walls planted with token trees that promptly die, or left as ugly cement strips."[4]

It is always difficult to tell whether seemingly good ideas get perverted by the ineptness, niggardliness, or conscious decision of developers. Is it lack of taste, the almighty dollar, or a calculated attempt to discourage public use of private buildings that created so many ugly plazas standing as divorced from their urban environment as if they were bounded by a chain link fence? Kenneth Halpren, in his discriminating book *Downtown, U.S.A.: Urban Design in Nine American Cities,* suggests one explanation:

> Once the developer sees through the camouflage and understands what the architect is doing or what it is costing the developer (in smaller profits), the developer is likely to take out his trusty pink eraser, causing many a stern-faced architect to weep.[5]

Whatever the answer, the plaza era has taught us two things: first, downtown developers will respond eagerly—almost irrationally it seems—to zoning incentives and, second, unless we can find some better way to define the response we want, we might be better off if the response were not half so enthusiastic.

Urban Design

Jonathan Barnett, in his book, *Urban Design as Public Policy,* ruefully observes, "I once heard an urban designer defined as someone who knew the answers to a lot of questions that no one is asking."[6] Barnett, himself an architect and urban designer who has been in the pit of urban design politics, knows that is not true, at least in New York. Indeed, in cities where "downtown" means something and has a call on the affections or investment of those who count, design control is *the* issue. If it also happens to embrace traditional zoning considerations, such as bulk, height, and setbacks, that is coincidental.

We should pause here for a moment to emphasize that an interest in quality of design in a city's commercial center appears to be directly related to the structure of the local business establishment. Architectural excellence is often a reflection of the ego of the person who is paying the architect's fee. In cities, such as Minneapolis, where there are many home offices, one may expect corporate management to initiate or to respond with sympathy to municipal calls for outstanding design. In such communities the incorporation of design policies into a zoning ordinance will be productive. (Yes, we know Cleveland, too, has many headquarters.) In cities where the corporate office is only a way station on the path up the organization, the only question may be the cost per square foot. San Diego is the prototype of the latter. No city, not even Los Angeles, has a track record of such undistinguished commercial architecture. San Diego does not even indulge in daring gambles in design, such as Ranier Square in Seattle's downtown. (After all, a design error in 1976 may be a historic architectural shrine in 2076.) We suspect the reason for this is that San Diego is not a headquarters town. No executive of a national concern chooses to erect a monument in that idyllic and isolated southwestern corner of this country. Architectural inspiration to produce results needs a patron, and the Medicis of this era are the corporate chief executives.

At least one former member of the Minneapolis city council does not believe zoning means much in the CBD but, he added, "if you're going to build a building in downtown Minneapolis, you darn well better spend some time at city hall." Minneapolis is design-sensitive, and that city may be threatening Chicago as the locus of imaginative urban commercial architecture, as the Windy City, mesmerized by Mies Van der Rohe, allows too many schlock imitations of his work. In Indianapolis no development can take place in the CBD without special design and site plan review. Boston, in contrast to Indianapolis, seems to have been quixotic in its design controls, allowing fast-food operations to peddle their grotesque marquees in downtown while carefully regulating their appearance in quaint areas such as Newberry Street. The

Boston Establishment, it should be noted, can become more agitated over the shadows cast by Park Plaza or the Hancock Building on an 18th-century pile than by the obvious inequities in its real estate tax system.

The focus on design has perhaps reached its high (low?) point in New York City, where the sterile response of the development community to the plaza bonus has produced proposals by the planners to tighten the zoning ordinance's plaza standards with new design provisions that, if they were to be seriously applied, would require all zoning inspectors to have a degree from the Harvard School of Design:

> [The regulations are] getting to be so esoteric and so arcane that it's beyond the ken of all but maybe six or seven people. Now they say there must be a drinking fountain and that it shall be no lower than one foot, six inches in height. The next step is to stipulate how far the water shall arc and at what temperature.... I understand the theory behind it but the regulations are getting so arithmetic that many good architects find that the regulations bind them.... You return to the old cliche: Can you quantify good design?

That statement comes from a responsible critic of the New York planning scene—not, by the way, associated with the building industry.

The second principal problem with urban design, and the initial public attempts to control it, is the tendency to focus on each building rather than on its qualities in relation to the setting. Again, Jonathan Barnett:

> While plazas have introduced valuable open space into the city, their proliferation has accentuated some of the defects of the underlying zoning, notably the tendency of the regulations to separate each new building from its surroundings.... The 1961 zoning regulations have had the effect of belatedly imposing this concept of modernism on New York City, creating towers that stand in their individual pools of plaza space.... Shopping frontages are interrupted and open spaces appear at random, unrelated to topography, sunlight, or the design of the plaza across the way.[7]

Why can't good urban design be more than the facade of one building? the architects are largely responsible for this weakness because, whether they admit it or not, they suffer from the LeCorbusier complex; they become so absorbed in their own creation they ignore the setting.

Later (see Chapter 20) we offer a proposal to correct both of these flaws because, despite the shortcomings of the initial efforts in this area, we believe design controls may be the most appropriate, if not the only practical, police power response to the market in the central business district.

Mixed Uses Downtown

The IDS Center in Minneapolis is, in many ways, an urban success story. Yet when fully occupied it will be a money-loser. It is a symbol of the continuing problems that face the downtowns of major cities. The building's office space is substantially occupied, the hotel is one of the finest in the city, and the indoor plaza is, during the day, full of people, buying, hustling through, or just dawdling. "A magnificient modern version of the ancient Greek Agora," *Fortune* magazine called it. But a small movie theater on the lower concourse level was a failure—three different operators gave it up—and IDS has taken it over as a space for seminars and conferences in conjunction with the hotel. In the evening, at movie going time, Nicollet Mall is usually deserted, and the IDS plaza is frequented by a few strollers from the hotel. The fate of the movie theater is symptomatic of the 8:00 A.M. to 6:00 P.M. style of most downtowns. The effort to reverse this endemic condition has led critics to alter the old zoning rules that sought to separate commercial from residential development.

There are a number of examples of what has been termed "vertical zoning." The Prudential Center in Boston has 1.4 million square feet of office space, 785 apartments, 1,285 hotel rooms, 32 stores, and an auditorium. Water Tower Place on North Michigan Avenue in Chicago has a retail area that is a Xanadu for shoppers, as well as office space, luxury condominiums, and a Ritz-Carlton Hotel. Indeed, Water Tower Place is the only structure in the world that houses both a Ritz and a McDonald's, which helps explain the number of mink coats in line at the heavily used fifth-floor hamburger stand. Olympic Tower at Fifth Avenue and East 51st Street in Manhattan has 28 floors of condominiums, 19 floors of office space, and approximately 40,000 square feet of retail area. Renaissance Center in Detroit, when completed, will contain a 70-story hotel, four 39-story office buildings, and 350,000 square feet of retail space. It has no residential units. In that latter respect, it is like IDS in Minneapolis.

A second type of residential development is also taking place in the centers of our larger cities. That is the conversion of older commercial and industrial buildings to residential (and other) purposes. Indeed,

Walter C. Kidney, under the sponsorship of the Society for Industrial Archeology, has recently written a book, *Working Places: The Adaptive Use of Industrial Buildings*[8] (for the uninitiated, an "adaptive use" is a "conversion" that you like), providing case studies of actual and planned conversions of industrial buildings. He points out that:

> Industrial buildings frequently offer easily subdivided interior space, housed within durable construction that yields higher quality and less expensive space than could be obtained in a new building of comparable size.[9]

Usually these buildings are converted for moderately priced rental units and often, but not always, are designed for the elderly under a federal subsidy program. Seymour Baskin, a lawyer turned developer, has done this very successfully with two buildings in the heart of Pittsburgh's central business district. Retail uses are on the ground floor. Ryan Elliot & Co. in Boston converted 115 Chauncy Street, an old commercial structure at the end of the retail area near the Combat Zone. The company has a waiting list, not all elderly but also young married couples and singles. The company is planning other, similar projects. According to Ralph Memols, of the Boston Redevelopment Authority, Boston's waterfront population has quadrupled since 1972, and 80 percent of the new residents are living in converted warehouses—some paying as much as $100,000 for the privilege.[10]

The conversion practice is more widely spread in the largest and older cities, such as New York. According to a New York and New Jersey Port Authority study, entire neighborhoods in New York City are shifting from manufacturing to residential use. In the Soho District in lower Manhattan, obsolescent industrial loft buildings were converted by imaginative artists into galleries and living quarters. The city sensibly responded by changing its zoning ordinance to permit residential and commercial uses in the same area. Now, as might be expected, rising land values threaten those whose life-style inspired the new regulations. Paul Goldberger, the *New York Times* architectural critic, reported on February 3, 1977:

> The conversion of old commercial structures into residence is a phenomenon that is reaching massive proportions right now—by conservative estimates, 50 to 75 factories, office buildings and hotels in Manhattan have recently been turned into apartments or are being renovated. And dozens more are being sought out by architects for conversion potential. . . .
> The spate of conversions comes as a logical outgrowth of several recent

trends in New York: the decline of manufacturing jobs in the city, which has freed a number of older structures for reuse; the city's recent expansion of the rules for its J-51 tax abatement program, which now offers tax abatements to hotels and commercial structures, that are converted to apartments, and the growing market on the part of younger residents for urban housing, provided it offers some sort of alternative to the standard new high-rise tower.[11]

In Chicago, the residential movement into abandoned industrial lofts near downtown is apparently proceeding with some vigor despite the fact, as pointed out in a *Chicago* magazine article on the subject, that loft living "isn't illegal in most instances, but it isn't exactly legitimate either."[12] Here is yet another example of urban land use regulation marching just a step behind the real world.

The Boston experience mentioned a moment ago may suggest a limitation on this "adaptive re-use" idea. In that city successful conversion appears to require a building that is oh so old. If 19th century is good, 18th is even better. It seems that even redevelopment enthusiasts may know the difference between something that is historic, or at least quaint, and something that is just plain old or, worse yet, obsolete.

A third type of residential effort in the center core is represented by such efforts as the Dearborn Park project on abandoned rail yards on the south edge of Chicago's loop, and Loring Park, a nine-block area that, when undertaken, will be the end of a four-block extension of Nicollet Mall in Minneapolis. Both of these will be attempts at massive housing projects (with some commercial facilities) for what it is hoped will be a mix of income groups.

Will all this work? One cynic in New York said, "We've just so many Arabs that will move into the Olympic Towers. If you're building housing in Manhattan, for upper middle income on down, you need a program. Mitchell-Lama is dead for the indefinite future; Section 8 [of the 1974 Housing Act] is a joke, an aptly named program." In the Loring Park Development, Minneapolis is acquiring the land and writing it down but is finding it hard to persuade private developers that there is a market for mixed income; there is a concern that it may go all low-income.

Another risk is that new close-in residential developments may generate resistance from organized neighborhood groups. Dearborn Park has produced a bitter response from its Spanish-speaking neighbors in the adjoining Pilsen area. "Distrust, skepticism and fear of [Dearborn

Park] will continue to grow among predominantly black and Mexican-American communities in the central area until the communities are permitted to actively participate in the plan's implementation." So the *Chicago Tribune* reported the attitude of Fidel Lopez, a Pilsen community leader. Cedar-Riverside, one of HUD's most trumpeted new-town-in-town projects, enjoyed success in its initial rent-up but has been stopped by angry neighbors who used the federal courts to enjoin more construction because of the project's failure to comply with the national Environmental Protection Act. The project has now joined the list of failed new communities. All this despite glowing reviews from HUD: "Accomplishments of the Cedar-Riverside New Community Program to date include: revitalization of the neighborhood, general physical rebuilding with minimal disruption, and socio-economic integration within apartment buildings." Nothing revitalizes a neighborhood like something to unite against!

The introduction of residential uses into or near the central business district is too recent a phenomenon for anyone to predict whether a trend is developing that will make the mixed-use and vertical-zoning concept a useful regulatory technique. The Urban Land Institute, in its 200-page Technical Bulletin 71, "Mixed-Use Developments: New Ways of Land Use," published in 1976, perhaps overstates the case when it says: "Mixed use developments are quietly reshaping much of American life." But there is no doubt that something positive is happening. Sometimes small signs of life are more telling than 200-page reports on the patient's condition: The decision of Marshall Field's and Lord & Taylor, the two anchor stores in Chicago's Water Tower Place, to open on Sundays, a practice since followed by Nordstrom's store in Downtown Seattle, is a strong indication that those market-sensitive companies have concluded that a measure of off-hours economic life has returned to the city.

While the development of these three techniques to deal with the problems of urban CBD's is again a sign of zoning's resiliency and adaptability in a city setting, it is interesting to note that none of them deals directly with what must be the most dramatic land use change occurring in the CBD of practically every medium and large city in the country: the significant decline of the CBD as a regional retail shopping center. In every city we studied, and in nearly every medium-sized and major city we know, the prognostication is more or less the same, but no one summed it up quite so well as Tom Roberts, a planner in Atlanta:

Oh, you still see a few little old ladies with blue hair who have come downtown to their favorite store for 20 years and, by golly, they're going to continue to come downtown. But downtown shopping is mostly for the captive who works downtown and is turned loose at noon, and for the conventioneer and the tourist. For the rest—it's out to the shopping center.

The success of the Rouse Company in Boston and Philadelphia may be an omen of better things to come, but so far those two in-town retail successes remain the exception to the rule. A recent HUD study, prepared jointly by the International Downtown Executives Association and Real Estate Research Corporation, surveyed the situation in 25 CBD's around the nation and documented the obvious: retail uses, the traditional cornerstone of the downtown economy, are rapidly being replaced by office, financial, and governmental uses. According to the study, CBD retail sales as a percent of city and metropolitan area sales declined 16.6 percent between 1963 and 1972, while service and office employment was growing in 4 out of 5 of the cities studied. In Chicago, for example, while office space increased 37 percent between 1971 and 1977, the Loop suffered a net reduction in total retail space.[13]

Unlike most urban land use problems, where the near impossibility of identifying the causes and cures makes development of an effective regulatory program difficult, here there is a readily identifiable culprit, the modern outlying shopping mall. A trustee of one of the largest estates in Hawaii said that after the Ala Mauana regional center was opened in 1965, rents on their downtown retail properties, which were based on a percentage of gross, were cut in half. The same dramatic effect can be seen in many medium-sized cities. In middle-range cities, the CBD is typically the only significant shopping center in the region until the new mall opens its doors; and it requires no market study to establish the direct, immediate, and drastic cause and effect relationship between the opening of the new mall and the death of the CBD as a retail center. While the process is somewhat less dramatic in large cities where the retail market is more spread out to begin with, no one doubts that the same thing is happening with the opening of each new outlying center. When Evergreen East, a new 120-acre regional center outside Seattle, was proposed, former Mayor Les Uhlman let out the following blast:

> The Evergreen East impact statement states that the project's financial success will come at the expense of Seattle and other cities in the region.

They estimate the center will create a loss of $20 million in retail sales for downtown Seattle alone by 1985....

This loss of business affects not only storeowners but will translate quickly into a loss of jobs for employees of local businesses.

A loss of business revenues also means a decrease in city tax revenues. We then will be forced to choose between increasing taxes or curtailing essential city services. Can a responsible mayor ignore these facts?[14]

Despite the clear problem, the obvious cause, the moral outrage of city leaders such as Uhlman, and the fact that there are some workable zoning responses to the situation, the zoning ordinance has practically never been called upon as a tool to protect the CBD's retail function. The simple zoning response is to refuse to zone areas to accommodate outlying centers. Of course, most major cities have no land use control over their suburban rings; but even where they do, as in Honolulu, Jacksonville, and Indianapolis, or in areas where only by annexation can developers receive sewer connections, they show little inclination to use their power to stop the outlying centers. Nor do city councils often attempt to use zoning to stop the construction of CBD-destroying malls within the borders of their own cities.

The reason lies in a combination of nervousness of the city attorney who has read half a dozen cases that parrot Edward Bassett's famous declaration—"Neither can distribution of business be forced by zoning... it is not a proper field for zoning... "[15]—and the queasiness of elected officials at the thought of so directly "regulating competition." We have some difficulty in understanding either attitude.

Bassett's edict, and the cases that repeat it, have nothing to do with the concept of regulating commercial development in the *public* interest. They deal with petty, private squabbles. The same rules don't make any sense when transferred to a game in which the objective is the preservation of the unique amassing of public and private investment and interest that makes a central business district a central business district. Ten years ago, the small borough of Tenafly, New Jersey, candidly denied development permission for an outlying commercial center because it believed it would have an adverse impact on the CBD. The court held that "the intention to preserve, rehabilitate and improve the central business area... " was the only possible justification for the ordinance, and it went on:

We hold that [Tenafly] has the right [to elect to preserve its central business district], and the fact that the ordinance may give the central area a virtual monopoly over retail business does not invalidate it.[16]

For many years that opinion stood alone, but the law and the judges have recently begun to show signs of understanding the problem.[17]

One can hardly be surprised that the law moves slowly. The common-law system is designed to avoid big mistakes by taking small steps. It is more difficult to understand the hesitancy of municipal zoning officials in this area. If, as Victor Gruen has said, the central business district is the heart of the city, it is essential to the vitality of the entire organism, and the police power has for two centuries imposed benefits on some private interests and detriments on others when in the public interest those consequences were believed to be justified. Zoning officials think nothing of telling people in the business of building and selling houses that, no matter what the market thinks, only so many houses will be built and they will be built by those developers who have met the community's standards and by no one else. They think even less of controlling the minutiae of everybody's existence through zoning ordinances that dictate the type, style, and size of people's homes. They define what is and is not aesthetically pleasing. They specify the type of living arrangements that will be tolerated in "single-family" neighborhoods. They regulate admittedly constitutionally protected, but locally disfavored, speech. They intrude into the privacy of abortion decisions that the Supreme Court has said shall be left to a woman and her doctor. In light of all that, it has always seemed odd that those same local officials find it immoral and beyond their proper sphere to regulate the size, type, and location of commercial shopping centers. Ah, well, this has always been an intriguing field.[18]

THE COMMERCIAL STRIP

Crime? Oh, the girls talk about it sometimes but I don't think anybody thinks it's worse here than any place else. The two big objections are the commercial strips and the schools.

—Resident of Chicago's South Shore

There is no more baleful aspect of the urban scene than the commercial strip. It may be a dismal reminder of a past era: a dreary stretch of vacant or marginal stores, boarded up movie houses, abandoned gas stations, and dirty parking lots. If it is still commercially healthy, it is probably also a tawdry succession of garish signs, fast-food operations shouting to outdo each other, and open-air uses with their debris scattered and blowing for half a mile in all directions.

The Obsolescent Strips

No city is without them, and few cities have come up with any good ideas to deal with them. Occasionally a city will, in the course of a comprehensive rezoning, cut back the seemingly endless commercial street-front zoning, established in the euphoria of earlier, more optimistic days. In 1957 the City of Chicago adopted a new zoning ordinance. It cut back more than 750 lineal miles of commercial zoning, much of which consisted of vacant lots where dreams of commercial values had long vanished and only billboards flourished. Such efforts are a start, but they do not solve the problem of dead or dying strips. Major surgery is necessary, and it will, in some instances, require a rejection of past practices. A few cities are trying new ideas—once again a portent that land use regulation may, if anywhere, find its inspiration out of the desperation of our cities.

An approach tried in a few cities is based on the idea of transforming the old strip into something that resembles a suburban shopping center. Minneapolis is undertaking just that at Nicollet and Lake Streets. Lake Street is an old commercial strip that runs from the river to Lake Calhoun. Nicollet is a major thoroughfare. K-Mart said that if the city would vacate Nicollet Avenue for two blocks in the vicinity of the intersection with Lake Street, K-Mart would build an 84,000-square-foot discount store. An existing grocery store agreed to expand its area. These two would serve as anchors for a number of smaller stores in a suburban-type shopping center with substantial off-street parking. Additional proposals call for more townhouses and an entertainment facility. The decision to take this step was not easy for the city council. The abutting neighborhood was concerned that traffic would clog the side streets (as it probably will), and merchants on Nicollet just north of the proposed center feared the loss of business when the traffic was diverted. The city council had to make a tough choice. It concluded that, on balance, the redevelopment was imperative.

In Seattle, Broadway is an aging commercial strip that cuts through a strongly organized Capitol Hill area. The perceived Satan on Broadway—or at least the devil concerning which something could be done—was the proliferation of accessory parking lots required under the old zoning ordinance. The lots broke up the contiguity of retail stores, the innumerable curb cuts were annoyances, if not hazards, to pedestrian shoppers, and too frequently the open lots were poorly maintained and handy depositories for trash. In 1974 the city added a new section to the zoning ordinance, titled "Pedestrian-oriented Business Districts." The purposes section reads as follows:

In order to preserve, protect and encourage the pedestrian scale and character of certain established business districts of the city, to provide continuous retail frontages uninterrupted by vehicular accessways and parking facilities, and to minimize pedestrian-automobile conflicts in areas of high pedestrian traffic, the council may from time to time, as warranted, designate such areas as "pedestrian-oriented business districts" by ordinance.

This was a floating overlay district that could be applied to any business zone by council action. When first adopted, it was simultaneously applied to portions of Broadway. In these districts, no off-street parking is permitted as of right; parking lots are conditional uses requiring special approval. That approval is subject to the following conditions:

(a) The size and location of such parking area shall be necessary to the successful operation of the use or uses served; and the number of parking spaces provided shall not exceed the minimum number of spaces otherwise required for such uses. . . .

(b) Driveways to such parking areas shall not be located across a sidewalk on the principal business frontage of such district, except where no other possible access to such parking area exists.

(c) The parking area shall not be located on the principal business frontage of the district so as to interrupt such frontage.

(d) All opportunities for cooperative and joint use parking facilities . . . shall be explored and employed.

(e) The conditions for conditional accessory parking areas in R zones as provided in the screening requirements shall apply only on street margins and such screening shall be set back a minimum ten feet from said street margin, which area shall be landscaped with grass, trees or hardy evergreen shrubs. The report of the director required by Section 26. 54. 050 shall include an inventory of the available parking areas, both on-street and off-street, serving such district and shall include a report of the city engineer as to the probable effect of such parking area upon traffic movements in the vicinity and any suggestions for mitigating any adverse impacts thereon. The director's report shall also discuss possible alternatives to establishment of such parking area such as the use of public transportation facilities and cooperative and joint use parking facilities, and shall take into account the nature, scale and character of the immediate vicinity and the district as a whole. The director shall also identify the area served by businesses in the immediate vicinity of the proposed parking facility.

Existing nonconforming parking facilities must be discontinued in two years.

Broadway does show evidence of rejuvenation, but this, in part at least, is attributable to the aggressive posture of the Capitol Hill organization in fighting undesired types of development along Broadway. The Seattle planners know that such measures cannot alone turn around a sick commercial strip, and programs to develop and fund joint use parking facilities are easier called for than done. The concept is probably workable only where there is a rather dense residential area within walking distance of the strip. The significance of this ordinance, however, lies in its break with past thinking that subsumed required off-street parking as a necessary component of any commercial area. It is one, but not the only, example of a new idea glimmering at us from the future: there are some situations in which you cannot successfully accommodate the automobile and so you should quit trying; life just may go on without it.

Baltimore has launched an aggressive attack on the decay plaguing some of its older commercial strips. In a widely publicized nonregulatory effort, the city has begun a "shopsteading" program in which it will sell abandoned storefront buildings for $100 to small businesspeople who agree to bring the buildings up to code and to operate a business in them for at least two years. Low-interest rehab loans will be made available. But even when a city decides to put its money where its problem is, allegiance to the zoning ordinance remains the sine qua non: residents have been given the right to decide what types of business are acceptable for shopstead properties in their neighborhoods.

In another program, Balitmore is working with residents and local businesspeople in a number of neighborhoods to revitalize sagging commercial strips through a combination of public and private investment and financing. Again, however, the regulatory power is brought to bear. Once 80 to 90 percent of the merchants are agreed as to the elements of the revitalization plan—things like signs, facades, zoning changes—an ordinance is adopted to compel compliance by the stragglers.[19]

The Garish and Vital Strips

At the other end of the spectrum from the old commercial strips that can't possibly survive are the new commercial strips that, to the dismay of many, show no signs of weakness. They are the product of America's love for the automobile, the fast-food franchise, and the plastic sign. They appear in almost every city over 15,000 population, are repeatedly photographed for Sunday supplements as Exhibit A to the case for American environmental decadence, and are the crown of thorns for urban designers. Only fools would allow any more to be built or waste their time trying to figure out how to exorcise those we already have. We predict that in time new market technologies (or, may we hope, new consumer attitudes) may make them obsolete; they will be cleared at a comparatively low cost to the public, and one of the species—as a sort of latter-day pop art—will be reproduced and sanctified in some outdoor museum. Period.

THE FUTURE?

We conclude our report on the current state of commercial land use in the cities by reporting on a new development. We are convinced it is significant, but we don't know whether to view it as a sign of hope for cities or as further evidence that existing commercial development faces a difficult and uncertain future in our urban centers. Perhaps it is both. The ambiguous omen of things to come appeared in early 1977 when K-Mart, whose decade-long blitz on the retailing world had remade the image of suburban shopping, opened its first store within the city limits of Chicago on the site of an abandoned brickyard.

The significance of the step should not be underestimated. From its comparatively modest roots in the Kresge dime-store chain, K-Mart's explosive growth has carried it, in just over a decade, to the point where only the ancient—and beseiged—Sears empire remains ahead of it on the list of the largest retail firms in the nation. All of that growth, however, has been in the suburbs. The first halting step of this new retail giant into a major central city was, in and of itself, cause for notice. But the true significance of the step became clear in less than a year after the project, known as the Brickyard Mall, opened its doors.

The following article by Jay McMullen appeared in the February 24, 1978, issue of the *Chicago Daily News:*

One of the most successful shopping center leasing programs ever executed in the Chicago area is drawing to a close at the Brickyard Mall. . . .

Spurred by reports of record sales in stores that opened in Phase I, prospective tenants for Phase II have already leased more than 90 percent of the available space.

Michael K. LaRue, vice president of the Harry F. Chaddick Realty Co., leasing agent for the Brickyard, said, "The Brickyard offers retailers an opportunity to get in a center where they don't have to wait for the population to grow up around it. . . ."

Phase I of the Brickyard with 14 stores in 230,000 square feet opened in March, 1977, and was an instant success. Chaddick later signed up J. C. Penny's and Montgomery Ward's for Phase II, which will have more than 600,000 square feet of retail space.

Sales are outstanding at the Jewel Food and K-Mart stores—"I understand they're already at the top of their respective chains in volume," LaRue said.

The Brickyard's growing success is bringing premium rentals. . . . "The average at the Brickyard is higher than any center except Water Tower Place on N. Michigan Ave.," LaRue declared.

The Brickyard is just a suburban shopping mall inside the city boundary. It may be evidence that major cities can slow the loss of retail sales and real estate taxes to the suburbs, but it will do nothing to revitalize either Chicago's Loop or its decaying commercial strips. Indeed, it may be the symbolic last nail in the coffin of retailing in the CBD and commercial strips. If it is, it won't be because zoning couldn't have prevented a Brickyard; it will be because society no longer had any desire or use for the traditional retailing modes being replaced by the Brickyard.

If we are witnessing the end of the CBD as a retail trade center, it should not be concluded that that means we are witnessing the end of the CBD as a regional focal point. The emerging new shape of the CBD and the new zoning techniques being developed to deal with it are subjects we discuss later (see Chapter 20). Some of the bright new ideas in urban zoning may yet sprout in the heretofore unproductive soil of the CBD.

FOOTNOTES

1. J. S. Kayden, "Incentive Zoning in New York City: A Cost-Benefit Analysis," Policy Analysis Series No. 201 (Cambridge, Mass.: Lincoln Institute of Land Policy, 1978).

2. *New York Times,* December 2, 1978, editorial.

3. *New York Times,* February 5, 1979, editorial.

4. *New York Times,* March 2, 1977, editorial.

5. Kenneth Halpren, *Downtown, U.S.A: Urban Design in Nine · American Cities* (New York City: Whitney Library of Design, 1978), p. 206.

6. Jonathan Barnett, *Urban Design as Public Policy* (New York City: Architectural Record Books, 1974), p. 19.

7. *Id.* at 41-42.

8. Walter C. Kidney, *Working Places: The Adaptive Use of Industrial Buildings* (Pittsburgh, Pa.: Ober Park Associates, Inc., 1976).

9. *Id.* at xi.

10. *Little Trib,* October 2, 1977.

11. .*New York Times,* February 3, 1977, pp. 31, 39.

12. *Chicago,* April 1977, pp. 115-116.

13. International Downtown Executives Assoc. & Real Estate Research Corp., *Analysis of Major Commercial Districts* (Washington, D.C.: U.S. Department of Housing and Urban Development, 1978).

14. *Seattle Times,* July 7, 1975.

15. Edward M. Bassett, *Zoning* (New York: Russell Sage Foundation, 1936), p. 53. Reprinted (New York: Arno Press, 1974).

16. *Forte* v. *Borough of Tenafly,* 106 N.J. Super. 346, 255 A.2d 804 (1969).

17. Clifford L. Weaver and Christopher J. Duerksen, "Central Business District Planning and the Control of Outlying Shopping Centers," 14 *Urban Law Annual* 57 (1977).

18. All of that was before *City of Lafayette* v. *Louisiana Power & Light,* 435 U.S. 389, 98 S.Ct. 1123 (1978), in which the U.S. Supreme Court held municipalities may be subject to anti-trust claims. It is too early to tell what *Lafayette's* effect on land use regulations will be. We know, however, that the test cases have already been filed. For some

preliminary thoughts on the matter, see Marlin Smith, "The Applicability of *City of Lafayette* v. *Louisiana Power and Light* to Municipal Land Use Regulations," 42B *NIMLO Municipal Law Review* 179 (1979).

19. Marie Nahikian, "Here's One City Where Commercial Rehab Works," *Planning,* July 1977, p. 14.

Chapter 6
The Industrial Areas: To Have Meat on the Table, Must One Keep a Pig in the Parlor?

*You can zone it for oil wells—but you
might not get any.*

—Fred Bair

There is something uncanny about the way healthy neighborhoods and healthy industrial districts, especially in the old industrial cities of the Northeast and Midwest, seem to crowd against each other in one or two areas of the city while, elsewhere, neighborhoods deteriorate and industrial tracts stand vacant. Given the need to preserve both city population and city tax base, when the confrontation comes at a boundary between a sound residential neighborhood and a sound industrial area, city planners face one of their most difficult land use decisions.

Such confrontations are typically resolved on a case by case basis. The agonizing that goes on is epitomized in a statement by Detroit's city council president, now a Michigan senator, Carl Levin. The occasion was a neighborhood request to downzone land adjacent to it from manufacturing to residential. Levin explained his vote in favor of the downzoning as follows:

> The local industry says that rezoning will eliminate the opportunities to expand and the possible loss of jobs. The residents say that *failure* to rezone will condemn their neighborhood to slow death.
>
> I believe that the City needs both its neighborhoods and an industrial base for jobs for its citizens. In a particular case, we freqently must go one direction or another but that does not signify that, on the overview and based on all the cases, council is insensitive to either goal. . . .

Jobs and neighborhoods—we must have both. Sometimes we must choose between them. This is probably *not* such a case since none of the businesses have shown any inclination to expand or even renovate. . . .

The St. Hedwig community has made an extra effort to create and preserve its identity and its beauty. We should respond to that effort.

But when General Motors came to the city council, Levin's reaction was different:

A year ago we were asked to stop the expansion of Cadillac Motor Car Company, which was going to build a plant to box the new mini Cadillacs. . . . And they needed to change the width of a berm or some damn thing. It wasn't a major encroachment, but they wanted to come closer to the road across the street from some residences. . . . We're talking about hundreds of jobs. We're talking about people, well organized, saying, "No—we made a deal with Cadillac 20 years ago; they were going to stop at a certain point with their plant and we want them to stop there." And the Council said, "Hey, we're sorry, we want that plant. . . ." If we had kept Cadillac from expanding, I think we would have been stupid.

Nevertheless, the growing strength of neighborhood power and the obvious importance of maintaining stable populations can, and most frequently do, compel rejection of even very attractive industrial proposals when they threaten viable neighborhoods.

Detroit again illustrates the point. It is a city desperately in need of tax base but, apparently in the minds of its leaders, more desperately in need of people. So much so that when the city had an opportunity to sell 26 acres of land it owned for a truck terminal in an area that already had a large chemical plant and an iron works, the city council bowed to extremely strong neighborhood opposition and refused to go ahead with the deal—even though the city planning commission had approved the plan.

Even where neighborhood opposition is not a problem, some cities simply have no room for industry to grow. Based on studies conducted by the Minneapolis Industrial Development Commission, Charles Krusel, executive vice-president of the Greater Minneapolis Chamber of Commerce, estimated that combining all of the vacant land in Minneapolis available for industrial development would yield only about 200 acres; clearing of blighted business areas for redevelopment might add another 500 acres. When you consider that that amount of acreage is scattered across the entire city in a variety of disorganized parcels and separate ownerships and that Minneapolis, like every other city, is surrounded by scores of well-planned, fully developed industrial parks and subdivisions with vacant tracts of all sizes ready for immediate development, the problem of expanding or even protecting an industrial base becomes overwhelming.

In larger cities, such as New York and Chicago, there is more industrial land available. Harry Chaddick, Chicago's greatest proponent of in-city shopping centers and industrial parks, estimates that Chicago has 7,000 acres of vacant industrial land and possibly as much as 8 million square feet of vacant industrial buildings.[1] An earlier survey put the figure at three times that much.[2] In Chicago and New York, there is some movement to assemble land for modern, in-city industrial parks. However, in the context of the amount of obsolete industrial development and land that becomes vacant every year in these cities, a few scattered industrial parks cannot be accepted as an ultimate solution. Between 1953 and 1973, New York City lost 38 percent of its manufacturing employment.[3] Since 1973 Chicago has had a net loss of 658 industrial concerns, about 10 percent of its 1978 total of 6,672 such concerns.[4]

The problem is so massive that no single solution can hope to deal with it. In some cities, most notably Atlanta, one senses an acceptance of what is viewed as an inevitable loss of industrial tax base. Several Atlanta officials and staff members all but said that the loss of industry was not something Atlanta was going to fight. If the suburbs want industry, that seems fine with Atlantans; they will be happy to become the white-collar service center of the South. It may be that even the traditionally industrial cities of the Northeast and the Midwest will have to eventually accept the same conclusion.

A recent study by the New York and New Jersey Port Authority of 266 manufacturing companies that left New York showed that, in addition to avoiding high labor costs and taxes, industries relocated because of the need to replace obsolete facilities and to find more room for expansion.[5] Between 1962 and 1970, Minneapolis lost 176 of its industries. The Minneapolis Industrial Development Commission conducted a survey of those firms and found that the principal reasons given for the relocation was a lack of space for expansion. Lack of local government cooperation was the second major problem cited.[6] A 1973 Urban Land Institute study in Baltimore showed that the average industrial site in that city was 17 percent as large as sites in nearby suburbs.[7] To compound the problem, much of the industrial development in major cities predated the time both of highly mechanized, large-scale manufacturing and of near-total reliance on the automobile and truck for passenger and freight movement. The result is multi-storied buildings with FAR's in excess of 1.0 crowded along obsolete rail and water transportation corridors.

Industry's need for one-story, sprawling plants on lots having 50 percent or more of their area reserved for truck loading, employee parking, and future expansion coupled with the high cost and scarcity of inner-city land in large parcels separated from residential areas may prove an impossible obstacle to overcome; but not many cities are yet willing to concede that.

In Minneapolis, for example, the Minneapolis Industrial Development Commission (MIDC) has launched an all-out assault on the problem of declining industrial base. Using a $400,000 appropriation from the city, it has instituted a land acquisition and reserve program; the city has also begun using one of the suburb's most effective industry-luring weapons, industrial development bonds, to finance construction and expansion of industrial buildings; MIDC is supporting the use of tax-increment financing to assemble large enough parcels of city land for industrial parks. Six parks are currently being developed in Minneapolis; the city is also seeking to restore the traditional advantage cities enjoyed as centers of economic transportation by developing a municipal harbor terminal that will permit the easy transfer of shipments between railroad and economic barge transportation; finally, MIDC is supporting a vocational training program to assure a supply of appropriately skilled laborers.[8]

In Philadelphia, the city and the Greater Philadelphia Chamber of Commerce established a quasi-public corporation known as the Philadelphia Industrial Development Corporation (PIDC). PIDC assembled and developed parcels totaling 1,100 acres. In several instances the city designated the corporation as redeveloper for industrial land cleared in renewal areas. Project capital was made available to developers through a revolving fund and low-interest loans. PIDC also undertook a $1.5 million, three-year marketing program to attract new business.

Chicago has created the Chicago Economic Development Commission, which has, in turn, produced the "Chicago Plan for Economic Development." Under the plan the following bale of incentives is available to industrial developers who locate in one of four "target areas":

1. Industrial revenue bonds, tax exempt, producing an interest rate savings of about 2% on industrial financing.

2. Property tax relief on industrial construction, a direct reduction of 60% in real estate taxes over a 13-year period on new construction.

3. Federally guaranteed loans.

4. Assistance in site assembly.

5. Direct savings in costs to companies and developers resulting from assistance in installing water, sewer, streets, parking, landscaping, and security improvements.

6. Sales and use tax breaks on manufacturing equipment.

7. Job training funds. A company receives half the wages of a new employee for up to a year.

8. Reduced carrying charges on industrial parks through joint venture. The Economic Development Commission will undertake limited joint ventures with developers in target areas.

Over $250 million in public and private money has been earmarked to implement the program.

These examples are enough to make the point about industry in the city: The economic disincentives to industry either remaining in obsolete city plants or building new plants in the city (coupled with other disincentives such as higher taxes, crime, and lack of skilled and semi-skilled labor) are so great that only massive, comprehensive programs involving the investment, in one form or another, of public funds is likely to enjoy even a glimmer of success in slowing the industrial exodus. When the suburban competition is offering a qualified labor force, lower taxes, plenty of cheap land located conveniently to modern transportation (and to the boss's home and country club), and is willing to finance the whole deal with industrial revenue bonds, one must begin to admit that notions of a police power response become all but fanciful. We wish we had a bright idea for a zoning package that would attract industry back to the city, but we don't. Part III, in which we offer our ideas, has no chapter on industrial zoning.

While we cannot suggest that cities abandon the effort to maintain their traditional economic base through non-police-power programs (indeed, we refer them to our discussion of "The City as Developer or Landlord" in Chapter 16), we would caution that in pursuing such programs, city governments keep an eye open to the possibility that they are consuming an undue amount of their limited resources and energy in trying to buck what may be an inevitable trend in the evolution of metropolitan land use patterns. Libby Howland made the point in her review of *Suburbanization and the City* by Thomas Stanback and Richard Knight:

> Municipal governments find it more politically rewarding to be responsive to their cities' lagging sectors, which however much in decline, are the employers of proportionately more resident-voters, than to be responsive to strategic firms and institutions.
>
> "Attention is focused on the region's weakness, and a generalized pessimism develops. As the city loses sight of its strengths, the vision of the city's future becomes blurred; the region turns against itself; sectors exercise their veto power with increasing frequency." The approach that concentrates on job retention schemes in the lagging sectors—plant expansion and attraction schemes—is simply buying time, because the "discipline of economic forces eventually wins out as local resources become exhausted."[9]

Of course, the fact that cities may not be able to win the war doesn't mean they should abandon the troops in the field. Inasmuch as major cities now have a substantial industrial base, there are a number of industrial zoning issues that should be addressed.

First, even if the zoning ordinance cannot be a major weapon with which to attract industry, it should at least avoid being a deterrent. What we say elsewhere about eliminating useless red tape, unnecessary delay, and pointless substantive regulations applies here with a special urgency.

We should also mention the issue of industrial performance standards, an idea which enjoyed great popularity in the two decades after Dennis O'Harrow first introduced it in 1951,[10] but whose time has, we think, all but passed. As everyone knows, the major trouble with industrial performance standards was always the cost and difficulty, for both industrialist and zoning officer, in knowing whether the highly technical standards were met. Administration and enforcement have been especially difficult in major cities where major industrial development occurred long before any regulations existed to control it. In Detroit, for example, city officials, fearful of hampering efforts to attract new industry with complex performance standards and faced with a fait accompli as to existing industry, rejected performance standards and established an Industrial Review Committee to evaluate proposals for industrial development. The committee is composed of a qualified representative from the City Plan Commission, the Detroit Department of Health—Bureau of Industrial Hygiene, the Wayne County Department of Health—Division of Air Pollution Control, the Mayor's Committee for Industrial and Commercial Development, and the Fire Marshal. Consciously opting for the discretion allowed by avoiding specific performance standards, the Detroit Code is brief in describing the duties of the Industrial Review Committee:

> When requested, the Committee shall review and investigate the site plan, the operating characteristics and processes, the type of machinery and equipment proposed, or any other facet of the proposed industry, especially as regards external emissions such as noise, vibration, smoke, odor, noxious gas, dust, dirt, glare, heat, or other discharge or emission that may be harmful to adjacent or surrounding land uses. The Committee shall submit its report to the Commission and recommend that the use be permitted, denied, or be permitted subject to certain changes or alterations such as the installation or deletion of mechanical devices or equipment, changes in construction details, provision of yards, fencing, setbacks, or any other change deemed desirable to properly blend the proposed use into the area.

Detroit's decision must certainly have been made easier by the realization that a variety of other government agencies would be enforcing specific pollution regulations. With the advent of increasingly sophisticated federal and state environmental regulations and enforcement mechanisms, the idea of costly local enforcement of local performance standards seems a needless redundancy for both the local government and the industrial community. Legally, such local efforts are, in any event, frequently pre-empted by federal and state laws and regulations. A few years ago, in Rochester, New York, the city devoted a quarter of its total budget for a new zoning ordinance to the development of performance standards only to conclude that newly adopted state legislation left the city with little authority and no reason to adopt them. As adopted, the ordinance contained relatively traditional permitted and prohibited use lists, along with use limitations that prohibited nuisance-type impacts; that assumed that high-impact industries would be segregated from residential, commercial, and low-impact industrial uses; and that required submission of permits from state and county pollution agencies as part of the zoning application.

Rochester's experience in preparing a new ordinance also highlighted what is perhaps the most troublesome of all the industrial zoning issues facing big cities. It is the issue with which we began this chapter:

what to do at the boundary where healthy industry meets healthy neighborhood. While zoning cannot remove the conflict, it can ease the tension by smoothing the transition and removing some of the more obvious irritants.

In Rochester, some of the city's strongest and best organized neighborhoods and some of the industrial giants around which the city originally grew and upon which its economy still depends stand facing each other across a thin zoning line. More than once, industry had sneaked across the line—first with a rezoning for a parking lot, then with a building expansion onto the newly zoned land. In its new zoning ordinance, commissioned largely at the insistence of a coalition of neighborhood groups and drafted in close consultation with both industrial and neighborhood leaders, the city included an array of special provisions and devices to keep both reasonably happy. Three separate devices provide for the encroachment of industrial parking into residential areas, but both the substantive conditions and the procedural requirements for approval get tougher as the encroachment gets more aggravated. Another pair of regulations applies special standards to lots on either side of the zoning boundary between residential and industrial. The ordinance also provides special screening, signing, and access regulations at such boundaries.

The industrial districts have special yard and landscaping regulations for industrial lots adjacent to residential districts. Many uses generally permitted in the industrial districts are prohibited within specified distances—which vary with the nature of the use—from residential districts. The general procedures in the ordinance assure that both individual neighbors and organized neighborhood groups will have early notice of, and ample opportunity to influence, requests for zoning changes.

In New York City, not unexpectedly, a special district approach to the problem is being tried. In effect, what the Special Northside Mixed Use District does is this: The area was inventoried; then an attempt was made to conciliate both the manufacturing and residential interests by designating as M(R) those neighborhoods where manufacturing was predominant and as R(M) those where residential uses appeared to be the principal characteristic. In R(M) districts, existing industrial plants, even though technically nonconforming uses, could be enlarged by 45 percent of existing floor area or 6,000 square feet, whichever was less. All would have to comply with environmental or performance standards established by the plan commission. In the M(R) district, existing homes could be improved as of right even though some improvements would customarily not be permitted a nonconforming use. New residential construction, however, requires special authorization by the plan commission.

We find the whole question of industrial development in major cities exceedingly troublesome. It is not so much the recognition that there is little that cities can do—short of massive public subsidy programs—to retain their industrial base that bothers us; there are any number of urban problems that cannot be solved by adopting a regulation to either decree or cajole them out of existence. Our discomfort as we conclude this discussion stems from the issue that underlies much of the debate about urban revitalization but that appears with special clarity when considering the future of cities as major industrial centers: is our ultimate goal to preserve cities in the form to which we have become accustomed or to recreate cities in some new but still socially and economically viable form. The choice of one goal or another is difficult to make, but the fundamental process could be dramatically altered depending on the decision. We cannot go on ignoring the necessity of making the choice.

FOOTNOTES

1. *Chicagoland's Real Estate Advertiser,* February 4, 1977, p. 4.

2. *Chicagoland's Real Estate Advertiser,* December 5, 1975, p. 1.

3. George Sternlieb and James W. Hughes, *Post-Industrial America* (New Brunswick, N.J.: Rutgers University, 1975).

4. *Manufacturers' News, 1978 Illinois Manufacturers Directory* (Chicago: 1978).

5. *Plants, Sites and Parks,* July-August 1976.

6. Minneapolis Industrial Development Commission, *Industrial Migration Study, 1962-73* (Minneapolis: 1973).

7. James H. Boykin, *Industrial Potential of the Central City,* ULI Report No. 21 (Washington, D.C.: Urban Land Institute, 1973).

8. David R. Goldfield, "Historic Planning and Redevelopment in Minneapolis," *Journal of the American Institute of Planners,* January 1976, p. 76.

9. Libby Howland, "City and Suburb—In It Together," *Urban Land,* February 1977, pp. 19, 21.

10. Dennis O'Harrow, "Performance Standards in Industrial Zoning," in *Planning 1951: Proceedings of the Annual National Planning Conference* (Chicago: American Society of Planning Officials, 1951), pp. 42-55.

Chapter 7
The Urban Natural Areas:
A Contradiction
in Terms?

*Any beneficent public policy, if prose-
cuted vigorously, is bound to conflict
with an equally beneficent public
policy.*

—R. F. Babcock and D. L. Callies

*The Environmental Impact Statement
is also inadequate in another respect.
The relocation of the Naval Oceano-
graphic Center ... raised obvious
disturbing questions about the availability of adequate housing and schools
for low- and moderate-income groups
and racial minorities. There is no dispute that such considerations are of
major environmental importance.*

—*Prince George's County* v. *Hol-
laway,* 404 F.Supp. 1181, 1186

The last decade has witnessed a remarkable turn around in American
values about growth and the preservation of the natural environment.
One must, however, start by admitting that the natural topography and
the preservation of open lands has not, even in recent times, been a
major issue in the cities. Most of the notable victories of the ecologists
and their allies have been in the countryside. Rarely does a lawsuit
challenging governmental or private action on environmental grounds
involve a major urban center. Only a few exceptions come to mind.
Perhaps the most dramatic was the lawsuit successfully challenging

the Los Angeles County zoning ordinance on the ground that it and the comprehensive plan on which it was based were not bottomed on an adequate environmental analysis.[1]

Most dramatic extensions of the police power in the name of environment have related to the protection of areas as yet comparatively undisturbed by man. *Just* v. *Marinette County*[2] has achieved national attention because the Supreme Court of Wisconsin said that there was no inalienable right to use one's land if, in order to do so, it was necessary to change the natural features of the land. It is not, said the court, "a taking" to deny a permit to fill a swamp if the filling would cause damage to the water system of which the swamp is a part. And the New Hampshire Supreme Court, in effect, told a complaining landowner: You paid swamp prices, you are not deprived if you are limited to using it for swamp purposes.[3]

It is a nice question whether the courts will show the same degree of concern for open space when property rights are attacked in our urban areas. There is, indeed, a pregnant footnote in an opinion of Justice Frederick Hall, the celebrated former justice of the New Jersey Supreme Court. The court was considering a zoning restriction that restrained the use of a portion of a city lot. In footnote 4, Justice Hall observed:

> The approach to the taking problem, and the result, may be different where vital ecological and environmental considerations of recent cognizance have brought about rather drastic land use restriction in furtherance of a policy designed to protect important public interests wide in scope and territory, as for example, the coastal wetlands act, N.J.S.A. 13:9A-1, *et seq.*, and various kinds of floodplain use regulation. Cases arising in such a context may properly call for a reexamination of some of the statements 10 years ago in the largely locally limited Morris County Land case.... See Bosselman, *et al, The Taking Issue.*...[4]

With a few exceptions, such as Honolulu and San Diego, when one thinks of a "city," the mind's eye pictures the antithesis of a natural environment. Yet, in most cities, some natural feature was largely responsible for the original location and growth of the city; and few, if any, cities exist—Indianapolis may be an exception—without some significant natural feature, such as the harbors of New York and San Francisco, the lakefront in Chicago, and the hills of Cincinnati. To date, the treatment of these natural treasures within our great cities has been less than ideal. Only Chicago among all the cities on the Great Lakes has a public and green lakefront. New York City, almost a century after the Burnham Plan in Chicago, is at last trying to recreate a waterfront of public amenity by the Manhattan Landing Special District. Access and views to great rivers have been all but obliterated by industrial development crowding the banks; lakefronts and bays have been filled; whatever water there was has been polluted beyond use; terrains that would not willingly accommodate development have been leveled. Still, much natural beauty remains in nearly every city. Some of it, like Chicago's system of lakefront parks, New York's Central Park, and Seattle's new Freeway Park, is man-made nature that rivals and improves the real thing; some of it, like Boston's salt marshes, Discovery Park in Seattle, significant portions of Staten Island in New York, and parts of the Chattahoochee River in Atlanta, remain in essentially their pristine conditions. One of the great challenges facing urban planners and zoners, especially in this day of the environment, is the preservation or, in many cases, the restoration of these sometimes striking natural features and areas.

Of course, it is far easier politically to save an estuary in Maine than the quality of water in the Cuyahoga River as it passes through Cleveland. Some of the success of the environmental movement in the virgin territories may be explained by the fact that the moose and goose lovers met no serious opposition from crusaders marching to different tunes. After all, it is less divisive to attack the spread of second homes for Boston stockbrokers in the New Hampshire Hills than it is to keep out, for ecological reasons, first and only shelters in Fairfax County, Virginia.

When environmentalists move into the city, however, their big green machine faces new obstacles in the form of competing and equally deserving values. Overton Park in Memphis has been (so far) protected against bisection by an interstate highway through the efforts of persons concerned with protecting a magnificent natural urban area. The result is that vehicular access to the Memphis central business district is far more difficult from outlying areas than is the case in, say, Chicago or Atlanta. And, heaven knows, the Memphis CBD needs, among other things, ready accessibility. This is not to argue against the efforts to fend off the concrete scar through the park; it is to suggest that legitimate and competing values often exist in an urban area where they do not appear when a six-lane highway threatens a Berkshire Hills landscape.

The same need to be sure of the rightness of our understandable and instinctive reaction against any proposal to build on precious open space appeared in a public debate some years ago in Chicago. That city has a number of large public open spaces, many of them within deprived areas. Some black groups proposed that Garfield Park be cut down in size by the construction on it of a school and some moderatecost housing. This would, they said, remove the necessity of demolishing existing housing in the neighborhood for a school and would limit the park's large crime-infested open area. The cry was long and loud from those who saw any taking of urban open space as a cardinal sin. Of course, most of those who protested had not walked through Garfield Park in 20 years and were not likely to do so. Bob Cassidy, former editor of *Planning* magazine, describes the use of another large urban park in Chicago:

> Every year the Hyde Park-Kenwood Community Conference sponsors a festival on Wooded Isle, a lovely island park behind the Museum of Science and Industry. Hundreds flock to the island that day to play games, see craft exhibits, ride ponies. But on the other 364 days of the year, Wooded Isle is a no-man's land. With the exception of a few bird watchers and some fishermen, the place is almost totally deserted. Crime—or the fear of it—has driven the public away. Wooded Isle, like many other fine open spaces in this city, is a beautiful wasteland. The situation is not unique to Chicago. In an Eastern city where I worked, people begged the parks department not to build parks in their neighborhoods for fear that junkies, bums, and perverts might be attracted to them.[5]

The following brief account of the efforts to preserve or reclaim open space in some of our cities, particularly through the use of the police power, should, then, be accepted as it is intended: with a recognition that in our urban areas, the need for adequate open space—perhaps even more urgent as a psychological amenity than in the countryside—requires a most difficult balancing of valid and often-competing interests. In cities, concern for natural environment must be tempered with an appreciation of the fact that natural environment is only one part of human environment. Whatever may be said for the virtues of preserving natural environments free of man (or at least free of the great mass of mankind) in the great virgin areas of our country, in cities, the challenge is to preserve, restore, and enhance natural environments for the use and the enjoyment of people. It might be said to be a natural law that the less the concern over preventing muggings, the greater the concern over preserving salmon.

In many cities, the challenge to balance natural environment with other values has not been easily resolved. The standout example of human values being overwhelmed by environmental goals has to be Honolulu, where, according to a series of articles in the *Honolulu Advertiser:*

> ... the problem goes like this:
> The most recent figures show that 3,291 families in inadequate housing were waiting for 13 vacant units administered by the Hawaii housing authority. . . . The waiting list for public housing is five to six years long.
> Less than 15% of the families on Oahu earned enough this year to qualify for a conventional loan that will buy a median-priced, $60,000 condominium.
> Less than 10% of the families on Oahu earned enough this year to qualify for a conventional loan that will buy a median-priced $83,000 single family home.[6]

Of course, the inadequacy of Honolulu's housing supply is attributable to a confluence of complex causes; nevertheless, the final cause, as Aristotle used that term, is the prevention of alteration of the natural environment. The sad irony of it all is that Hawaii's and Honolulu's zoning policies and practices have not only created human hardship; they have also, in those areas where urban development is permitted, allowed the almost complete destruction of everything that was worthwhile about the Hawaiian environment. Thus, with some happy exceptions, Oahu is fairly characterized as a place that has no environment where it has people and no people where it has environment. One could have hoped for a happier accommodation of both resources.

At the other end of the spectrum stands Detroit, a place where people problems have become so critical that a concern for environmental aesthetics is all but overwhelmed. Senator Carl Levin, then president of Detroit's city council, said:

> We just have approved a housing development on the river front. The developers of the housing were very, very clear. They didn't want public open space between their development and the river. Now Chicago would never permit it, and we shouldn't permit it either, theoretically. The trouble is, we need housing—desperately—downtown. We've got to turn the tides. We may be making the same mistake we made 70 years ago when we let the railroad use all of our river front for rail yards and warehouses. We may be making the same mistake this time using it for housing instead of requiring that it be a couple of hundred yards away—using the river front for a park. Having it accessible to everybody, like Chicago. I think we

are making that mistake. I think that we are probably doing it consciously because it is the lesser to two evils. It may be that the only way we can attract developers, in the condition that this city is in, is to give them a piece of our river front.

Levin's reaction on the Renaissance Center was less ambivalent:

With Renaissance, hey, a guy comes in and says, I'm going to put $600,000,000 on your river front. We desperately need Renaissance in this town. The psychology of this town is terrible. We need something to point at and say, "You say downtown is dying all you people out there, but see Renaissance over there, you're wrong." I mean it's a very tangible, physical thing desperately needed to try to turn around the negative psychology of this city. So who is going to tell Henry Ford, when he makes the offer, "Hey, Henry, we think you ought to leave a green space along the river front for people to walk by."

In between is just about everything else. Most cities have something to save or something to rehabilitate and some hope of being able to do it.

In New York, 4,300 acres of wetlands, slopes, and wildlife areas on Staten Island have been designated as the city's first Special Natural Area District. The natural area designation is intended to apply to any area with significant geological, topographical, aquatic, or other natural features meriting preservation; and, within such areas, all development requires planning department permission. The city has also provided for the establishment of special scenic districts where existing views must be protected. In keeping with its belief that cash is as legitimate a trade-off for development permission as are plazas, New York also offers a developer in the Little Italy Special District in lower Manhattan additional floor area if the developer contributes to a fund to purchase mini-parks in the district. Perhaps more realistic is the requirement that developers on Fifth Avenue across from Central Park, in order to obtain additional FAR, pay into a fund to help maintain the park.

In Chicago, the Lake Michigan and Chicago Lake Front Protection Ordinance designates a wide swath of public and private property along Lake Michigan as the Lake Front Protection District and requires special reveiw by city departments, including the Department of Environmental Control, and a public hearing before the city plan commission before any public or private development or any public acquisition or sale of land can occur within the district. Of course, the green and open lakefront in Chicago has a long tradition and a civic sentiment that provides a rallying cry for otherwise diverse interests. The Montgomery Ward covenants designed to preserve the east side of Michigan Avenue between Randolph and Twelfth Street have resisted most attempts to subvert them—most but not all. The Art Institute on the east side, between Monroe and Adams, was first built because Ward gave his waiver and consent. In more recent years, the Institute was able to construct additions over the cries of objectors who alleged the construction violated the covenants. The objectors, said the Illinois Supreme Court, were wrong because the additions were "monuments," not buildings.[7] On the other hand, a proposed $1 million grant to the Park District to build a bandstand was not accepted because consents could not be obtained to waive the covenants. No matter that the would-be donor was the Montgomery Ward Foundation.

In Atlanta, the Atlanta Regional Commission must approve all construction within 2,000 feet of the Chattahoochee River, and no impervious surface may be constructed within 150 feet of either bank. Approximately 1,200 acres of the river corridor is now in public ownership.

In Rochester, New York, significant portions of the Genessee River frontage in downtown Rochester have been redeveloped with plazas and walkways open to the public. The newly enacted Rochester zoning ordinance protects the river and encourages its rehabilitation as a natural asset by requiring site plan review and approval of proposals for:

> Any development or redevelopment in the [CBD] which develops, redevelops, rehabilitates and expands any use of property abutting or facing, whether or not separated by a public right-of-way, an existing or planned public park or plaza, or an existing or planned walk, mall, arcade, pedestrian bridge or tunnel, or any other kind of pedestrian system improvement plan contained in the Comprehensive Plan or the Official Map. Only that rehabilitation or expansion work which adjoins or is related to such open spaces and pedestrian routes requires site plan review.
>
> Any development or redevelopment on any lot in the [CBD] abutting any publicly owned land, easement or right-of-way which parallels the Genessee River.
>
> Any development or redevelopment on any lot abutting the Genessee River.

In addition, the ordinance establishes a special zone applicable to all public open space in the city. The purpose clause of the district provides that:

> The O-S Open Space District is intended to preserve and enhance Rochester's major open spaces and recreational areas by protecting the

natural amenitites they possess and by encouraging only that development which respects and is consistent with those natural amenities. Open Space Districts are intended to apply to all public open space of notable quality and to all cemeteries.

The Boston Redevelopment Authority has identified 143 sites, encompassing 2,000 acres, as "urban wilds." Consideration is being given to the adoption of special zoning districts for these natural areas and also to a variety of programs for public acquisition of such sites. Sites already owned by the city may be transferred from Boston's Real Property Department to its Conservation Commission for preservation as city park land.

Pursuant to Washington State's Shoreline Management Act of 1971, Seattle has adopted a shoreline-management ordinance that requires a special permit for any "substantial development" occurring in, on, over, or within 200 feet of any significant body of water or any wetland within the city. Seattle's Freeway Park, even though it involved no issue of zoning or land use regulation, deserves special mention as an imaginative effort both to create environment in an urban setting and to do so in a fashion that ameliorates some of the environmental and social disruption created by other human efforts. The park, designed by the San Francisco landscape architect Lawrence Halprin, is a man-made environment that spans Interstate 5 as it comes into downtown Seattle. What the expressway once split asunder it rejoins with winding pedestrian paths. As it passes over the freeway, the park creates canyons, complete with waterfalls, by descending into the median strip. Once in the "canyon," the only reminder of the fact that this is environment in a city is a window behind a sound-deadening waterfall where cars are momentarily captured in view as they pass. The park provides proof positive of the fact that, with a little bit of imagination, even the most destructive of our urban needs can be satisfied without total loss of natural beauty and environment.

San Diego provides a fitting conclusion to this catalog of efforts to preserve and protect pieces of nature in an urban setting. It has, like Honolulu and unlike most other major cities, a natural environment that is pervasive, more an ambience than an area or feature. As described in *Temporary Paradise?*, an analysis of San Diego's environment by Kevin Lynch and Donald Appleyard:

> This is an arid coast, with a dry mild Mediterranean climate. If you add water, and prepare the soil, this land will bloom. But its natural vegetation

is, for the most part, low and dully colored. At a distance of 20 miles, bold rocky mountains parallel the sea coast, a handsome backdrop for the landscape. Through the intervening races, small streams and deep valleys carry the intermittent mountain water back to the sea from which it came. . . .

The ocean shore is a long arc of sand, which foots bold bluffs, or seals off the dune-sheltered salt lagoons into which the rivers empty. This is still a clean ocean: the undersea fauna are luxuriant, the lagoons and bays full of life.[8]

As the same report notes:

. . . the fine climate and dramatic sight are not yet destroyed. Large open areas remain: underused military and industrial lands, numerous airports, flood plains, steep slopes, discontinuous urbanization, farms, wastelands waiting for development. San Diego is not yet committed, not yet seriously congested.[9]

Certainly, the challenge to preserve this environment is one that should be met. That is not the issue; the issue is how and for whom. Lee Hubbard, understandably biased after his unsuccessful 1976 campaign to unseat Mayor Pete Wilson, nevertheless reflects the concern of many that an unrealistically narrow dedication to things environmental and aesthetic may leave San Diego a very pretty place for a very few people:

[People have] given up; they won't fight city hall. By the time they go through the subdivision review board and the planning commission and everything else, it's months and months on end. . . . It is true that we're building more and more units than before, but they're going to be costing so damn much in rent because the people paid so much for the lots. . . . The cost is unbelievably high. The end result is that, yes, there is money available; yes, there are places to be built; but who is going to be able to afford them, that's the question.

While the tension between environmental values and other human values is most evident in cities like San Diego and Honolulu, which enjoy both superlative environments and considerable growth pressures, the same basic issues face every city. On the one hand, we have at last recognized and resolved to deal with the tendency of this society to destroy the very environments it finds attractive. We now recognize that we must make a conscious effort to preserve and protect those aspects of the environment that are important or pleasant. If cities are to be livable places in the future, they too must show some concern for their environment. As this chapter's resume of efforts around the country indicates, there is no particular difficulty in devising zoning schemes to protect or create urban environment; no bright new ideas are needed to assure the goal is met. In pursuing that goal, however, what must be remembered is that environment is a hollow concept in a city reserved for the rich and a meaningless concept in a city abandoned to decay. The social and economic realities that limit most cities' ability to pursue any goal as though it were all-important may mean that environmental values are sometimes sacrificed to, and frequently tempered by, concerns for other important goals.

FOOTNOTES

1. *Coalition for Los Angeles County Planning in the Public Interest* v. *Board of Supervisors of Los Angeles County,* L.A. County Superior Court, No. 63218, 8 ERC 1249 (1975).

2. *Just* v. *Marinette County,* 56 Wis.2d 7, 201 N.W.2d 761 (1972).

3. *Sibson* v. *State,* 336 A.2d 239 (N.H. 1975).

4. *AMG Associates* v. *Township of Springfield,* 65 N.J. 101, 319 A.2d 705, 711 (1974).

5. *Chicago Tribune,* March 20, 1977.

6. *Honolulu Advertiser,* December 27, 1976.

7. *Art Institute of Chicago* v. *Castle,* 9 Ill. App.2d 473 (1956); *Stevens Hotel Company* v. *The Art Institute of Chicago,* 260 Ill. App. 555 (1931).

8. Kevin Lynch and Donald Appleyard, *Temporary Paradise?* (Cambridge, Mass.: Massachusetts Institute of Technology, Department of Urban Studies and Planning, 1974).

9. *Id.* at 3.

Chapter 8
Pornography and Other Bothersome Things: Is That All There Is?

We police ourselves very carefully.
Have lots of big boys that stand
around. In fact, we chase girls down
the street. "Get away; go away; shoo";
just like vermin.

—Public Relations Counsel,
Washington Street Merchants
Association

You know, you can't be nice about
zoning.

—Neighborhood Leader

Fear of crime is a lonely fear in our cities. It does not often generate a coalescence of response. Except when busing is on the agenda, the school board cannot count on an audience for its deliberations about our children's education. In contrast, that proposed home for the elderly intended to be put in our block, or the refurbishing of an abandoned movie theater to run X-rated films, is the occasion for angry assembly. These outbursts more often than not concern issues that bring wry grins to the faces of the uninvolved or bemused reactions from professionals who like to view "the whole picture." This chapter is about such noncosmic things.

PORNOGRAPHY

Back in the early 1950s, a small city in downstate Illinois was revising its zoning ordinance. The consultant proposed that the city tighten up the controls over boarding and rooming houses in single-family districts. When this proposal was submited to the city council, the mayor became agitated. Such regulations, he confidentially advised the consultant, would make existing whorehouses nonconforming uses. He did not take well to the suggestion that all that was needed was to relax the restrictions on nonconforming uses.

Twenty-five years later, the regulation of commercial sex via the zoning ordinance has become a cause célèbre in our cities. Of all the bothersome uses, sex is, lately, the most thought about, which may hardly be news to many readers. The American Society of Planning Officials reported that in 1976 its Planning Advisory Service had more inquiries on "controlling pornography through zoning" than on any other planning question. The issue of local taxation ranked in sixth place, the role of the planning commission came in 12th, and problems with planned unit developments were tied for last.[1] By contrast, Harvard's School of Design proposed to hold a two-day conference in 1976 on "Adult Entertainment Districts." It was cancelled because of lack of interest. What this says about the Cambridge types we cannot begin to suggest, but out in the streets of most cities, sex is the biggest thing to hit zoning since the U.S. Supreme Court agreed to rehear *Euclid* v. *Ambler Realty Co.*[2] The efforts to use zoning to deal with the spread of pornographic uses extends far beyond Boston's notorious Combat Zone, Detroit's "spacing" ordinance, and New York City's recent attempts to restrict and gradually amortize massage parlors. Cities like Rochester, New York; Sioux City, Iowa; and Memphis, Tennessee, also debate the appropriate zoning technique to handle the crisis, as do many suburban communities in major metropolitan areas.

One reason that the zoning ordinance is becoming a popular vehicle in this instance is the ticklish First Amendment issue. Even now, in this heyday of the local community standard as the test of what is criminally obscene, prior restraint is still a constitutional no-no. Until someone thought of zoning sex, you had to wait until the movie or the book or the whatever was thrust into the community before you could nab the purveyor. Even in Boston, systems for banning books without first reading them never managed to get by the First Amendment. Banning *bookstores* because they sold books you hadn't read seemed unthinkable.

But if these uses are regulated by zoning just as are gas stations and advertising signs, what, as the argument goes, is the big deal with free speech? After all, the logic continues, bookstores can be zoned out of residential districts without fear of constitutional restraint; and in spite of the express constitutional prohibition against interference with religion, a church may have to provide a minimum number of parking spaces before it can be built in a given zone.

The other conceptual problem with commercial sex is that often much that is openly regulated in the name of zoning is illegal under state obscenity or anti-prostitution laws. The circumstances are reminiscent of federal court decisions during World War II that wartime price ceilings were enforceable against illegal moonshiners.

In various circles, the focus on pornography and its regulation by government is viewed either as silly or as a sign of the decay of society or as a threat to civil liberties.

Those who regard the current agitation as a cause for harmless titillation would relish the following book review in the November 1959 issue of *Field & Stream:*

> Although written many years ago, *Lady Chatterly's Lover* has just been reissued by Grove Press, and this fictional account of the day-by-day life of an English gamekeeper is still of considerable interest to outdoorminded readers, as it contains many passages of pheasant raising, the apprehending of poachers, ways to control vermin, and other chores and duties of the professional gamekeeper. Unfortunately one is obliged to wade through many pages of extraneous material in order to discover and savor these sidelights on the management of a Midlands shooting estate, and in this reviewer's opinion this book cannot take the place of J. R. Miller's *Practical Gamekeeping.*

J. Richard Foth, chief judge of the Kansas Court of Appeals, reminds us, in a recent article in the *Journal of the Kansas Bar Association,* of another view of that novel:

> "The matter was debated in the House of Lords," Judge Foth states, "where one peer, on being asked whether he would not object to his daughter reading the book, replied that he had no such objection, but that he had a strong objection to the book being read by his gamekeeper."

More pretentious observers, such as Sydney J. Harris, the national columnist, offer more cosmic conclusions, such as: "Our periodic outbursts of civic indignation at pornography are as foolish as they are futile, and they, actually, I believe, prevent us from examining the ethical roots of our social order...."[3]

Those observers who, like the ill-fated Larry Flynt, publisher of *Hustler,* have been closer to the action and pinched harder by the regulation conclude that society has gone mad and that liberty is lost down the tube. After his 1977 conviction and sentencing to 7 to 25 years in prison for pandering obscenity in Cincinnati, Flynt is reported to have grumbled something to the effect that: "Murder is a crime and writing about it isn't; sex isn't a crime but writing about it is."

If pornography is illegal, it is, so it is said, a victimless crime and one that simply reflects the degeneration of our society. But there is a victim—the neighborhood—and neither fatuous observations by insulated commentators nor the outrage of the Civil Liberties Union will persuade the resident who sees these intrusions as a threat to his or her place of living. Commercial sex may aggravate more in the United States than in Europe, not only because of a more virulent American strain of puritanism but also because of the different locational characteristics. In this country, even in such large ports as Boston and New York, the salacious frequently shows up in or near important dowtown commercial centers or in small neighborhood business areas within a few hundred feet of residences. In places like Hamburg and Amsterdam, to the contrary, such activities are isolated at the waterfront, where they can be played without offending other citizens.

These operations tend to congregate just as do other, less offensive uses. In Minneapolis, a liquor license was refused in a small neighborhood commercial area because it was across the street from a hardcore movie theater. The neighbors saw the liquor store as the second of what would be a series of disruptive uses. When the theater stopped showing dirty films, the liquor license was issued. In St. Paul, one neighborhood that witnessed the growth of streetwalkers after some pornography outlets came resorted to a billboard to try to scare off what they believed to be a largely suburban clientele. It read:

Dear "John,"

Warning: Tricks May Be Hazardous to Your Health.

                    The Ramsey Hill Neighborhood Organization

In Manhattan, "physical culture" establishments increased from 16 to 49 between 1961 and 1975 in and adjacent to the Midtown theater area. A 1975 report of the staff of the Office of Midtown Planning and Development asserts:

> While serving a limited clientele, aggressive hawking of such establishments adjacent to the premises is conducted at subway station points and on pedestrian thoroughfares to the annoyance of residents and the many users of the central business district. . . . Although such uses represent only a small percentage of the land area, the common perception of these uses is out of all proportion to their square footage.

The same report stated that the Hotel Manhattan, a 1,314-room structure in the area, had closed down. It was "unable to attract European package tour groups because of the changing nature of Eighth Avenue." The $95-million Uris Building at Broadway and 50th Street faced foreclosure, the report alleges, implying that location was a significant factor. Directors of a large YWCA on Eighth Avenue and 50th Street said they had to cease operations due to "the fast-changing character of eighth Avenue and the surrounding neighborhood." A recent consumer survey in Chicago indicated that the greatest perceived threat to safety in Chicago's Loop after business hours lay in the numbers of people attracted to pornographic bookstores and movies.[4] A member of the Detroit corporation counsel's office said, "I don't see them as particularly bad, but people do."

We will examine briefly the alternative techniques employed by Boston and Detroit and proposed for New York. They have received the most attention, and other cities will probably choose from among their approaches.

Boston's Adult Entertainment District, inserted in the zoning ordinance in 1974, is commonly known as the "Combat Zone," a term, incidentally, that predates its present publicity and goes back to World War II, when it was an area of almost continuous skirmishes between sailors and the shore patrol. The district is only 5.5 acres in size, and its spine is the lower end of Washington Street, which, a few blocks north, is a principal downtown retail trade area.

Successive Boston administrations had wrestled with what to do with the Combat Zone. When the Park Plaza renewal project was first proposed downtown, the plan was to bulldoze the district. Then, when Park Plaza became bogged down in controversy, someone—probably a number of people—evolved the idea of giving the Combat Zone a special status under the zoning ordinance. Undoubtedly, there was an entente of sorts between the residents of Beacon Hill and Back Bay (who perceived the threat of spreading pornographic uses into their graceful precincts) and the operators in the Combat Zone who saw an official sex ghetto as a way to cut down potential competition. (Zoning is a bagful of bizarre alliances.)

The regulations creating the Combat Zone are straightforward. They provide for an Adult Entertainment District overlaid on an underlying zoning district. In the district, entertainment and recreation facilities that exclude minors are permitted uses; in all other districts, they are prohibited.

Has the zone worked? Has it cut down crime, stopped the spread of pornography, and encouraged the operators to spruce up, if not clean up, their operations? Different folks have different opinions, but by any of those measures the idea, in our opinion, would have to get a C— grade at best. The energetic public relations agent for the Lower Washington Street Merchants Association told us in an interview in April 1976:

> *PR:* ... of course you're going to have more petty larceny. The hookers do take wallets and that is that. But murder? Rape? Car theft? The six biggies— armed robbery—we don't have that here. This is, you know, not to say that it's wonderful; we only have little crimes; but in comparison to the victim crimes, we're very low. And in my humble opinion, if a man is foolish enough to walk into an alley-like street at two o'clock in the morning, up to two strange women he never saw before, with $200 in his wallet, he ought to get it stolen, or have his head examined, one or the other, because surely there are enough ads in newspapers like the *Phoenix* who would gladly entertain for money; they needn't go to a street hooker and risk disease and defamation, etc. So comparatively speaking to the kinds of crimes that exist in the city of Boston, their law enforcement money and time would be far better spent cleaning up business problems; clearing up murder, rape. We have, what, three rapes a day in the city of Boston? An average of something like that.

> *RFB:* How many do you have a year here in the Combat Zone?

> *PR:* We had one in 1974.

> *RFB:* When was the last time you had a murder in the area that's defined as the Combat Zone?

> *PR:* One in 1974.

Dan Ahern, until his untimely death the gadfly of the Boston Establishment and executive director of the Back Bay Association, offered this explanation for the remarkable record.

> ... it means nothing. You see, what happens in the Combat zone is this: Try it, by the way, I mean, maybe you could figure this out for yourself. Here's the zone—it's very small. Now let's suppose that you're in the Two O'Clock Lounge at one o'clock at night. And you're a little tipsy. You've been there long enough. You come outside and you're as safe as a baby. No place in the world that you're safer. The street is brilliantly lit. There are cops. There are plain clothes. Not only that. The people who run that place want you to be safe. So you go get your car over there and get killed on the way. But if you get murdered, 85 feet away, it doesn't matter, you're not in the Zone. I'll tell you, the Two O'Clock Club is the safest place in the world. If you go down there and get absolutely smashed, I mean everybody's watching you, but you can't stay there forever. At some point you'd get out and walk away, and when you turn the corner—pfft.

On November 16, 1976, two members of the Harvard football team were stabbed in the Combat Zone, and one subsequently died from his wounds. There were plenty of other felonious assaults on that day in Boston, but only the stabbings in the Combat Zone were reported in the national press. Prostitutes accosted the students and stole the wallet of one. The injuries were inflicted in the ensuing street fight on LaGrange Street. The Zone line runs through LaGrange Street, and we were warned to stay clear of LaGrange Street at any time—even high noon. "These girls are unreal. They'll come at you four and five at once. One gets the watch, one the rings, one the wallet, while the other entertains you." The sex merchants in the Combat Zone are genuinely concerned about the concentration of street solicitation, but it was predictable when an officially sanctioned sex magnet was created in the form of an Adult Entertainment Zone.

Has the blessing of City Hall led to a toning up of the zone? We were told the merchants have their own code of standards:

RFB: Does the Washington Street organization attempt to exercise some kind of indirect control over what they might regard as, to their mind, "offensive"?

PR: We have an unwritten code in the kinds of film that we do show. . . . We don't allow, at least those people that belong to the Association don't bring in animals, bestiality films, necrophilia, children in films, those things that would probably be obscene to 99-44/100% of the population. They bring in straight sex. It might be they have films with three black men and one white girl, or groups of people and maybe a little bit of bondage where a woman is tied and brutalized, simply sexually brutalized. And just plain—a man and a woman. They do have women in women's films; don't have men in men's films. You find that many men like the women in women films, so they put those in. And we keep out whipping and chains and blood and gore and a woman attacking a horse and that sort of thing. Now those films are sold in book stores.

RFB: Supposing, however, I decide that there's a big market in that, and I find some space?

PR: We have that right now.

RFB: You've got that situation?

PR: We have that right now, and it's very interesting. The Pussy Cat—which is at the end of Washington Street, five feet from Stewart Street—so that the box office is within the Zone but the theater where the film is showing is outside of the Zone.

RFB: In that forty foot buffer?

PR: Right. Within that forty feet, and they have been showing SM films. We've had them busted five or six times and got them in court now, and I've complained to the Boston Redevelopment Authority, and we are having a hearing on whether or not they're within the boundaries.

RFB: Are you claiming that they are in violation of the zoning ordinance?

PR: Yes. And Dan Ahern will tell you that I'm a terrible nit-picker for getting—for being allowed to get away with that in the press....

RFB: But suppose somebody wanted to locate one of those—where they're going to focus on bestiality or things like that, children—and they were clearly located within the Zone?

PR: Number one, they couldn't do it.

RFP: Why not?

PR: Well, the theaters that are in the Zone are all run by the same people right now, and they wouldn't change. And they own the buildings that the theaters are in. So they wouldn't change that. If they did, we would just create a stink. And it would have to be someone who had oodles of money to waste because I would have every film busted immediately upon showing, and we could do that. That you can do. Anytime you want to give the police something bad to do, they'll come help you.

RFB: But there's nothing in the zoning ordinance—I'm asking the question now—that makes a distinction?

PR: Nothing whatsoever.

The Pussy Cat theater has an odd zoning problem. Tufts Dental School is just across Stewart Street from the Adult Entertainment Zone.

Because of pressure from the school, the boundary of the Zone was moved 40 feet back from Stewart Street, so the entrance to the Pussy Cat is within the Zone but most of the theater is outside the Zone. The Lower Washington Street Merchants Association charges in court that the theater is in violation of the ordinance because most of the theater lies outside the Zone. They protest because the owners of the Pussy Cat are, they say, showing films the Association regards as obscene. True? Not according to Dan Ahern:

> *DA:* ... they want the city to close these people? They're crazy. Absolutely out of their minds.... That place is 97% inside the zone. You buy a ticket, you're on the edge of the Zone; if you turn right and go in one door you may be outside. If you go in the other door, you're inside. You walk down the line, if you turn left to your seat you're in the Zone. The projection booth might be outside the Zone. You know, they just want to really knock off the competitors.
>
> *RFB:* The other merchants claim they're trying to get rid of that one Pussy Cat because it's showing the kind of stuff that they don't want shown.
>
> *DA:* Yes, because it's better than theirs. And I'll tell you this: go see it. They buy the crappiest movies from the cheapest dealers in New York—I mean they're grainy films that are upside down—this guy has got "Sodom and Gomorrah" which apparently—I never saw it but it's made with real actors.... When it came to Boston it came at the end of the street in the Pussy Cat and these clowns—its laughable—this one group tried to put another one out of business. The fact of the matter is the guy who runs the Pussy Cat, who was a garment dealer in New York or something, built the only hard-core porno theater that doesn't smell.... It's a fixed-up place. And he buys expensive hard-core films. The rest of these guys are peddling junk.

The Merchants Association alternates between being upset that "really weird stuff will be shown" and being concerned that with all the national publicity the Combat Zone will become too respectable. Its PR agent wagers that on some nights half the audience in the Two O'Clock Club is from the national media. ABC was shooed off one night because CBS had disrupted a show the same week.

The Boston Redevelopment Authority (BRA) believes the Combat Zone can stand some sprucing up. It created a mini-park in the heart of the Zone known as Liberty Tree Park. One critical article responded: "BRA built the expensive brick-lined, brightly lit Liberty Tree Park as a 'catalyst for investment' and they got three more dirty book stores and a strip club."[5] BRA designers suggest ways for the merchants to improve their facades. But in the view of some, it will take more than that: "The atmosphere is gaudy, raunchy and sleazy. . . . BRA purports to be creating a little bit of Copenhagen in the middle of Boston. . . . Meanwhile, the Danes are cracking down on the original product."[6]

Has the Zone cut down on the spread of porno to other areas of Boston? Probably, but the industry, as with all cartels, has its problems policing competitors, even with government support.

The Boston Backgammon Club on Boylston Street, Ahern said, is an adult entertainment operation. In another operation outside the Zone, Ahern recounted this experience:

> I told [the entrepreneur] he was opening an illegal strip club and he said: "belly dancers." We went up there at one o'clock at night. He said, "Look, it's a chess club." So we go stumbling by the stage, through the bar, and he's got a chess table. I said, "Let's see the pieces." There were nine white ones and ten black ones. And I said: "You can't play chess without 12 pieces on each side." "Oh," he says, "I didn't know that."

Detroit chose an opposite strategy from that tried in Boston. Long before adult book stores and hard-core movies had become a hot issue, Detroit's ordinance contained an "anti-skid-row" provision that required minimum distances between unattractive uses such as secondhand bookstores, bars, and transient hotels. Spacing provisions between gas stations are almost as old as zoning itself. So it was plausible for Detroit to go that way.

In November 1972, the city council amended the skid row zoning ordinance by adding definitions (themselves nearly obscene) of four new skid row uses—adult bookstores, motion picture theaters, minitheaters, and cabarets—and by prohibiting the location of any such use within 500 feet of any building containing a dwelling or rooming unit or within 1,000 feet of any other use on the list of skid row uses.

The movie operators, including Pussy Cat Theaters of Michigan, took the city to federal court. The trial court held the ordinance valid in the face of the assertion that it violated the First Amendment to the United States Constitution. The circuit court reversed and held the ordinance violated the equal protection clause of the Fourteenth Amendment. The United States Supreme Court reversed the circuit court and upheld the ordinance.[7] After quoting Voltaire ("I disapprove of what you say, but I will defend. . . ." etc., etc.), Justice John Paul Stevens, writing for himself and three other justices, observed that "few of us would march our sons and daughters off to war to preserve the citizen's right to see 'Specified Sexual Activities' exhibited in theaters of our choice." Stevens' opinion explicitly concurred with the view of the trial court on the impact of these uses upon neighborhoods. The trial court had said:

> They attract the kinds of people who frequent these places and drive away those who do not. This contributes to the decline of a neighborhood. A concentration of such businesses also causes the neighborhood to appear to be declining and this causes a lack of neighborhood pride, resulting in a further decline. Nor is it possible to set aside certain areas where these business uses are to be concentrated, as is done with industrial uses, since the businesses, like other commercial uses, must have some proximity to residential areas and access to a suitable market.[8]

Justice Lewis F. Powell, who may yet be remembered as "the fifth on the fence," concurred in the result reached by the Stevens group but filed a separate opinion in which he disagreed with Stevens' rationale but nevertheless concluded that the ordinance could be sustained as simply "an example of innovative land-use regulation."

Three justices joined Justice Potter Stewart in his dissent in which he said:

> I can only interpret today's decision an an aberration. The Court is undoubtedly sympathetic, as am I, to the well-intentioned efforts of Detroit to "clean up" its streets and prevent the proliferation of "skid rows." But it is in these instances where protected speech grates most unpleasantly against the sensibilities that judicial vigilance must be at its height.

Those who choose to follow the Detroit example should remember that this was a 4-1-4 decision.

A 1976 New York zoning amendment, enacted prior to *Young* v. *American Mini Theaters,* was designed to control pornographic uses in the Special Theatre and Clinton zoning districts. Under it, physical-culture establishments, even where permitted by the underlying district regulations, would have to meet specified requirements, such as being part of a hotel or commercial facility with at least 200 rooms or being associated with a regulation-sized sports facility such as a swimming pool of at least 1,500 square feet. That raised the problem of the pristine YWCA down the street or the proper squash club across town. Every time the ordinance imposed a limitation on "physical culture or health establishments, including gymnasiums, reducing salons, massage establishments or steam baths," it had to add, "[h]owever, this provision shall not apply to gymnasiums used exclusively for the following sports facilities: basketball, handball, squash or tennis." One could already see the new marquees going up on West 42nd Street: "Tennis, Anyone?"

All nonconforming establishments were to be eliminated within one year. Over 30 massage parlors in these areas were closed down. In 1978, the idea was applied citywide via a zoning amendment barring future heterosexual massage and requiring existing uses to close one year from its effective date.

A more ambitious adult-use zoning amendment proposed in 1977 and patterned on Detroit's model failed of enactment. All "adult establishments" were banned within 500 feet of residential zones. Even where the ordinance permitted such establishments, it provided that no more than three (two in outlying commercial districts) could be within a 1,000-foot radius of each other.

The staff report that recommended the ordinance concluded:

> The proposed zoning text is not a panacea, nor should it in any way be viewed as a substitute for vigorous enforcement of the penal law against criminality wherever found.

The proposed ordinance seemed destined for certain adoption, until, on the day of the hearing before the Board of Estimate, the headline on the *New York Post* proclaimed: "Porno Zone Set Up in Manhattan." As our brief description of the ordinance indicates, the headline was incorrect; but as so often happens in such emotional fracases, one thing led to another and the Board of Estimate never adopted the ordinance. Norman Marcus recounted the whole mess in great detail in his article "Zoning Obscenity: The Moral Politics of Porn."[9]

New York's proposed ordinance represented the third-generation model of porn zoning; its fate represents the second generation of citizen response. From active support for some zoning solution in Boston and Detroit, the trend seems to be toward an attitude that any official action that recognizes the pornography industry—even if it is action to limit it—amounts to some sort of official approval; and the citizenry is not about to put up with that. It is hard to say whether the new attitude amounts to just a rekindling of the Victorian idea that if we don't talk about sex maybe it will go away, or to a new perceptiveness about the problems of trying to deal with the porn industry through zoning. There is, however, something to be said for thinking carefully before jumping on the bandwagon. Here was Dan Ahern's hindsight on the Combat District zoning:

I wanted the thing to go through very badly and I had to lobby for it. I'm not sure whether it was a good idea or not in retrospect. . . . One of the things I told all of these people was that if the area was zoned it would be upgraded, which turned out not to be true; it's a hell of a lot worse right now than when they zoned it. It's a stink pot. The BRA doesn't even know that and they couldn't care less. They don't give a shit what happens down there. It's a dump. Why is it worse now? I'll tell you exactly why it's worse now. Before the zoning, everybody, including the owners of the strip clubs, bookstores and the rest of these people kept a very low profile. They got kicked around by public agencies and they always were sort of indefensible. Once the zoning went through and the publicity unrolled, they came to the top. They became absolutely arrogant about the whole thing. I mean, you can't touch those people. If I'd go down and talk to the kingpin of the whole place and tell him that the public authorities are going to get on his tail, he laughs. He figures he's got the BRA in his pocket. . . .

So, cities can take their choices. Perhaps they might find compatible the solution suggested by Russell Baker in the *New York Times* of December 14, 1976:

> Most of the problems created by New York City's booming sex industry result from the city's reluctance to treat it as an industry. Everybody concerned wants to deal with it as a problem in constitutional law or moral philosophy. This high-toned approach leads to some very elegant arguments and some splendid emotional speeches, some of them entertaining, some edifying and all useless.
>
> This sterile approach has now led the city to propose regulations which will forbid the industry to concentrate in one community and force it to spread its shops at considerable distance from each other. What can City Hall be thinking with? The answer, obviously, is: lawyers. . . .
>
> The sensible approach is to concentrate the sex industry in its own district, as the garment and the financial industries have done. Unfortunately, however, the sex industry is no more welcome in most communities than a rendering plant would be. It may be, as some feminists argue, that *femina Americana* has a constitutional right to vend her bones wherever she pleases. It may be, as civil libertarians insist, that sex vendors have a constitutional right to proclaim the excellences of their goods all over the public ways. Right or wrong, these arguments do not change the fact that most communities do not hail the arrival of the sex industry with the welcome wagon. . . .
>
> What the city should be doing is finding them a community of their own. There are two obvious possibilities.
>
> The first is the Wall Street area. A district now almost entirely abandoned at night, it could be infused with round-the-clock life by encouraging the sex industry to move in late in the day as the brokers move out. When the financiers depart, Wall Street has no neighborhood left to be resentful, and

the nocturnal nature of mercantile sex makes it the ideal industry to locate in an area now unused more than half the day.

The other solution is to locate the entire industry in one of the giant agglutinations of empty building space which now depress the city tax rolls. West 42nd Street has a set of completely empty, unrentable apartment towers near the river which could easily absorb every trader in sexual goods from Eighth Avenue to the East River, with whole floors left over for clients of the most extravagant taste.

A combination of both the Wall Street and single-structure approach might be provided in the World Trade Center, which has acres of floor space waiting. Everything could be kept way up in the air, miles from everything else. The World Sex Center, we could call it, and point it out to the children as we skimmed the city, and in that day, with the problem sensibly solved at last, they might even ask, "What is sex?"

This is an area where humor is easy—and fun. But it is also an area with potentially significant meaning for the future. One cannot help asking why the United States Supreme Court would get involved in this issue in the first place and, having gotten involved, why it would conclude that cities may base zoning classifications upon the content of speech that is admittedly protected by the First Amendment. The answer, we think, lies in a growing awareness of the need to protect city residential neighborhoods from any potentially deteriorating influence and a growing appreciation that the strongest tool for that purpose may be the zoning ordinance. Justice Powell's concurring opinion in the *Young* case put it most succinctly:

> Nor is there doubt that the interests furthered by this ordinance are both important and substantial. Without stable neighborhoods, both residential and commercial, large sections of a modern city quickly can deteriorate into an urban jungle with tragic consequences to social, environmental, and economic values. While I agree with respondents that no aspect of the police power enjoys immunity from searching constitutional scrutiny, it also is undeniable that zoning, when used to preserve the character of specific areas of a city, is perhaps "the most essential function performed by local government, for it is one of the primary means by which we protect that sometimes difficult to define concept of quality of life." Village of Belle Terre v. Boraas, 416 U.S., at 13 (Marshall, J., dissenting).[10]

It is difficult to disagree with that ringing sentiment, but, on the other hand, one occasionally gets the feeling that Big Brother is alive and well and hiding in the zoning ordinance. In those moments, Justice Harry A. Blackmun's dissent in *Young* sounds pretty sensible:

We should not be swayed in this case by the characterization of the challenged ordinance as merely a "zoning" regulation.... By whatever name, this ordinance prohibits the showing of certain films in certain places, imposing criminal sanctions for violation of the ban.[11]

OTHER BOTHERSOME THINGS

Pornography may be the most publicized land use pariah, but it is only one example from a long list of bothersome uses that agitate urban residents and send them scurrying to the zoning ordinance for protection.

It seems that no one likes all-night food stores, gas stations, billboards, and drive-in restaurants. If any of them is part of a national chain, the strength of the opposition can be expected to rise. It is almost as though the uniformity of design that is so important to corporate identity and the routinization of operation that is so important to high volume and high profits heighten the impression of intrusion. They prevent any hope of the sort of neighborhood identification that might make such uses an acceptable part of a residential environment.

Of course, the national franchises have never really demanded that we love them; all they ask is that we eat their chicken and buy gas only with their credit card. They have succeeded not by being loved but by being convenient. There may be limits to success based on little more than pandering to the American mania for being able to do everything quickly, efficiently, and without turning off the engine, but those limits are by no means evident. Only recently, United Press International reported that, after failing in Florida and Arizona, the concept of a drive-in funeral home has begun gaining acceptance in a small town in Louisiana. According to the UPI report, the enterprising funeral director:

... wanted something for working people who didn't have time to dress up but wanted to show their condolences and sympathy. It's so nice to know someone cares.[12]

So now, in Louisiana you can even care from your car. A plate glass window affords an ample view of good old what's-his-name—lighted, appropriately enough, by the soft blue glow of a neon cross. A guest book located conveniently at window height lets you memorialize the depth of your feelings.

In cities and suburbs, while gas stations, all-night food stores and drive-ins of all sorts will continue to raise the ire of the citizenry, they will, because we continue to demand and use them, no doubt remain among us. So will billboards—but not for the same reasons. Attempts to banish them from the nation's highways have been plagued by loopholes and diversionary tactics. In cities, too, the strong sign lobby continues to frustrate—and sometimes to frighten—the determined opposition. The following is a neighborhood leader's description of a conflict in Minneapolis:

> Probably one of the most violent battles that we had in Minneapolis was about signs and billboards along the freeways. . . . Minneapolis now has an outright ban on billboards within 330 feet of limited access highways. . . . That went on to be the bloodiest, the meanest, the loudest, and to my ears the most dangerous sounding thing we ever did. . . . They dragged the unions in in great numbers. It would just scare us. They wrote scurrilous letters. . . . When we walked into the public hearing, it was the only time I was really frightened at the Planning Commission. There was an atmosphere of intimidation in the room. And a couple of years later we had to sit up all Christmas—we had to be down at the City Council on New Year's Eve because some of those councilmen were under pressure to water down the ordinance.

Our draft of a new comprehensive zoning ordinance for Rochester, New York, passed the city council by a unanimous vote of nine— subject, however, to a separate vote on the billboard provisions, which imposed new, more stringent limitations on the industry. Those sections, which had already been considerably watered down in the review process, passed 5 to 4.

Opposing porn shops, drive-ins, and billboards is easy. As Howard Gossage, a San Francisco ad man, once said of billboards:

> It is so strange that billboards exist at all that the current controversy about whether outdoor advertising should exist along federal highways achieves the unreality of a debate on whether witch-burning should be permitted in critical fire areas.[13]

There is, however, another class of these bothersome uses that do not permit the same free-spirited opposition from the neighborhoods in which they seek asylum. These are the uses that—at least according to the most recent social theorists—have a clear social utility but also have undeniably adverse effects upon a residential environment.

Part of what makes a city a city is that it accommodates and attracts a wide diversity of people, life-styles, and land uses. While there are, in every city, neighborhoods that demand as pure a land use pattern as any suburban neighborhood, cities by their nature, and city neighborhoods by the nature of those who reside there, generally display greater tolerance for diverse land use patterns. People who choose to live in urban neighborhoods frequently show a willingness to accept a degree of diversity that would be absolutely shocking to someone accustomed to the sterile uniformity of most suburban neighborhoods.

Nevertheless, diversity in the urban neighborhood is acceptable only so long as it is controlled. The regulation of diversity may well be the most significant challenge facing urban zoners. The historic develop-ment patterns of most cities, which frequently place residential neigh-borhoods hard against commercial and industrial areas, combined with the tendency of cities to attract a wide range of both residential and nonresidential uses, means that urban neighborhoods are constantly under pressure from uses that, if they are not totally unacceptable in a residential environment, are acceptable only on a limited and control-led basis.

Most characteristic of this group of Jekyll and Hyde land uses, and most troublesome to handle, is the assortment of special-purpose resi-dential uses that gained wide acceptance among professionals in the past decade. Like the electric substation of old, these uses require a residential setting but do not fit easily into any kind of residential area.

The most controversial member of this group is what is customarily referred to as the "halfway house." Whether they are called that or "decentralized social service facilities" or "transitional service facil-ities" or "after care facilities," they are essentially live-in facilities in-tended for the care and treatment (or, as is sometimes charged, ware-housing) in a residential neighborhood of previously institutionalized mental health patients, criminals, juvenile offenders, invalids, elderly persons, and other assorted individuals deemed fit neither for institu-tionalization nor independent existence.

National and state pressure—and funding—for the "de-institutionali-zation" or "normalization" of a variety of previously institutionalized persons is largely responsible for the proliferation of such facilities in urban neighborhoods across the country. An excellent article by Laur-ence Kressel in the *New York University Review of Law and Social Change*[14] chronicles the legal and social development of the belief that persons involuntarily committed to institutions for care and treatment have a right to be provided for in the "least restrictive setting" possible. Commencing with the adoption of the National Community Mental Health Centers Act in 1963,[15] law and practice have developed so as to make substantial federal and state funds available for the payment of care in such community-based facilities.

In most cities, the zoning ordinance makes no special provision for such uses and they are either permitted or prohibited as rooming houses, boardinghouses, nursing homes, and institutional uses, as well as under a variety of other headings never intended to embrace them. Where they have been permitted entrance into a neighborhood, that permission has frequently been abused to the detriment of the neighborhood. The first halfway house is typically followed by a veritable parade of similar institutions. The pattern is exaggerated only slightly in a transplanted Nebraskan's letter home from New York:

> I'm really tired today for some reason. There was a rather spirited meeting down in Chelsea last night which I attended. It seems the State of New York is putting a mini-prison for 150 convicts right in my neighborhood and then there was some talk about somebody opening up a half-way house for the criminally insane right in the next block (that would be right around the corner from the half-way house for the mentally retarded adults and right across the street from an ex-offenders program run by one of the churches, all of which is down the street from the mini-prision).[16]

Many city neighborhoods have, as a result, become in the words of Seattle Hearing Examiner Bill Snell, "institutional ghettos." Twenty-two of St. Paul's 66 halfway houses, for example, are located in one neighborhood.

The path of least resistance has typically led the halfway housers to concentrate their facilities either in some of the better, rediscovered city neighborhoods, where a returning young liberal population is sympathetic to the social goals of the program, or in declining city neighborhoods, where no cohesive opposition exists. The result in the former situation is a serious threat to neighborhoods struggling to come back; in the latter, the result is an acceleration of the decline. In both cases, not only does the neighborhood suffer, but the very purpose of the community-care concept is defeated by the erosion of the residential ambience.

A number of cities have reacted to the abuses of overconcentration by establishing some type of quantitative or spacing control over the location of such uses. In Rochester, New York, intermediate-care facilities require a special permit. One of the conditions that must be evaluated is the concentration of existing facilities of a similar type in the area. In Detroit, Seattle, and Minneapolis, ordinances have been adopted requiring a minimum spacing between such uses. Minneapolis also places a limit on the percentage of the total population of an area that can be persons living in intermediate-care homes. In New York City, areas are classified either as "impacted" or "not impacted" by an overconcentration of such uses, and no additional intermediate-care facility can be constructed in an impacted area without a special permit from the city planning commission. Portland, Oregon, has adopted an ordinance that melds licensing requirements with a conditional use zoning approach that requires consideration of a variety of traditional land use parameters as well as the issue of overconcentration.

Whether these urban attempts to control the abuse and problems of intermediate-care facilities while at the same time recognizing their social utility and avoiding blanket prohibitions will succeed remains an open question. The quantitative and anti-concentration regulations that many cities are adopting run counter to traditional zoning theories, and heavy-handed state pre-emption of the field threatens to make city neighborhoods a dumping ground for these uses. (That aspect of the problem is addressed in Chapter 15.)

Halfway houses, with their perceived—if not well-documented— threats of anti-social behavior, are the most visible, but not the only, quasi-residential uses that have recently come to trouble city neighborhoods. Housing for the elderly may seem innocuous enough, but it is not at all unusual to find severe opposition to it, as in Detroit, where senior citizen housing in high-rise, high-density buildings has encountered stiff opposition. An undue concentration of elderly housing in another city produced the following reaction:

> There were too many. There are elderly walking the streets with their pants down—literally. They foul the neighborhood. Oh, we like elderly people but, my God, this is too much. I mean, look at the size of these facilities. They are opening next to houses.

At the other end of the age spectrum, day-care centers run into increasing opposition from neighbors concerned with the traffic and noise associated with such facilities. Even typical neighborhood uses like churches and schools are no longer immune from protest. As churches and synagogues have changed from places to which families walked one day a week into day-in, day-out social centers and traffic generators, their place in the residential neighborhood has grown less sacred. Schools bring, at the very least, noise and congestion; at worst, they bring large congregations of rowdy, loitering teenagers—sometimes from neighborhoods on the other side of the tracks. Even neighborhood parks are perceived as pariahs by some people. A request by one group that the city provide a little park for neighborhood kids is likely to be met by another group's protest that all the rowdies from the entire city will descend on that particular park to harrass the good citizens who live around it.

The same schizophrenia plaguing urban neighborhoods in response to nontraditional and special-purpose residential uses is beginning to also affect neighborhood thinking about nonresidential uses. The monotony of suburban subdivisions has little attraction for many urban dwellers. It may yet be a while before someone stands up at a big-city zoning hearing to say, "Hey, you can't keep that convenience food store out of my neighborhood; I left a nice house in the suburbs because I had to drive 15 minutes to get a loaf of bread. I don't want to see that sort of thing happening here." Nevertheless, growing numbers of urban residents share the questions and concerns expressed to us by a United States district court judge:

> We used to think that we would put all the residences up here and all the shops down here. I am not too sure that it's not more human, more fun, more intimate, more satisfying to have the shop downstairs and our rooms upstairs; to live above it and be able to reach out your front door and shake hands with the guy across the street. Now you have to have a 40 foot wide highway and you have got to have so many feet between the buildings and you can't build within so many yards of a property line and you can't have anything but a residence in this area—you can't have a business in there. Why can't you? Why can't you have a doctor's office in his home? We've ·zoned ourselves into a style of living that nobody is very happy with. . . . We thought, oh, this is great. All one-family houses, all separated from each other so you can't hear the mama and papa making love in the back bedroom or the kids squalling in the front room. And it turns out that that is not very human.

Holly Mull, a resident of one of Atlanta's reviving neighborhoods, noted the trend back to what we used to consider not only convenient but charming:

> You know, one of the beauties of our older neighborhoods is the diversity of land use that developed before zoning came into being. . . .

There is an increasing trend for the young professional people that have moved into my community to establish their business, not downtown where it used to be, but either in their own home or by buying or leasing a small commercial building and establishing their business within that area. . . . And I think that's good.

Ms. Mull is right. The trend toward diversity in our urban neighborhoods is good. It not only capitalizes on the elements of urban living that seem to be attracting people back to convenient and cosmopolitan city neighborhoods; it also maximizes the range of opportunities for the rehabilitation and reuse of those neighborhoods.

In the end, however, the question is whether an urban zoning ordinance can be drafted to permit a diversity of residential and nonresidential uses in a neighborhood while at the same time controlling and regulating that diversity to ensure that it does not overwhelm the residential environment that is the essence of a neighborhood. Can a neighborhood have a mom and pop store without having a bar? Can it have a bar without having a strip joint? If it has a restaurant, must it have a drive-in? If it tolerates a home for unwed mothers, must it accept ex-cons, mental patients, and a day-care center on the same block?

While no city that we studied yet has good answers to the questions being raised about the extent to which diversity of uses is healthy and acceptable in neighborhoods and the mechanisms to ensure that such diversity does not become destructive, the fact that the questions have become important issues in city neighborhoods is, we believe, a hopeful sign of renewed urban vitality.

FOOTNOTES

1. American Planning Association, *PAS Memo,* February, 1977.

2. *Village of Euclid* v. *Ambler Realty Co.,* 272 U.S. 365 (1926).

3. *Chicago Daily News,* March 7, 1977.

4. Chicago Association of Commerce and Industry, *Chicago '78: A Consumer Perspective* (1978).

5. Daniel J. Ahern and Helene Johnson, *Downtown as an Arts Center* (Boston: 1976, Unpublished report prepared for the Park Plaza Civic Advisory Committee).

6. *Id.*

7. *Young* v. *American Mini Theatres, Inc.,* 427 U.S. 50 (1976).

8. *American Mini Theatres* v. *Young,* 373 F. Supp. 363, 365 (1974).

9. Norman Marcus, "Zoning Obscenity: The Moral Politics of Porn," 27 *Buffalo L.R.* 1 (1977).

10. *Young* v. *American Mini Theatres, Inc., supra,* n. 7, at 80 (Powell, J. concurring).

11. *Id.* at 96 (Blackmun, J., dissenting).

12. *New York Times,* January 31, 1977.

13. Joseph E. Illick, "Signs of Our Times," *Sierra Club Bulletin,* November-December 1970, p. 11.

14. Laurence Kressel, "The Community Residents Movement: Land Use Conflicts and Planning Imperatives," 5 N.Y.U.R.L.S. 137 (Spring 1975).

15. National Community Mental Health Centers Act, 42 U.S.C. §2681-87 (1963).

16. Kressel, *supra,* n. 14, at 139.

Chapter 9
Special Districts:
Breakthrough
or
Band-Aid?

*[Zoning] has always seemed a very
dreary subject, of little relevance to
any creative endeavor. As a result of
our experience with the Theater District, we came to realize that zoning
could be made into one of the basic
methods of designing cities.*

—Jonathan Barnett

*A special district legalizes the values of
whoever is running the area at the
time.*

—Another New Yorker

Most urban zoning ordinances are a stew of the old and the new. The
same ordinance that contains a definition of "family" or "home occupation" that was in the ancestor act enacted in 1922 will have provisions
for transfer of development rights or incentive bonuses for plazas. It is
also significant, and not as anomalous as it might appear, that the oldest
and most traditional provisions are generally applicable to the younger
areas of the city, while the older areas of the city, both residential and
commercial, are the ones in which zoning innovations are most often
applied. It is no surprise, for example, that Queens, the youngest and
most suburban of New York City's boroughs, is the only borough in
which there are no special districts.

The history of zoning, of course, is a story of repeated efforts to break away from and yet still cling to the so-called Euclidean envelope for bulk and use. The consequences of this love-hate relationship have been evident through each decade. Such devices as conditional uses, contract zoning, floating zones, planned unit development, performance standards, and vertical zoning, to name a few, are evidence that, with the important exception of healthy, substantially developed single-family areas, the old rules do not make much sense in the city in the last years of this century. The recent and widespread popularity of the special district is the latest illustration of this trend.

Special districts are not new; only their pervasiveness is a recent phenomenon. Special districts for hospitals and universities have been in zoning ordinances for many years, and special districts of a sort preceded zoning, some successful, others meeting with defeat in the courts. Before comprehensive zoning, height limits in areas of Boston, block ordinances, and efforts to restrict the location of Chinese laundries were attempts to place regulatory controls on selected areas of a city or to single out some uses for special treatment. Lowry Hill in Minneapolis and Summit Avenue in St. Paul trace their origins as special areas back to the early years of this century. Historic districts such as Boston's Beacon Hill and New Orleans' Vieux Carré have for many years enjoyed special dispensation, either from the state legislature or the state constitution itself.

While historic districts have been with us for some time, it is only within the last few years that they have moved from a few traditional seacoast locations. A clear reminder that we are entering the final years of this century is the movement of such districts up the Mississippi, across the Alleghenies, and into precincts identified not just with 18th- and 19th-century America but with our century. There is a historic district in Rochester, New York, that seeks to preserve the flavor of George Eastman's posh community. Meridian Street in Indianapolis is, between about 38th and 58th Streets, a historic district designed to preserve and protect old piles of mansions built in the 1920s. (If that works, we may expect the Charleston craze to rise again.) In San Diego, a post-World War II boom city, there is an Old Town Historic District where, one cynic claims, if you can find a picture showing that there was a used buggy lot on your property in 1890, you can get a permit to establish a used car lot.

Historic districts can be fragile. If it is a commercial area, too heavy a focus on tourism can reduce the area to an artsy-craftsy ghetto similar to Chicago's Old Town and Atlanta's Underground; or, as they realized in New Orleans, the rush of tourists to see the Vieux Carré can result in a spate of motels that may destroy the scene that lured the tourists in the first place.

Historic districts can also be threatened by neighboring development. An example is Pioneer Square in Seattle, one of the most impressive efforts in this field but one now threatened. It is near old Skid Road, where logs were once run down to the mill and where human derelicts came to hang out, thereby giving a generic term to sleazy areas of the nation's cities. Pioneer Square is cheek by jowl to downtown and therefore enjoys not only a brisk tourist trade but also the market created by the location of thousands of workers in nearby government offices and banks. The achievements are many. The following is a description offered by the Seattle Department of Community Development:

Results of Preservation and Controls

In the two and a half years that the Pioneer Square Historic District Preservation Ordinance has been in effect, the wisdom and foresight which encouraged establishment of appropriate controls in the Historic District have been well evidenced by the following developments:

1 Greater attention and interest ... in maintenance and repair. ...

2 Demolitions ... for parking lots have been discontinued.

3 Approximately sixty street level businesses have been expanded, improved or established.

4 At least six new restaurants ... have been established.

5 Many new offices ... have been located in the upper floors of renovated buildings.

6 A branch of a major bank was opened. ...

7 One new building has been built. Fourteen major buildings have been or are being rehabilitated and restored.

8 Seattle's first sidewalk cafe has been established. ...

9 Median planting strips ... have been completed.

10 Street lighting, unique to the District [has been installed].

11 [T]he expansion of Pioneer Square and the development of a new park [have been acomplished]. ...

12 Increased emphasis for additional city programs, land use controls, guidelines for the area ... [are being developed]. ...

But there is a real threat to the vitality of Pioneer Square, and, as is often the case, it arises from an equally legitimate public decision, namely, to locate an enclosed 50,000-seat stadium near to the historic district. The potential threat to Pioneer Square was apparent. The stadium was an invitation to a proliferation of parking lots and fast-food franchises. Two steps were taken to mitigate any adverse impact. First, in another bold refusal to accommodate the motor vehicle, Kingdome was designed with only 1,800 public parking spaces. The ticket holder just does not have much choice: a shuttle bus system from downtown is heavily used when there is an event at the stadium. Second, because the historic district ordinance was concerned with architectural design, not use, an overlay ordinance creating a special review district was superimposed to control use and to limit the market that otherwise would have been stimulated by the stadium.

Even with these efforts, the impact of Kingdome remains unclear. Although the stadium has helped the restaurants in Pioneer Square, a couple of art galleries have given up, some believe because season ticket holders to NFL football games are not the type who come to browse on a Sunday.

Historic districts generally have a common and single purpose—to preserve an ambience and architectural style of a bygone era. The origins and purposes of other types of special districts are, on the other hand, almost as numerous as the districts themselves. They may be intended to contain a use regarded as a social pariah, such as the Boston Combat Zone (discussed in Chapter 8); or to influence the type of commercial development, such as New York's Fifth Avenue District; or to protect a moderate-income, ethnic area from threatened intrusion; or to encourage, by incentives, the regeneration of a desired use; or, as in some transit-stop districts, to combine prevention of private wind-falls with the protection of public facilities. And, it must be said, such districts are sometimes created simply to accommodate some special interest. LaJolla Shores in San Diego, for example, is a nice, upper-middle-class residential area. Why it has anything unusual to deserve a special district classification is hard for the observer to fathom. One resident of San Diego offers the explanation that the LaJolla Shores special district was created just to give residents a greater leverage on any new development:

> The primary reason for the adoption of the ordinance—stripped down to its most simple terms—was to regulate half a dozen vacant lots. The locals

said they wanted to have control over their destiny. What they really meant was they wanted to have some control over what the guy was going to do with that vacant parcel on the corner.

But the neighbors aren't the only ones who know how to use the device for their own parochial goals. Special districts proposed for Washington, D.C., and Honolulu allegedly illustrate a similar use of the special district concept to further the special interests of, respectively, a developer and an ensconced group of hotel operators.

McLean Gardens in the District of Columbia was for many years the "Friendship Estate" of Mrs. Evelyn Walsh McLean. During World War II, the federal government bought the 33-acre estate for emergency housing. A major share of the units were 1,188 dormitory rooms; 723 apartments were built for families.

In 1976, CBI Fairmac Corporation bought the property. The dormitory rooms have been vacated and are in the process of being demolished. Fairmac had considered continuing to maintain the remaining 723 units, but they are over 30 years old, have no air conditioning, and have 1940-era bathrooms and kitchens. Substantial renovation appears uneconomical without significantly increased rents, which probably would involve substantial displacement of tenants. And so the developers, in a display of civic thoughtfulness, proposed the creation of a new special district, the Planned International District, to solve a currently troublesome public problem in the nation's capital. One supposes that it was only by coincidence that the new district would also solve the developer's problem.

There is a crisis for space in the district for foreign missions. Over 120 foreign governments have missions in Washington (the decolonization of Africa shows up in the Washington zoning ordinance!), and Congress has severely restricted their right to locate in residential areas. To get around these difficulties, the zoning commission has been resorting to a planned development approach. The consequence, according to the application of the drafters of the Planned International Zone, "has been a largely unplanned intrusion of chanceries into single-family residential areas. . . . It is not surprising that this ad hoc approach has caused substantial citizen concern." The Planned International District proposal is intended, its proponents say in their application, to "represent a constructive solution to an intricate and vexing land use issue . . . that thus far has defied solution." The special district would allow, based upon an approved plan for the entire designated area, embassies, chanceries, and residential units on the same parcel solely for employees of a foreign mission. By special permit, residential units for nonmission persons would be permitted, but the area for such could not exceed 25 percent of the total area of the district. While the district technically would be a floating zone available for mapping anywhere in the city, one must doubt that this example of corporate civic commitment will find much use beyond the borders of the Fairmac property.

This statement was made by a participant in Honolulu politics:

> Waikiki is sort of a rolling abortion. They've done nothing there but make mistakes and every now and then they'll go into a great fret and do something—usually wrong. In '67—I think it was '67—the council passed an amendment which would lower density and they, in their usual infinite wisdom, put a 6 months' hiatus on the effective date so that every fast buck artist in the country came flying in and got a building permit. That's Waikiki. That shows great foresight. A bunch of dumb-dumbs . . . or maybe they intended to do that, which is more likely.

Waikiki is today, after literally years of politicking and maneuvering, the location of a Special Design District, the latest attempt to "do something." As with McLean Gardens, this was a privately inspired proposal, the child of some existing landowners and hotel operators on Waikiki Beach known as the Waikiki Improvement Association. According to Donald Bremner, planner for the Association, it was calculated that, if the area of Waikiki Beach (seven-tenths of a square mile) was built up to its capacity under the zoning regulations, there would be somewhere near 68,000 hotel rooms (there are 24,000 now) and a daily population of 175,000 people, equivalent to the population of Salt Lake City, Utah, or Spokane, Washington, each of which has about 50 square miles of land area.

In 1970, the Association proposed a Special Design District for Waikiki under which allowable bulk, density, and height would be reduced and all development would be subject to special review *by the city council*. The idea was caught in a power struggle between Mayor Fasi, the city council, and the state legislature. The Mayor wanted to impose a use tax on hotels that would be passed on to the tourists, and he tied his support of a special district designation to endorsement by the Association of the tax. The hotel operators wanted no part of such tax. The hotel owners were charged with trying to use zoning to cut down further competition while wrapping their economic motives in the pious cloak of environmental protection. One participant in the struggle said:

> They've got theirs now. They didn't want any such restrictions in '69. Those were the big boom days. So they stopped it then. But now all the big stuff is taken care of. 26,000 hotel room limit? Fine. Then we can jack up the rates and that's the game. . . . There's certainly a good understanding among the council and the hotel industry.

The ordinance, as originally proposed, would have required at least 10,000 square feet of lot area in order to build a hotel or multiple-family units. The charge that the whole concept was to protect existing business gained some credence when it was asserted that there were 570 property owners in Waikiki with parcels smaller than 10,000 feet.[1]

Honolulu's then planning director, Robert Way, said the proposal was a power grab by the city council. "By setting up these interim measures," Way was quoted as saying, "which are really only zoning tools with a gimmick—we'll have the zoning tail wagging the planning dog." Way claimed he had been trying for years to get $300,000 to do "the kind of comprehensive planning that is needed for Waikiki. How do you justify clamping some arbitrary population ceiling on Waikiki without sufficient planning?"[2]

Probably the answer is that the justification lies in the fact that something is *done* instead of being interminably planned. Other possible solutions to the crisis of Waikiki cost money or are of dubious legality. Bremner again: "There were other proposals to deal with Waikiki, and that was a bit strange to me because I felt they were very questionable on a legal basis, but I knew that zoning could handle it, and we had to get that point across to the decision-makers."

The moral? Biblical advice to the contrary notwithstanding, it is sometimes prudent to pour new wine into old bottles. Zoning is, indeed, an old bottle.

It is as pointless to talk about special districts without a focus on New York as it would be to discuss the steel industry and ignore Pittsburgh and Chicago. The New York City Plan Commission, these last ten years, has been cranking out special districts as though they could be used to redeem anemic municipal bonds. One has a mind's picture of New York City's planners and architects at their drawing boards at 2 Lafayette Street drafting a special district a week, oblivious to the drums and cymbals of the municipal Götterdämmerung outside. There are—at our last count—33 special districts in the New York zoning ordinance and more are being proposed, the latest we recall being a district along Fifth Avenue opposite the Metropolitan Museum of Art and an Upper East Side Historic District.

One critic has dismissed New York's special district kick as "the penicillin effect":

> First the miracle drug is invented for a specific purpose and it works. Then all want it prescribed for their illness, when it's not needed or it won't help.[3]

That may be a harsh judgment considering the available alternatives in land development policy in our cities. It is instructive to note the variety of purposes and diversity of techniques employed by New York.

The first nonhistoric special district to receive national attention was the Theater District between Sixth and Eighth Avenues and from 40th to 57th Streets, the general area of New York's theater industry. A 1975 study of some New York special districts by the New School for Social Research points out that the last theater was built in 1934 and that legitimate theaters in the area had diminished from 100 in 1900 to 68 in 1930 to 30 in 1950.[4] The 1961 comprehensive zoning resolution had created a FAR of 18 in the neighborhood, a provision that did lower previously allowable densities but was sufficiently generous to reflect the boom market of the early '60s. Clearly, the raw land was worth more than the old theater that stood on it. To make matters worse, the adult entertainment business was moving rapidly into the area, and some legitimate houses were now purveying hard-core films.

The New York planners accepted the inevitable but, they concluded with eminent good sense, if the market was going to rape the area, why not be seduced—for a price. So a bonus was offered to any developer of office buildings who would include space for a legitimate theater in the office building: one theater, an additional 20 percent of allowable floor area. This was purely at the developer's option; there was no compulsion. This meant that the base FAR had to be sufficiently low to tempt the developer to opt for the bonus. Permissible densities in the area were not lowered when the special district was created. Four new theaters have been added to new office buildings since the district was created. The conclusions reached by the New School study are mixed.

The concept may have produced new theaters, but it has not prevented the continued destruction of the ambience of the Theater

District; only the depressed real estate market slowed that trend. And the character of the area is not enhanced by a new theater somewhere inside a 45-story office building. Only a *tout ensemble* approach, as in the Vieux Carré, could have dealt with that bleak trend. The New Orleans city council, for example, finally put a stop to any new hotels in the French Quarter. It would, however, have been unthinkable or, if thinkable, politically naive to expect similar drastic tactics in New York. It is one thing to consider draconian measures against the shadowy establishment that operates the impinging sex marts; it would have been a threat to a different, more established Establishment to have lowered the FAR in 34 blocks of mid-Manhattan to, say, 8.

The Fifth Avenue District created in 1971 between 38th Street and 58th Street for the frontage on both sides of Fifth Avenue was another attempt to use zoning to reverse what appears to be an inevitable market trend. The image of Fifth Avenue as a posh retail area was seen to be in trouble, and zoning was called in to try to affect the market. (Some students of zoning will recall that zoning received its first impetus in New York in the second decade of this century when Fifth Avenue merchants feared an invasion of their sidewalks by the Seventh Avenue garment district.) By 1971 retailers occupied only 55 percent of the frontage along Fifth Avenue between 34th Street and 57th Street. Banks and travel agencies occupied 21.4 percent of the frontage. Airlines—particularly government-owned foreign airlines that were not troubled by high rentals—were moving in. These "walk-in billboards," as someone aware of the economics tagged them, were creating vast blank areas in the avenue's retail facade. Retail users could not compete for space in the rental market with these institutional or subsidized uses.

The design of the Fifth Avenue Special District was in part bonus and in part mandate. In new construction in the district it is required that there be a minimum FAR of 1 of retail space, starting on the ground floor. No setback is permitted at ground level. Banks and airline offices in a new building are limited to no more than 10 percent of the ground floor area nor more than 15 percent of the total linear frontage on or within 50 feet of the Fifth Avenue street line. The bonus part of the new provisions, as in the Theater District, is intended to encourage desired uses, in this case hotel or residential uses. Then there are the amenity bonuses of additional FAR, not new in New York, for interior plazas, subway connections, covered pedestrian spaces, and other perceived public benefits. The district does not touch the existing nonconforming uses, which, at ground floor, constitute 45 percent of the street frontage. Olympic Tower, on the northeast corner of Fifth Avenue and East 51st Street, took advantage of every bonus offered in the new district. Its 52 stories above street level contain offices, retail shops, and condominiums. Another new office building across Fifth Avenue from Olympic Tower, while not utilizing bonus factors in excess of FAR 18, does comply with all mandatory design and use features of the district, including retail uses at ground level.

Norman Marcus, the skilled and imaginative general counsel to the New York City Planning Commission, asserts that the Clinton Area Special District is "an example of a very political use of the special district concept." It was a trade-off between City Hall and an infuriated neighborhood. The anger of the locals was sparked by a proposal to build an enormous convention center on the Hudson River between 44th Street and 47th Street. The Clinton convention center site, as now proposed, is shifted about 10 blocks to the south, outside the special district area, but the Clinton District is still in the zoning ordinance.

The Clinton area is between Eighth Avenue and Twelfth Avenue, from approximately 43rd Street to 56th Street. It is a mixed-use area of moderate-income whites (over 90 percent), many of whom work in the area. Three-quarters of the buildings are pre-1901 Old Law Tenements, mostly four- and five-story multi-family dwellings with ground-level retail. For some reason, almost half of the retail outlets in the area are food and drink outlets or food suppliers.

If many neighborhoods are believed to deteriorate because of population movements, falling real estate values, and degenerating public services, some are also threatened by what the real estate industry would regard as the "upgrading" of a slum. (The fears of the residents of Cabrini-Green, a less than successful public housing project on Chicago's north side, are exacerbated by a paranoia that real estate developers will tear down the crime-infested buildings in order to expand the Gold Coast.) Clinton saw itself in precisely that confrontation. Office development, satiated on the east side of Manhattan, was coming west and moving up Eighth Avenue; and old residences were being demolished, if not for a high rise then for a parking lot to pay taxes while waiting the spin of the market's wheel. The battle line was drawn with the proposed convention center. The residents could see a rippling effect in high rises, hotels, and traffic that would send them packing or make life intolerable. The Mayor had no choice but to offer some apparent protection, and, in November 1974, the Clinton Special District came to be law. A preservation sub-area was designated between Eighth Avenue and Tenth Avenue. In the preservation area, the FAR was lowered to the prevailing densities. A perimeter sub-area was established adjacent to the preservation area on its southern and eastern flanks. Here new development would be encouraged.

The Clinton District contains both mandatory and incentive provisions. In the preservation area, no building may be demolished without a special permit from the Plan Commission, or unless judged unsafe by the Department of Buildings. If demolition is permitted, the number of units demolished has to be replaced within the district. In the preservation area, existing parking lots could continue only until November 1979. Thereafter, they require a special permit from the planning commission. Presumably, the intent is to stimulate (compel?) construction of low-rise residential units.

In the perimeter area, high rises are permitted and a bonus of 20 percent FAR may be granted in exchange for improvements *in the preservation area.* So much additional FAR is allowed for each room rehabilitated in the preservation area, but the number of rehabilitated rooms cannot be greater than the number of rooms that existed prior to rehabilitation. In addition, a maximum rent is set for each room. (Rent control via the zoning ordinance!) An additional bonus is granted for each square foot of park—whether on site or off-site—that a developer provides *and agrees to maintain.*

Some observers believe the concept cannot work. One who is knowledgeable in the New York home building market said: "There's no way in hell to rehab and maintain those old tenements at a reasonable rent." Another described the Clinton District as "novocaine for the neighborhood."[5]

The list in New York seems endless; three more deserve brief mention. The Little Italy District south of Houston Street (for the uninitiated, it is pronounced "Howston," not "Hewston") is an area where Americans of Chinese descent outnumber those of Italian descent 38 percent to 30 percent, but the plan was drawn by the Italian-Americans. The New School report quotes one resident's views: " . . . Little Italy is showing a unity that we needed in the area to combat growing infiltration of other nationalities,"[6] a sentiment denied to be the motivation for the district by the executive director of the Little Italy Restoration Association. The scheme has some of the off-site redevelopment features of the Clinton District, and it smacks of a romantic attempt via zoning to resurrect a depressed ethnic area. The proposal is vintage Jane Jacobs and is endorsed, of course, by Ada Louise Huxtable.

The Greenwich Street District was created to accommodate the Bankers Trust Building on Greenwich and Washington Streets. Here incentives are offered for pedestrian bridges and decks, shopping arcades, contributions to a fund to improve adjacent subway facilities, and a bundle of other trade-offs. Bankers Trust even obtained an additional 488 square feet of floor space in return for 16 trees. The most significant provision, however, is in the administrative section. The developer can build as-of-right provided the developer's proposal is certified by the chairperson of the planning commission as meeting the standards. No special permit applications and no public hearings are required. Whether the Board of Estimate would be willing to short-cut the potential process in other districts remains to be seen. The Greenwich Street District is a testament to the days when the office boom seemed unending. Whether it ever will be used again is doubtful. As Norman Marcus puts it: " . . . it's difficult to give up the grand dream and, in this case, the grand dream is on the zoning book."

One of the more recent special districts is the Central Park District, which affects property on the east side of Fifth Avenue facing Central Park. Setbacks are forbidden, and an additional FAR is offered in exchange for payments to a fund to help maintain the park. In essence you pay money for a bulk variance, and we suppose New York is to be congratulated for declaring that when such payments are offered they will at least be above the table.

New York City is already learning one problem with freezing a pile of special incentives and privileges into its zoning ordinance. Today development is raging in the central Manhattan District as though no one recalled the slowdown of 1975-76. And one can predict it will be overbuilt by 1981, affected by a slowdown and recession in 1982, and so on. As the *New York Times* editorialized on February 5, 1979:

> New York is a boom or bust town. After a decade of office building glut and no new construction, there is now an office shortage with rentals at record levels and a rush to build. The cycle is as predictable as the seasons.
> Unfortunately, the city's response is equally predictable. It might be called too much, too late. At the construction low-point, New York provided special economic incentives to entice developers. Builders began receiving tax abatements and other favors just as the market was turning into the best of real estate worlds. . . .

The developers are not to blame; they simply play the game they know. It is the job of the city's planners to control and direct building patterns sensibly; they seem to have defaulted. The Planning Commission's most useful act now would be to shift those tax incentives away from the desirable and healthy core. It needs no help right now and is even endangered by the density of the new projects. Why can't planners respond appropriately to market forces . . . ?

It is an easy assignment to criticize the problems and the proliferation of the special districts, to say that, Canute-like, they are futile efforts to stem the inexorable tide of the market or that they are the antithesis of comprehensive planning or the effluent of self-serving commercial or ethnic interests. Sometimes they may backfire, as was the case of the Yorkville area of Manhattan, where, in an effort to preserve the "mom and dad" commercial character of the neighborhood, a maximum size was placed on each business establishment that, in turn, spurred the intrusion of fast-food franchises, which could do very well, thank you, with a limited floor area. In some instances, notably some historic areas, the special district may be viewed as an official blessing to the dispersal of blacks by young whites returning to the city or as a device to push the poor out, whatever their racial makeup.

Nevertheless, we are persuaded that they are not only a sign of the ability of the zoning concept, after a half-century of life, to respond to marked changes in the urban scene but also a groping toward a realization of the absolute necessity to recognize the modern city for what it is: a collection of villages that will insist upon differing treatment and yet will require a central governmental system if they are to survive.

FOOTNOTES

1. *Star Bulletin,* December 18, 1975.

2. *Honolulu Advertiser,* November 13, 1975.

3. *New York Times,* June 6, 1975.

4. Robert E. Davis and Jon Weston, *The Special District Concept in*

New York City (New York: Center for New York City Affairs, New School for Social Research, 1975).

5. For one case in which the concept seemed to be working—until a developer sued—see *Middlesex and Boston Street Ry. Co.* v. *Board of Aldermen of Newton*, 355 N.E.2d 1279 (1977).

6. Davis and Weston, *supra,* n. 4, at 83.

Chapter 10
The System:
Some Opening Thoughts
on the Process
and the People

Whate'er is best administer'd is best.

—William Cowper

... persons who must deal with the Code ... are continually frustrated by procedural niceties which bear no relationship to the results of action contemplated by the Ordinance. Substantively, the Code does not even attempt to resolve the practical administrative difficulties which are manifested by the dispersion of authority among various departments and individuals located throughout City Hall, while the express language of the Code omits all explanation of the function of these numerous administrators.

—*Procedural and Administrative Problems Under the Seattle Zoning Ordinance*

Everything that can be said about zoning administration is an oversimplification.

The existence, in almost every city, village, and town, of a legislative body, a plan commission, a zoning board, and a professional or technical staff projects a false picture of uniformity. In fact, the impact of personality, politics, and petty jealousy quite normally overwhelms the apparent uniformity dictated by the widespread adoption of the original standard state enabling acts. The result is that it is impossible either to understand or to revise or reform zoning administration in any city without some considerable study of the personalities and politics pervading the system. Nevertheless, in approaching any discussion of zoning administration, it is useful to bear in mind three basic approaches that can be taken to the subject.

The first, and perhaps most prevalent, is simply to ignore it completely. The great majority of zoning ordinances ever written make no serious attempt to define and regulate the actual day-to-day operation of the administrative structure. Scores of pages are devoted to establishing substantive regulations, and then, almost as an afterthought, some few pages are devoted to a bare bones description of the administrative processes by which those substantive provisions are to be given life.

Two factors probably operate together to make this approach so popular. In the first place, drafting administrative regulations is dreadfully dull. Neither the citizen zoners nor the planners who advise them find it easy to get worked up about how the ordinance will work. Frequently, the lawyers that advise them don't understand the system and its goals well enough to capture them on paper. As one planning director said:

> A great deal of the problem is that the attorneys have not been trained to the subtleties in this area. ... In addition, there is a fair amount of professional laziness on the part of the planner who may not really understand enough about some of the subtleties of how you do put together an ordinance or an administrative procedure. ... The same kind of ignorance has existed for a long time on the side of the attorneys. There hasn't been an awful lot of interplay. Both the planners—hell, all of the professions—in their arrogance, and I think that the planners' level of arrogance may not be as high as the guys in the highway business, but I think the lawyers are pretty stand-offish and pretty arrogant when it comes to making comments about things like zoning. ...

The second factor that makes the say-nothing approach to zoning administration popular is that the officials and the administrators responsible for zoning most frequently do not wish to be encumbered by a zoning ordinance that too-clearly spells out how and on what basis they are to behave. Procedure checks power. To the extent that the administrative structure and the standards governing it can be kept nebulous, the power of those who control the process is enhanced. For this reason, among others, procedural reforms have come slowly to zoning—in both suburb and city.

As always, there are exceptions. Seattle's hearing-examiner (discussed in Chapter 13) raises procedural protection to a high level and seems to be working well. In Hawaii, reform of the state Land Use Commission's procedures seems to have gotten somewhat carried away. According to one participant:

> The procedural thing has gotten tight to the point of almost being outrageous. For example, there is a procedure that is drawn directly from the rules and practices of the legal fraternity in terms of evidence and in terms of examination of witnesses, cross-examination and the whole bit. It has really gotten a little bit ludicrous. . . . It was an attempt on the part of the public to tighten up the excesses of the land use commission. They have, in the tightening process, almost aced themselves out of it. . . . It has gotten to be a very rigorous process. Only now are we beginning to realize how many implications there are. . . . We had a hearing last Friday, for example, where a citizen protester had to establish that he had the rights of a party. The only way it seemed that the land use commission could permit him to testify was to waive the rules.

In Detroit, after being "slapped down" several times by the courts, the zoning board has begun to take a more rigorous approach toward its findings. A member of the staff thought the requirement for stated findings was severe enough to eliminate some of the emotionalism. A practitioner before the board, on the other hand, felt that, while the findings were stated with more completeness, the justice was still rough. In San Diego, a requirement for more complete findings imposed by the California courts simply resulted in the lay boards making the same sort of decisions they always did and then instructing the winning side to come up with some detailed findings to support what the board had done.

Frequently, hearings are approached more as a matter of discovery for a later appearance before the city council or the judge, or as a forum where the emotions on all sides can be vented, than as a meaningful part of the decisionmaking process. Frequently, cross-examination is not allowed or, if allowed, not used. Swearing of witnesses is sporadic. The use of experts is, except in extreme cases, all but nonexistent.

To a greater or lesser extent in practically every city we visited, zoning is still conducted on the basis of influence and politics—a situation that seems to suit just about everyone involved. Jacksonville,

Florida, provides an especially striking example because influence and politics continue unabated despite some of the most rigorous "government in the sunshine" legislation and case law one could imagine. The result so far, as best we could discern it, is fairly reflected in the following conversations:

> *CLW:* The courts keep pressing the Sunshine Act farther and farther. Has it made any real difference in the way zoning matters are conducted?
>
> *Developer:* I know that it has. I know that it has. I think you really have to be more careful. Not to get caught! ...
>
> *CLW:* In your experience, has the Sunshine Act changed the way, practically, zoning is accomplished?
>
> *Staff Member:* No, it is still being done in the back room—just more carefully. You know goddamn well that people are calling people on the zoning board and people are calling the councilmen. Hell, they're even going up to the tenth floor and talking to them.
>
> *CLW:* Just not two at once!
>
> *Staff Member:* Never two at once so the press doesn't have to be there.

Nor is it just the developers who believe that the best arguments are made off the record. In Detroit, where opinions of Justice Levin of the Michigan Supreme Court threaten to impose much more rigorous administrative procedure standards,[1] an experienced practitioner told us that no one, neither developers nor neighborhood groups, thought much of the idea. One Atlanta neighborhood leader freely admitted that the tactic of neighborhood groups was to go after council people, one at a time. In another city, a citizen described citizen participation this way:

> We get what might be called a real good workout with the zoning review board, but it is really just the warm-up. If we don't like that decision, or if we still feel there is some chance on it, I can call up the council person and talk directly.... In being organized, we can get a hold of some council people.

Despite the widespread support for quietly ignoring zoning administration, it is possible to identify a second fundamental approach to the subject. This alternative is most frequently sponsored by reformers who believe the only way to make zoning work is "to get the politics out of it" and turn it over to the professionals and technocrats who are able to understand it and administer it "in an objective manner." This reflects the view, widely held by planning and zoning professionals, that planning and zoning have become too complex to be trusted to laypersons and that what the world of zoning needs is a new commitment to professionalization of the process. Tom Shuttleworth, then Atlanta's zoning administrator, characterized Fred Bair's approach to zoning administration in words that could well become a rallying cry for this group:

> Now Fred's theory is that "If the ordinance is worth having, and it takes two PhD's to administer it, then get two PhD's."

That view, of course, is not popular with those who espouse the say-nothing philosophy of zoning administration. They are quite content with the way the system now functions under their benevolent thumbs and most often view professionals as intrusive know-it-alls who really do not understand what makes either a city or its zoning function.

There is, finally, a third basic approach to zoning administration. Its advocates join the say-nothing group in being somewhat skeptical of the idea of "professionalization" as a cure-all. Their hesitancy, however, proceeds from a commonsense distrust of utopian schemes contructed on unrealistic assumptions. Myron Thompson, a trustee of the Bishop Estate in Hawaii, captured the essence of this viewpoint:

> Any system which needs perfect or even unusually talented men and women to operate it is sure to fail. One does not need to endorse the doctrine of original sin to recognize that human beings lack perfection. So remember when the next scheme which requires perfection for its implementation is proposed, it will be operated by your not quite perfect next door neighbor.

The goal of those who share Thompson's concern is to create a system that is understandable both to those who must administer it and to those who must be administered by it; a system where the rules are, to the maximum extent possible, stated up front and where checks and balances operate to ensure fairness to both the public interest and the private applicant. Their problem lies in accomplishing that without creating a sea of red tape that defeats the goals.

No one of these views can be summarily dismissed. Each of them has some merit; each of them has deeply entrenched and persuasive advocates; reconciling them is no easy matter. Nevertheless, none of them has yet produced a system of zoning administration that has any significant merit. Administration remains "the running, ugly sore of zoning."[2] It is, however, a sore cities can no longer allow to fester. While a strapping and healthy suburb yet in its vigorous youth may be able to survive with a system of zoning administration that is more productive of arbitrariness and red tape than progress, cities cannot.

If development and redevelopment are to be encouraged and attracted, the importance of creating a fair and open process that responds to the legitimate concerns of private citizens and developers without needless delay cannot be overemphasized. San Diego planner Lou Quinney reflects a common theme among business people and developers:

> I think it will be very difficult for the City Staff to come up with incentives that are meaningful to the people for whose use they are intended. Most people on City Staffs are not in an environment where they recognize what an incentive is. They might feel, for example, that a 10% density bonus may represent a great concession on their part because of the fact that philosophically they are actually relaxing the zoning ordinance. . . . But from the builders' point of view, that might mean very little in the absence of other more meaningful incentives such as, well, I think an incentive the developers would respond to much better would be a vast shortening of the process time.

In Atlanta, Dick Fleming, then vice-president of Central Atlanta Progress and now general deputy assistant secretary of the Department of Housing and Urban Development in charge of neighborhood revitalization programs, had this to say on the subject:

> The answer is to make the process sensitive to the realities of the marketplace. You have to have a guy in the City government with the power and the tools to sit down and make it happen in a way that the developer can function. . . . On the point of how many developers would object to decreasing the FAR, they probably wouldn't mind. . . . But a bureaucracy that requires every developer to tag 2% onto any land he goes to Connecticut General for, then that's a problem.

A major downtown developer pointed out the special problems of delay in many urban development projects:

> In the downtown situation, nobody can live with that sort of delay. Due to the overexposure a developer has on the front end. . . , he has to execute that thing as fast as he can or he's going to go broke! At best, he'll go broke. You can't make money in the downtown development unless you can execute that thing and move with it. . . . You can't stand the battles that go on for years like they do in the suburbs.

Developers everywhere echoed those sentiments. And no wonder, if one can believe the following account, hilarious if it were not true, by Samuel H. Lindenbaum, a distinguished Manhattan land use attorney:

A fellow came in to see me the other day with an idea to do something at the Queensboro Bridge, and I thought it was a hell of an idea. But I had to tell him what he was up against. The Queensboro Bridge is owned by the City of New York under the jurisdiction of the Department of Highways and for real estate purposes it's under the control of the Department of Real Estate. If you wanted to lease any portion of the Queensboro Bridge for any commercial venture, you have to go to the Department of Real Estate besides having the approval of the Department of Highways. In addition, the Queensboro Bridge happens to be on 59th Street. South of 59th Street is Community Board 6, north of 59th Street is Community Board 8, and since Community Board 6 can see, hear and smell what happens across the street, they feel they have a vested interest. In addition, several months ago a Task Force was created to study the whole 59th Street problem, so there's a 59th Street Corridor Task Force. Then there's the mayor's office of Midtown Planning and Development that would have to be spoken with. The Queensboro Bridge is a landmark so you'd have to go to the Landmarks Preservations Commission to get their approval of anything you propose to do. You'd have to go to the planning commission; it would have to be sent out to community hearings; the Board of Estimate would end up holding a hearing; and if this was something that by virtue of the procedure had to go to public bid, the Department of Real Estate would then have to offer for public bid, and even though you spent $100,000 developing your plans, you might lose out to somebody else altogether.

Now this fellow sat here, and he said, "You're kidding." And I said, "I really, truly, really, truly wish I was kidding. I'm not giving you all of this to tell you what a hard job I'm going to have to do. I'm really trying to discourage you because I want you to know what's ahead of you if you decide to go ahead." Plus, I didn't mention SEPA of course. If we touch that bridge there'll be a question of air emission and stuff like that.

Of course that project touched a public facility, the Queensboro Bridge (reflect on what would have been the process if that monument the Brooklyn Bridge were involved), but it is only a slight exaggeration of the endemic and pervasive influence of delay. To cut that knot is the greatest area for incentives in the zoning ordinance of a city.

Somewhat surprisingly, while some city officials and administrators recognized the counterproductive and inequitable features of zoning systems that create delay and uncertainty for developers and hopeless confusion for citizen-applicants and objectors alike, few showed much sensitivity to the need to eliminate what Louis Wolfsheimer, president of San Diego's plan commission, characterized as the "nonsense of going through 27 hoops and over 16 logs and through 8 burning infernos...." We heard repeated complaints of "apathy, indifference, red tape and unnecessary demands." Even in the more desperate cities where one might expect a more accommodating attitude, the process is often painfully cumbersome. As one planning director told us, the process of getting a simple zoning change was "lengthy" because:

> ...the application is received by the City Council, referred to this Department for initial investigation and report, we submit that report to the City Council, they forward our report and the application to the City Planning Commission ... for their investigation, public hearing and recommendation. If both of our recommendations are favorable, the council automatically introduces the matter and sets its own statutory public hearing. That is where the time comes in. We keep it for two to three or four weeks. City Planning keeps it for three to four to five weeks because they have to have time to set up a public hearing, obtain the addresses of owners of property and residences and businessmen within the 300 foot radius, take it under advisement, make their decision the following week, send it to the City Council. Then they introduce it after receiving the formal ordinance from the law department, set their public hearing three to four weeks later, make their decision and, unless there is an emergency [seemingly, a contradiction in concepts in this setting], the decision doesn't become effective until one month after that. ... On the kind of thing where there is a directive from the administration ... to process thoroughly but rapidly, ... it still is a minimum of three months' process.

That, of course, is a cakewalk compared to some cities, such as San Diego, where the processing time is measured in years rather than months, or Honolulu, where the common unit of measurement is the half-decade.

Is all that processing necessary? Clearly, it is possible to do it in less time. In Jacksonville, for example, where dedication to growth and development is high, developers and officials alike agree that the process is streamlined, efficient, and free of delay. The ordinance is structured so that even applications requiring hearings before several bodies can be processed in 35 days. According to developers, six weeks is the average for a routine application. A 1,600-acre planned unit development was approved within 60 days following the application; the developer did six to nine months of prepatory work before filing. A 9,000-acre PUD spanning two counties and requiring development of regional impact approval took only 12 months.

Most suggestions for reducing processing time and red tape are rejected on the basis that it would require a sacrifice of quality. It is, however, difficult to detect terribly significant differences in the quality of development from city to city depending on whether the process takes a month or five years. Elimination of red tape, at least within very broad limits, should not require a sacrifice in the quality of development control and regulation; what it may require is the sacrifice of both the quantity of control exercised by some of the zoning bureaucrats who have found their way into the system by election, appointment, or employment and the opportunities for influence now cherished and jealously protected by applicants and neighborhood protestors alike. That is the real rub.

Everybody bemoans the delay and points to everybody else as the guilty party, but most proposals to shortcut the process are greeted with suspicion from all sides. Everybody wants a look and a say at as many points in the process as possible, and if that means letting the other guy hang on to the same privilege, well, it could be worse. The staying power of an administrative system so maligned by so many can perhaps be explained only as a classic case of preferring the devil you know. There is, to be certain, a need and a role for elected officials, lay boards, professional staff, and citizen advocates in the urban zoning process, but there is also a need to define the proper limits of the role each should play. In the following chapters, we examine the current roles being played by each of these groups, the criticisms and credits they each attract, and the emerging forces that pose significant challenges to the continued role of these traditional actors. It should be said, however, that the more one listens to each party involved in the process idly complain about all the others, the more one thinks Edward Vallis Hoch, one time governor of Kansas, may have been right:

> There is so much good in the worst of us,
> And so much bad in the best of us,
> That it hardly behooves any of us
> To talk about the rest of us.

FOOTNOTES

1. *Sabo* v. *Monroe Township,* 394 Mich. 531 (1975); *West* v. *City of Portage,* 392 Mich. 458 (1974); *Kropf* v. *Sterling Heights,* 391 Mich. 139 (1974; Levin, J. concurring).

2. Richard F. Babcock, "The Chaos of Zoning Administration: One Solution," *Zoning Digest,* January 1960, p. 1.

Chapter 11
The Elected Official:
Politics or Perspective?

*We must remember that the machinery
of government would not work if it
were not allowed a little play in its
joints.*

— Oliver Wendell Holmes, Jr.

*"Jacky, come give me your fiddle,
If ever you mean to thrive."
"Nay, I'll not give my fiddle
To any man alive."
"If I should give my fiddle
They'll think that I'm gone mad
For many a joyful day
My fiddle and I have had."*

— Mother Goose

With rare exceptions, like Boston, where the Boston Redevelopment
Authority has all but supplanted the Boston City Council in zoning
matters, and Indianapolis, where the Metropolitan Development
Commission has, as a practical matter, the final say on zoning matters,
city councils in cities across the country cling to their zoning power
with a jealousy that raises questions about motives. (New York, too,
could be cited as an example of a city where the council has lost all
control over zoning. But there the loss of the zoning power is simply
one small part of a larger movement that has, in the words of one New
Yorker, resulted in "the Council's greatest responsibility being the
renaming of the streets.")

Surely, some elected officials are motivated to retain power over
zoning by considerations of less than the noblest nature. Old-fashioned
money corruption undoubtedly motivates a few, but our impression is

143

that the lust for power, more than the lust for money, is what drives most elected officials to hang onto their traditional zoning functions. The power inherent in the ability to give zoning is clear enough; however, it pales in significance next to the power to withhold zoning in response to the outcry of citizen-electors. Zoning is people-oriented in the extreme. Its impacts are direct, visible, and significant. Control over it gives a politician the politically invaluable power to "save" his or her constituents' neighborhood by denying zoning approval for an unwanted use. (For a practical demonstration of the importance of such power to politicians, reread the Chicago scenario in Chapter 1.)

Another, very human, factor should not be overlooked in trying to understand why a busy city council appears so often determined to waste valuable time on comparatively insignificant zoning matters. Elected officials may well wish to retain their zoning power simply because zoning is to them a familiar and comfortable function in a world of increasing complexity. When many of the problems of cities seem beyond both comprehension and solution, it must, on occasion, be nice to worry about whether or not the lot at the corner of Commerce Boulevard and Cottage Lane should be rezoned for a pizza parlor.

No one seems so upset by the politician's role in the zoning process as do the professionals that populate city planning departments. It is a fair and accurate generalization to say that city planners see the city council as an unprofessional body interferring in an area it does not understand for reasons purely of politics and power, using both terms in a perjorative sense. One former staffer told us: "We have twelve council people with ward responsibilities and they can literally become some kind of king maker or hero or whatever else because they are holding the line." In another city, a staffer explained the city council's displeasure with a charter admendment that reduced its role in the zoning process this way:

> The charter change has removed a lot of headaches from them. It has removed also, though, a lot of exposure to citizens that they had before. A politician likes exposure. He likes the chance to express his opinions verbally, maybe loudly, especially if he knows that they are the same opinions as the 100 or 200 people that are sitting there from his neighborhood. I'm sure they miss that. They miss the glory. I'm sure they don't miss the headaches.

(One of the ironies of the reawakening of neighborhoods and neighborhood power in cities may be that it once again makes zoning such an important issue that city council members will be more reluctant than ever to release control of it to anyone, including neighborhood groups.)

It is not surprising that the city planning professionals should have that view; nor is it surprising that the same facts and circumstances take on a wholly different tone and quality when seen through the eyes of those who sit on the city council. While planners could hardly be called scientists and while city council members are not quite properly characterized as administrators, the difference of their perspectives is explainable in terms of C. P. Snow's classic description and differentiation of the roles of the scientist and the administrator: "To be any good," Snow said, "... a scientist has to think of one thing, deeply and obsessively, for a long time." But, he cautioned those scientists, "Administrators are, by temperament, active men. Their tendency, which is strengthened by the nature of their jobs, is to live in the short term, to become masters of the short-term solution."[1]

One councilman to whom we spoke said it less elegantly, but no less effectively: "The difference is that they are planners, they are not operators. We operate the government."

Charges that the zoning process is "political" are, to the politicians, hardly a source of embarrassment. Carl Levin, then president of Detroit's city council, rose to that issue as follows:

> It depends on what you mean by political. ... For me, it's not a dirty word. Zoning decisions should be made by either elected officials or people who are sensitive to the pros and cons of their various public policies. ... I don't think we ought to stop Renaissance because there is not enough green space. Now maybe a professional would say, "Screw it! Play poker with Henry Ford!" I'd rather that that decision be made by someone who is closer to bearing the responsibility for his decisions. Which really means the political process.

In Atlanta, Councilman Richard Guthman put it this way:

> Zoning can make or break an area. If anybody is going to have discretion, then I would want it to be the elected official because he is responsible and he has to think about what is good for both the neighboring people as well as the area as a whole.

In another city, a neighborhood leader turned elected official saw the same need for a "political" balancing of the disparate factors that frequently characterize zoning issues and verbalized what others seem to feel: "I would just be afraid of turning zoning and land use matters over to government without the participation of elected officials."

The elected officials are not alone in believing they belong in the zoning process. Applicants and opponents alike are all but unanimous in their desire to keep "politics" in zoning. Claude Petty, an Atlanta-based developer with experience in several cities around the country told us elected officials belonged in the process because "... you want, you need, to have an arbitrator who can say, 'Well, the staff has done a good job on this but I can see that over the long haul what is planned here might have value.'" We posed the same question to a developer in Florida:

> *CLW:* What do you think of the idea that zoning should be more professional and less political—the idea that zoning is something on which there can be a rational, professional answer?
>
> *Developer:* I don't think that's true. I used to think that. But, after meeting the city planners and the city engineers, I now have more faith in the city council than I do in them. Politicians tend to be in favor of "progress" as long as not too many people object. Whereas, the planning board can have a lot of theoretical objections. Pie in the sky type of thing. And your public works people ... and so forth are just lazy. So, when a developer is restricted to the city agencies, he is going to run into incompetence, laziness and idealisms.

Gerald Dake, a member of Jacksonville's Stockton, Watley, Davin, one of the country's largest mortgage bankers, didn't mince any words either:

> I don't want a group of appointed citizens making a final legal decision involving my property. I want my elected officials, in the democratic process, making that decision.

Developers aren't the only group afraid to take politics out of the process. As neighborhoods have become more organized, they have become more adept at the application of political pressure and seem, increasingly, to be content to rely upon the influence they know they can exert. According to a neighborhood leader in Honolulu:

> We are more at home with the political process than we are with the professional at this stage of our growth. We don't think we can trust the professional. We have watched the professional planning consultants come and go and all of those studies are gathering dust. To get something done on our agenda, the City Council is the only place. We have to go down and bombard them with numbers—reminders to our elected officials that we'll remember them, one way or another, come the next election.

Even in Seattle, where the hearing examiner idea has caught on in a big way, to the apparent satisfaction of just about everyone, the neighborhood groups are still sensitive to the problem of keeping the professional under control:

RFB: Are the technocrats in charge of Seattle now?

Citizen: No, I wouldn't say they are. They are more in charge now than they were, but up until now, they have had their cages rattled pretty constantly by the mayor's office and by the city council. As long as the council has been responsive to citizens, and the citizens have known how to get the attention of the politicans, the technocrats really haven't had too good a look in. We are very wedded to the ascendancy of the amateur—the good government people.... That has made government very responsive. It has made life pretty tough on bureaucrats, and I think rightly so.

It is impossible to discuss the role of the elected official in zoning without pausing briefly to consider the system of "aldermanic courtesy." If "politics" is a bad word in urban zoning, aldermanic courtesy may be the reason. It is blamed by many Chicago observers for the periodic scandals that plague the administration of zoning in the Second City. It is reputed to have made many aldermen wealthy. It is a matter of public record that it has sent several packing off to federal prison. The following account appears in *United States* v. *Staszcuk,*[2] a case involving a conviction for a bribery in a zoning case:

In September, 1970, William Harris planned to build an animal hospital on property located in the 13th ward of the City of Chicago. As then zoned, such a use of the land was prohibited. Harris therefore paid $5,500 to Al C. Allen, who had acquired a reputation as "the zoning man";* Allen talked to defendant Staszcuk, who was then serving as alderman of the 13th ward; on September 15, 1970, an amendatory ordinance was introduced in the City Council.

*The witness Prokop referred to Allen as "the zoning man." (Tr. 174) When asked to explain how she heard about Allen, she stated that she had read about him in the papers and she went in to see him "because he was always zoning." (Tr. 177)

As it is practiced in Chicago, aldermanic courtesy makes each alderman a zoning czar within the ward from which he is elected. If he wants a zoning application granted, his compatriots on the city council generally grant it; if he wants it denied, the applicant might just as well prepare for judicial review.

There seems little doubt that, in every city where the ward system of council elections exists, some form of aldermanic courtesy likewise exists. Despite its potential for abuse, there are things to be said in favor of the idea. As one former councilman said:

> There is a great deal of aldermanic courtesy. But downtown has always been treated separately for aldermanic courtesy because it affects the whole city.... In theory, it makes a certain amount of sense. What does anybody else in the city care or know about proposals in an outlying neighborhood?

In Jacksonville, a city councilman pointed out that the system enables him to short circuit zoning lobbyists and to devote more attention to other business of the city:

> My first impression is that I'm against the zoning if the councilman is against it. It stops a lot of traffic in here. It helps you to operate. You get lobbied on these things. If the councilman of the district is willing to say no, if it's bad zoning, he'll say no, I can say, "Listen, the district's councilman is against it, and you are going to have to show me strong reason why I'm not to follow his lead." So that is the position that I have taken on it. I don't know whether it's good or bad.

The answer is that it may be all right if the district councilperson is doing a good job with zoning and isn't corrupted by the power. The same Jacksonville councilman explained his approach toward the problem of aldermanic courtesy becoming a corrupting influence in the zoning process:

> I will never vote for a zoning because a councilman was for it in his district, but you would have a hard time getting me to vote for a zoning if the councilman was against it. If the councilman is for it, you ought to look at it and do what you think is best. I won't vote for any zoning because the councilman is for it.... That is one of the biggest areas for curruption in government and we have to guard against it. But when you are against the zoning, it doesn't normally have that kind of effect.

Several Jacksonville developers confirmed that this is the way aldermanic courtesy operates in Jacksonville: a yes vote of the local councilperson will not carry the day for the applicant, but a no vote will veto the project. The strength of the veto is illustrated by a staff member's description of one project:

> The staff recommended rezoning to CPO. The zoning board recommended CPO. The urban affairs committee recommended CPO. But, when it got to the full council, it was pulled from the consent agenda and the district councilman made the statement that he thought it was bad zoning. And they killed it! The goddamn thing went to court and got reversed so damn fast it would make your head spin.

Where aldermanic courtesy provides that strong a veto, there must still be some concern about its corrupting influence even in the form it takes in Jacksonville. But in the day of demands for more attention to neighborhoods and their problems, the ward system of government has its attractions. The concept of an elected official charged with both citywide and special neighborhood responsibilities having a strong voice in zoning matters in that neighborhood is not an idea to be scrapped without some consideration of how it might be legitimatized. Is it possible to legislate a system of aldermanic courtesy? What would happen if a zoning ordinance formalized neighborhood power to the extent of saying that, if the neighbors could convince their council-person to protest a zoning change, some extraordinary vote of the council would then be necessary to approve the change? Perhaps any city that considers the idea ought to start by having two councilpeople elected from each ward. Atlanta zoning lawyer Clifford Oxford noted that the negative aspects of aldermanic courtesy gave him less concern back in the days when you had to convince two aldermen of your position in order to qualify for the courtesy.

Before leaving the subject of aldermanic courtesy, neighborhood groups should be warned about a variant of the practice that operates in at least some cities. The growth of neighborhood organizations has frequently made it vital for a councilperson to support the neighbor-hood in its opposition to even those rezonings the councilperson favors. In such cases, the variant system permits the district council-person to register a public vote against the rezoning with the private assurance that the rest of the council will see to the passage of the rezoning over his protest.

Despite what can be said in favor of an honest and rational role for "politics" in zoning, city councils across the country are under increas-ing pressure to relinquish substantial chunks of their zoning authority. In later chapters we deal with the attacks on city authority from the neighborhoods below and from federal, state, and regional policies above. As if those were not enough, city councils now find themselves under attack from within the city government itself.

In city after city, we found a growing division between the city administration, led by the mayor, and the city legislative branch repre-sented by the city council. In some cases, the split between branches is the result of politics, a mayor from one party with a city council controlled by another; in others it is largely a matter of personality, as in the city where a city councilman described the mayor, who was a member of the same party, as a "show horse," and the mayor described the city council as "a bunch of pay off artists"; in others, the movement appears to proceed from good government notions about the need for executive/legislative checks and balances within city government. Whatever the cause, the widening split between city administrations and city councils is producing visible tensions within the system that do not portent well for a rational implementation of land use and zoning policies.

In Honolulu, the inability of the administration and the city council to get along brought development to a practical halt. The scope of the problem was reflected in the following statement issued by the administration's chief planning officer on Febrary 17, 1976:

> STATEMENT BY ROBERT R. WAY
> CHIEF PLANNING OFFICER
> DEPARTMENT OF GENERAL PLANNING
> CITY AND COUNTY OF HONOLULU
>
> I will no longer process proposals for amending the general plan which expand the current urban boundaries at the cost of converting agricultural lands. This policy will be in effect until the city council sets an overall policy for future growth. I submitted such an overall policy . . . to the council for adoption . . . in November 1974. . . .

The response of the Honolulu city council to such assertions of authority by the administration was typical of that found in several other cities:

> About two years ago, . . . the council got itself a legislative reference bureau and began to staff it. They have planning, they have some lawyers—good people. Once that happened, they said, now we are going to try to capture and properly meet legislative responsibility. . . . And so now, for instance, just recently, there has been a situation where somebody made a request for a change in the general plan and the planning department arbitrarily and administratively determined that they were not going to process it because they didn't like the direction it proposed in relation to their new proposed general plan. . . . The council didn't like the implication of that, just on an academic basis, of who the hell is the administration—some functionary—to decide that. It's a policy thing. They've got to process it, they shouldn't be afraid of it, they can give us the evaluation, we'll make the decisions. So, in the new charter there is a provision that allows council to initiate plan changes and zoning changes. Summarily, to give this guy his day in court, they initiated the process, and they are

getting all kinds of flak from the administration: "Dirty guys, aha, there must be some skullduggery going on with this guy...." Council doesn't care. They're processing it and they are going to make a decision....

A similar phenomenon is clearly observable in Atlanta, where one city councilman had this to say about the staff:

No, they're not totally sensitive and they're not generally always that efficient in providing the kinds of facts that we need. The staff advice is inadequate—especially if it's going to embarrass the planners or embarrass the administration. The decision maker should have some other alternative in terms of developing their own information.... I mean, the Council is another branch of government. They sit over there and we over here and those guys make policy and decisions. In some instances, their attitude is that, "We'll give them what we want them to have...." I've seen that happen—deliberately withhold information.... It got to that point. We do have subpoena power and we can subpoena information.

As in Honolulu, the result is frustration and action without planning background:

I'm so frustrated about this issue,... that I'm ready to introduce an ordinance and say, dammit, we're going to do it and here's a time frame to do it in, and here's some of the ingredients, and you [administration and staff] put it together.

In Detroit, too, the shift to a strong mayor form of government has produced noticeable tensions between the administration and the city council. The result, again, has been an apparent degeneration of efficiency in the planning and zoning process. In Detroit, as in Honolulu, the city council concluded that it needed a staff separate and apart from the administration's city planning department. One councilman offered the following explanation:

Well, public servants are beholden to those who pay their salaries or who hire them. If the administration hires all the planners, well, then, that particular planner is going to be beholden to them. The planner might be giving opinions which are—which reflect the desire of the administration. So you need a counter in the traditional checks and balances function of government. You need a counter balancing force.

"Counter balance" is a deceptively gentle way to characterize the relationship. A member of the city council's new staff confessed absolute ignorance as to what the administration's staff was doing:

We really don't actually know what the administrative agency is doing. So I don't know if we should be frustrated or not by what they are approving or not approving. They can be approving almost anything. There is no monitoring. We don't really do monitoring of what they are doing. We take it that they are doing things in good faith. We hope.

On the other side of the divide, a member of the administration's planning staff admitted that the division between administration and council was thwarting any possibility of increased professionalization of the Detroit zoning process:

Staff Planner: Detroit's city council is reluctant—because our department is an administrative department under the mayor—to give final authority on land use consideration items to the administration. It's not that they don't trust our current mayor, it's not that they don't trust the current staff. They don't trust the unknown as to what might be in the future.... I can see why they would want to have their own staff. But it certainly is a duplication and a waste of taxpayer's dollars to have two agencies reviewing everything.... The city planning commission is under the city council. It is even called the city council's planning commission.

CLW: And you do not staff the city council's planning commission?

Staff Planner: They have their own staff.... We work together on an informal basis rather than on a formal basis. Sometimes we duplicate, sometimes we work for and with. But it is an informal basis—staff to staff. I don't think that a formal basis would be tolerated.

The tensions faced by the poor city planner in all of this are obvious. According to a member of the planning department in St. Paul, another strong-mayor city:

The question always comes up: What is our relationship to the council? It's a very strange relationship. There are some councilmen who feel that we ought to be more responsible to them. However, we are in the mayor's office, so in effect the mayor sets the policy. Now, that has its advantages and disadvantages. The advantage, of course, is that we have direct access to the mayor and can influence city policy. The disadvantage, of course, is trying to feel our relationship with the council which really, as you know, passes all the laws and so forth.

An important item in the "and so forth" is, of course, the planner's salary and the appropriations for the planner's programs.

Across the river in Minneapolis, the so-called weak-mayor form of government still prevails. However, even there, the city council is, at least according to one observer, literally under siege by the administrative bureaucracy:

RFB: I have the impression that the Minneapolis city council has retained a pretty strong hold over zoning changes.

XXX: I don't know. It depends on the council. Legally they have. But as a practical matter, the bureaucracy in City Hall controls it.... Council is constantly fighting the bureaucracy just to hold on to some semblance of what they consider reality. The bureaucracy on the other hand, ... if they don't want a particular alderman, they give away the store just to win the election. So there is a lot of tension between the two, and who is running the show depends on who is on the council and who is on the staff at that time.

And so it goes with the poor, beleagured elected official. The property owners and developers see him as the least unattractive of the alternatives; the citizens enjoy the power their votes give them over what he does; and he believes he brings important balance and perspective to a system where sharp conflicts of fundamental policies are a daily occurrence. But those who compete for his attention, his job, and his power all threaten to consume him. Through it all, he at least has the comfort of knowing he is in the system pursuant to the will of the people. In the next chapter we turn to the lay boards, which have no such comfort.

FOOTNOTES

1. C. P. Snow, *Science and Government* (Cambridge, Mass.: Harvard University Press, 1961), pp. 72, 83.

2. *United States* v. *Staszcuk,* 517 F2d 53, 56 (1975).

Chapter 12
The Lay Boards:
"Sticks and Stones . . ."

A man was killed by a circular saw; in
his obituary it was stated that he was
"a good citizen, an upright man, and
an ardent patriot, but of limited
information regarding circular saws."

—Anonymous

THE PLAN COMMISSION

Some things are hard to explain. Over 10 years ago, *The Zoning Game*
concluded that "the plan commission, except, perhaps, in the smallest
communities, is a dodo. It is, as a growing body of criticisms suggests,
neither expert nor responsible."[1] That volume quoted politicians, lawyers, planners, and developers on the many evils of the planning commission: "The executioners of the master plan"; "neither fish, flesh, nor
fowl"; "the worst device that has ever been invented by man. . . ."[2] One
would have expected the institution to wither under that assault. It has,
in a few places, begun to show signs of weakening. To a surprising
degree, however, it continues to flourish. It even has found a few
defenders.

In Indianapolis, the planning commission (albeit somewhat con-
cealed behind the pseudonym "Metropolitan Development Commission") has become, by law, far more powerful than even the city council
in zoning matters. In Indianapolis, if the plan commission turns down an
application for rezoning, the applicant doesn't even get a day before the
city council. The only recourse is to the courts on the constitutional
issues, and the Indianapolis lawyers to whom we talked offered no

encouragement on the chances of succeeding with that sort of challenge. If, on the other hand, you are blessed with an approval of the plan commission, it is next to impossible for the city council to do anything about it. Pursuant to Indiana statute, the matter can get on the city council's agenda only if a majority of the city council agrees to call the matter up. Once the matter gets on the agenda, it requires a two-thirds vote of the full membership of the 29-person city council to reverse the plan commission decision. The politicians in Indianapolis continue to grumble about their plan commission, but annual trips to the state legislature have not as yet resulted in any relief.

In San Diego, too, the plan commission has considerable power by law. It is the final authority, subject to appeal, on a variety of special approval matters like planned developments and conditional-use permits. Beyond that, however, the moral authority of the commission runs high. As its president, Louis Wolfsheimer, says, "In this city, if you can't get a project by the planning commission, you might as well pack it in." Wolfsheimer estimated that the council followed the commission's recommendations 95 percent of the time. While the politicians put the percentage slightly lower, they agreed that the council normally followed the recommendation of the commission except in those cases where the commission itself had rendered a split decision.

The moral force of a well-run plan commission should not be underestimated. Following is a forceful plan commission chairman's description of how his board bootstrapped itself into a meaningful role in the zoning process:

> When we started out, our track record in terms of whether our recommendation ultimately got through council was very poor. We would make our decisions based on whether it is good zoning. We have sort of a general policy on what is going on. The council members, on the other hand are interested in their own little district, you know, and then you find this power playing of trade-offs between councilmen. What we have been able to do is to cut through that kind of thing. . . . I went to the mayor after about six months of serving as chairman of the board, and I said, "Mayor, this board is going to function either as a viable committee that is going to make some sort of injection into the whole zoning process or you are going to lose all of them, including me, because I don't frankly have the time to waste running a public hearing that the councilmen ignore. Now, if I am going to have to be subjected to that, I would rather not be involved." I mean it just came right down to that kind of thing. That meeting went into the council's zoning committee and ultimately to

council and they were made aware of the fact that we were pissed off. The Mayor took a stand and said, you know, we are going to have to stand up and respect what the Plan Commission recommendations have been.

We requested, as a matter of fact, a track record. . . . We are running maybe at 80%, maybe more than that, but 80% approval. Before that, we were running about 50-50. I think council members are now respecting the powers we have because we look at the city as a total kind of thing. They say, "Well, maybe these guys do have a handle on what should be done."

The strength of plan commissions in these few, scattered cities may, however, be more explainable in terms of either an unusual set of political circumstances or an unusual strength of leadership on the commission. In a number of other cities, both the city council and the staff seem intent upon eliminating the plan commission's role as an intermediary between politician and professional. The following brief interchange with a member of the Minneapolis planning staff captures the essence of the movement:

RFB: Well, when the planning commission has to make the recommendation, can't they look to staff for analysis and background?

Staff: Yes, they do, and we provide those services for them. But what if they don't like the services that we're providing? They complain to the council and the council says, "Well, we think they're doing all right. They're giving you just as much information as we want them to give you."

The squelching of the planning commission by the politicians and professionals in another city was even more extreme. The planning director there characterized the plan commission's role as ". . . almost exclusively advisory. That's all—it almost got eliminated at the last charter." In describing the relationship between the commission and the staff, the bureaucrat said:

We strongly and vigorously force these issues to the board. I think there is a lot more executive or professional—executive input into our planning commission. We really shove it to them pretty good. And so, that kind of constrains, in a professional sense, the area of their purview.

A lay observer of the process noted that the plan commission had been blessed with a full-time staff executive who had all but taken over the commission:

Of course, he is anxious to get the point of view of the planning department across. And I've seen him badger, almost, some of the commissioners, who are lay people, and he sort of pushed them into a decision in
the direction that he desires.

Despite all the evidence suggesting that the politicians and the
planners had no use or respect for the plan commission, the official
establishment persisted in the pretext that the commission provided a
valued "forum for public participation." The participating public,
however, wasn't exactly blind:

> *CLW:* The plan commission here seems to have gradually become a
> weaker part of the system.
>
> *Citizen:* It's a bullshit organization. The plan director gets his way. . . .
> We wouldn't waste our time going to the planning commission. Maybe
> that's bad to say it that bluntly, but it's never on our agenda to check
> them out. We'll deal with the administration, the elected and the highly
> appointed officials, and then work with the city council. We try to
> simplify everything. We don't have that much to work with. They'd love
> us to take the time and energy to do all this process work.

The effect of the rise of neighborhood power on the role of the plan
commission should be interesting to watch as we push into a new
decade. On the one hand, the formal and informal organization of
neighborhoods tends to eliminate one of the last excuses for a lay·
board in the zoning process. A member of the Seattle Department of
Development, another planning department that is now directly
accountable to the politicians rather than the plan commission, put it
this way:

> The plan commission is less important today. They were sort of a
> formal citizen participation process back in the days when citizen par-
> ticipation really would insulate politicians in the case of land use deci-
> sion making. . . . Here, today, in this city, we have citizen participation
> coming out of our ears.

On the other hand, the growth of the citizen voice may demand the
revitalization of the plan commission as a legitimate (as opposed to
phony) forum where that voice can be heard. Despite the frequent
complaints about plan commissions, a surprising number of politicians, developers, and neighborhood leaders agree that, when given
the chance, the plan commission can serve a valuable purpose in the

process. From the politicians' point of view, the plan commission is a way to permit and yet structure and control citizen participation:

> The plan commission is one of the most effective ways of getting citizen involvement in the government, and that is what I mean by structuring citizen participation. The zoning process is a real model in my estimation of what citizen participation ought to be about. It is structured, they understand that theirs is a recommendation only.... I think unquestionably there is a value in having that screening process prior to getting to the decision making level.... The other alternative would be to have the mayor hold the public hearing, which is physicially impossible, or have him designate certain staff people to hold it, which is undesirable in my estimation.

From the citizen's point of view, even though the plan commission may require another massing of opposition and even though it may sometimes be ineffective, it is nevertheless a place to discover the developer's case and to have a dress rehearsal of the neighborhood opposition. Where the plan commission has a meaningful role, citizens' groups frequently seem to prefer it to the city council as a forum because of a feeling of greater rapport between the citizen group and the nonprofessional, nonpolitician citizens who compose the plan commission. Similarly, developers, despite their frequent disenchantment with the interjection of a lay board in the process, are never quite sure they want it abolished. They, too, enjoy the opportunity it provides to discover what their opposition is. And they like the idea of having a body that insulates the final decisionmakers from the screaming protests of the electorate.

In the end, the only group that is rather uniformly certain that the plan commission ought to be abolished is composed of the professional planners for whom the plan commission is an insulting interference. As planning consultant Patrick Crowley put it:

> You have the planning experts here operating, providing input to the lay planning decision makers, but the lay planning decision makers really don't do their homework. They really fiercely point to their ignorance and lack of sophistication as their strong point. That's what makes the whole process "democratic" and it also makes the entire fact finding process and the planning that goes into whether a project is approved or not go right out the window when it hits the planning commission. And this is really one of the things which caused me to leave the architectural profession to study city planning. I really could not believe the attitudes and action of the planning commissions.... I am convinced that it would be difficult to

derive a less efficient method of arriving at rational land use decisions than a planning commission.

ZONING BOARD OF APPEALS

If the plan commission is thought to be ineffective and useless, the zoning board is usually attacked as being downright dangerous to any rational system of land use regulation. Politicians, planners, and neighbors alike have for years berated the variance practices of zoning boards across the country. From the time that the variance power was written into the first zoning ordinances as a sop to constitutionality, the battle has been to devise a way to prevent the tail from wagging the dog to death.

To some considerable extent, boards of appeal seem to have been brought under control in many cities. In Honolulu, for example, staff planners, politicians, private planners, and neighborhood leaders all agreed that the zoning board was completely under control. Not surprisingly, the only exception to that chorus came from the professional staff of the zoning board itself, which was not yet satisfied with the extent to which the board followed its direction.

In New York City, the traditional power of New York zoning boards to dismantle a comprehensive zoning scheme has been nipped by a charter amendment allowing both the community involved and the plan commission to appeal, to the Board of Estimate, any variance granted by the Board of Standards and Appeals. The result, according to Norman Marcus, is that " . . . at the moment, the board is not a lever, not a fulcrum, a place where you can reverse policy. The board is very well behaved these days and they do what they should do. . . . I really can't fault them." According to a report in the *New York Times* on December 22, 1978:

> Since the revised charter went into effect on Jan. 1, 1977, there have been 600 decisions by the appeals board. The Board of Estimate has chosen to review 41 of them, at the request of community boards, civic associations and individual abutters. In 20 cases the appeals board was reversed.
>
> Of the 20 reversals by the Board of Estimate, 19 were cases brought by a community board. In only one case did the Board of Estimate sustain the appeals board when the community board objected to the decision.

And so it goes—in most cities; as always, there are exceptions. In Boston, the variance has all but replaced the amendment, which seems to have been relegated to a device used only by neighborhood groups seeking to downzone their community. In Detroit, the applications for rezoning per year are counted in the tens while applications for variances are counted in the hundreds—lots of hundreds. Detroit's ordinance is filled with sophisticated zoning techniques. According to the planning staff, those techniques are not used, in part because people ask for, and get, a variance instead. If they can't get the variance, "they are more apt to seek another location than they are to ask for a change in zoning."

What has brought the board of appeals under control in most cities? Why does it remain a problem in some cities? Some of the answer to the latter question is that ordinances simply are not drafted to impose meaningful controls on zoning boards. The usual three- or four-part formula for assessing the merits of a variance is all but meaningless when applied to most cases that come before a city zoning board. The result is that zoning board members, having no meaningful standard, fall back to acting in light of what they perceive their role to be, that of a board of equity sitting to do rough justice in difficult cases. Frequently, the zoning board sees itself as the protector of citizens against the professionals. A former director of the Jacksonville planning department recounted his frustration in trying to arrange for his staff to meet with the zoning board to discuss planning principles and approaches: "Frankly, they didn't want that. They felt that we would be making them biased toward a decision."

In part, too, the inability to control zoning boards results from the fact that the administration of amendments, special permits, and other supposedly "rational" zoning tools is frequently larded with so much administrative delay that the variance, by default, becomes the path of least resistance. In Detroit, it takes three to five weeks to get a variance and that many months to get a rezoning.

Finally, the zoning board abuses its power simply because it has long been neglected by the politicians and the administrators. Only in recent years has the zoning board been given access to any kind of staff assistance. Even now it is a rare city that feels the zoning board's function justifies both a planner and a lawyer at its meetings.

But more interesting than questions concerning why some zoning boards still abuse their power is the question of why many do not. Some of the answer is that the problems recounted in the preceding paragraph have been addressed in many cities. More significantly, the answer lies, again, in the advent of neighborhood power. In Atlanta, the general attitude of the zoning board was characterized as follows:

> If somebody comes in and says, "Well, my filling station is sort of over at the hill and I have to put up a sign that is 200 feet tall and I want it to rotate, and just think of all the wonderful things it will do for the travelers on the interstate, and we'll sell all that gas to those Chicago people going to Florida because they can see my sign." Well, they will grant that. Just like that. And it doesn't matter about the implications.

But if the neighbors object, the story is different:

> My impression of the Board of Adjustment is that it doesn't matter how perfect the variance situation is, you know, there are perfect ones that come in. The classic, blackboard example comes in and if there are five people standing to raise hell about it, they'll turn it down.

In Detroit, despite the laxity of the zoning board in general, Avern Cohn, one of the city's leading zoning lawyers, said this about the outcome of a typical "hardship" case in the face of neighborhood opposition:

> *CLW:* What if you are just a widow that needs to rent out a room to get by?
>
> *AC:* And you end up over there? And your neighbors come in and oppose it? You're going to get turned down unless your case catches somebody's fancy on the board of zoning appeals.

In discussing an attempt to tighten up the substantive and procedural limits on the power of the Detroit zoning board, a member of the planning staff reacted the same way to the same poor-widow hypothetical:

> Without neighborhood opposition, the widow's request would have been granted under the previous system—and it would still be approved under today's procedurally tighter system.

It appears that, having in most places brought the zoning board under control, neither the politicians nor the neighbors are much interested in the "final solution" frequently urged by the professionals—abolition of the institution. In Jacksonville, a move to drastically cut the jurisdiction of the zoning board produced, and was defeated by, a citizens' uprising. That reaction, and the following description by Jerry Hillis, a land use lawyer, of a similar event in Seattle, are typical of what any reformer who suggests a significant cut in the jurisdiction of the zoning board is likely to encounter:

Hillis: The zoning board is, in some respects, ill-conceived in terms of what it has come to be, but it has become a sacred cow. Variances are like magic, and when zoning reform occurred in this town we talked about going to a different kind of system, . . . and people just could not conceive of not having variances. They couldn't conceive of it, and they couldn't conceive of not having a board of adjustment. There was no reason to keep it.

RFB: Well, you could still have variances but they could be handled by the "technocrats" or the "professionals."

Hillis: There was a discussion, there is still now, of having minor variances, major variances, and to do that kind of thing, but the board of adjustment lasted. It has lasted in King County which has a very extensive hearing examiner system. People who are on it, I think, look upon themselves as filling a gap between the technocrats and the elected officials, on the one side, and the citizens, on the other, providing what they are supposed to provide—relief. That is the way they look on themselves and the way they act.

MEMBERSHIP

An issue on which no one seems to agree is what criteria ought to be used in selecting members for lay boards. Atlanta's official community is noticeably proud of its legally mandated system for staffing the Zoning Review Board to ensure geographic representation. Beyond that, it is obvious that race and sex are consciously considered. As pleased as the establishment is with its accomplishment, a developer who has to deal with the board dismisses it as "cosmetically" staffed.

Some real estate and development types complain if the lay boards are staffed with laypersons who know nothing. Others complain if they are staffed with professionals who have a competitive interest in which projects are approved and denied. Neighborhood leaders shout conflict of interest every time someone who knows anything about real estate and development gets on a lay board. One neighborhood leader went beyond charges of conflict to charges of incompetence:

The lay board has a real estate developer mentality . . ., they ruined the theatre district. They don't care about the theatre district. You know why? First of all, none of those people have ever gone to the theatre. They go to hockey games. You have to go down about 4 levels in the staff before you can find anyone that is literate. . . . So the theatre district is a frightening mess. Frightening. I'll tell you another thing, the Symphony Hall is going to go down the drain. . . . What the christ do they give a damn about Symphony Hall. They want to build more projects.

One city official, on the other hand, bemoaned the overrepresentation of neighborhood types on a lay board, saying, "They don't know as much about business as I know about how to operate on appendicitis." The result, he complained, was that the narrow views of the neighborhood were having devastating effects upon the long-term viability of the city. While neighborhood leaders may not want professionals on the board, they frequently complain that the lay people chosen for the board don't know enough about zoning (presumably, you have to be part of a neighborhood organization to know enough about zoning).

The solution, one supposes, may have been found in San Diego, where the president of the plan commission described the membership as follows:

There used to be two attorneys, myself and another attorney who was black, but he resigned to take a state position. We have one attorney; one real estate broker who is also, also has had income tax background working for the IRS; and land appraisal. We've got one guy who is a Mexican insurance broker, our Chicano member. We have an architect, a very valuable member of the Commission. We have a housewife who is very active in the League of Women Voters. We have a Vice President of the local telephone company. We have just appointed a black woman and she has been very active in many civic things.

That such a group can agree on anything—including (perhaps especially) a place to eat after the meeting—is a tribute to the art of compromise.

If there is a conclusion to be drawn, it is that the citizen's board is, like just about everybody else with a role in the zoning process, probably going to suffer with—but nevertheless survive—a continuing steam of criticism from various forces and sources that question the legitimacy of its role. The temptations to join again the chorus of those deploring that situation must be tempered by the reality that such bodies, despite continuing professional criticism, survive and prosper and, when threatened, are jealously defended by most of the nonprofessional participants in the zoning process. One suspects there must be some reason.

The reason may find its roots in the continuing unease experienced by most people when they try to decide whether zoning should be a political process or a professional process. If lay boards are neither fish, flesh, nor fowl, it is perhaps not surprising to find them so deeply engrained in a process that is subject to the same schizophrenia. The instincts of those involved in the process seem to tell them that they ought to have guidance from someone more knowledgeable than an elected politician but more sensitive than a hired technocrat. The lay board is supposed to fill that function and, indeed, frequently does. When all is said and done, the lay board is perhaps not such a bad idea after all. In any event, anyone who really believes that plan commissions and zoning boards will quickly fade from the scene is advised to read the discussion in the next chapter of what happened when Seattle reformers tried to give the zoning board the bum's rush in favor of a professional hearing examiner.

FOOTNOTES

1. Richard F. Babcock, *The Zoning Game* (Madison, Wis.: University of Wisconsin Press, 1966), p. 40.

2. *Id.* at 39.

Chapter 13
The Staff: Professional, Policymaker, or Pawn?

Whereas, the penguin is
aesthetically pleasing in design; and
Whereas, everything about the
penguin is clearly black or white; and
Whereas, it could never fly; and
Whereas, it has an elegant
stance; and
Whereas, it faces all decisions with
cold feet and huddles together in
groups; and
Whereas, it has few friends except
those of its own kind; and
Whereas, it is considered to be a
strange bird;
Therefore, be it resolved that we do
hereby recommend the adoption of the
penguin as the official bird of the Ann
Arbor Planning Department.

— Resolution of the Ann Arbor,
Michigan, Planning
Commission

Of all the official participants in the urban zoning process, the city's professional staff is the most maligned, the least defended. (Perhaps that is only fair because they are, typically, also the most critical of other participants in the process.) It is not surprising that, where the staff has taken the most affirmative role, it has been subject to the most criticism.

The staff, of all groups in the process, has the broadest range of people to keep happy. Staff is always in the middle: between the council and the administration, between the city and the citizens, between the neigh-

167

borhood groups and the developers. That they survive at all is a tribute to the depth of their dedication and the indestructibility of bureaucratic systems.

Honolulu's professional staff is as well-developed and highly visible as any in the country. The reactions to it from all sides are, as a result, more extreme and more readily observed. They are, nevertheless, typical. One apparently impartial observer characterized the staff as "very good" and not "gooey-eyed or starry-eyed or anything else—but very practical." Others, while generally supporting the staff, excuse its failings on the basis that the tremendous pressure for development in Honolulu has never permitted the time necessary for the professional staff to catch its breath and demonstrate its true capabilities. Still others are confident in their own minds that Honolulu's development scheme is all the better for having been controlled by a professional staff and could have been even better had the politicians given the professionals "more latitude to do their job as they professionally see it should be done."

The staff's detractors, however, see the situation in a different light. The following criticism by a long-term observer of Honolulu's politics and planning is an articulate expression of the essence of the single most common complaint about planning staffs everywhere:

> We now see city council taking the lead in planning matters where we would ordinarily expect planners to take it. I think what has happened is that the planners have gotten too academic, too theoretical. There just isn't time. By the time they arrive at decisions to produce their pretty plans, the neighborhood is all built out. . . . Planners must recognize that they have to take a position at some point. They have to take it even though they don't have all the information that they would like to have. There has to be a pace to the planning process comparable to that of the political decision making pace. . . .
>
> The Mayor of this city asked the planning department how long it would take to prepare a scenic district ordinance to preserve Diamond Head. They said three years. Well, there were proposals that were on the shelf to be considered by the City Council within the next 6 to 8 months. There would be no need for that ordinance by the time they came out with it. . . . The planning profession must recognize the impatience that results from that kind of pace. Developers are considered as the protagonist for a negative point of view in the eyes of the planning department. . . . Developers with long term investment potential and desire . . . have just been rejected—kept at arms length until the entire island's comprehensive planning is redone. . . .

The root cause of the often-heard criticism of staff planners as "pie-in-sky . . . do-nothing . . . dreamers" is to be found in the peculiar circumstances of their existence as professionals functioning in a political environment. One seldom encounters criticism of staff planners insofar as they are charged with review and analysis of specific development proposals; generally, developers, officials, and citizens agree they do a pretty good job in that context. Nor are staff planners criticized as being incompetent to develop and administer tools designed to implement a specific policy decision. Rather, the principal grumbling about staff planners concerns their inability to produce final, workable, and meaningful plans for what the city will look like in the year 2000 or for how specific areas "should be" developed in light of strongly competing political or social demands. Examples are self-evident and common to practically every city: whether growth should be "controlled," "directed," "dispersed," or "concentrated"; whether an "ethnic enclave" should be sacrificed to, or saved from, an expanding commercial or industrial neighbor; whether significant concentrations of commercial and office use should be allowed outside of, and in competition with, the CBD; whether future plans should accept or discourage automobile use as a principal means of commuting; whether environmental, scenic, and aesthetic considerations should have a higher or lower priority than tax base or housing.

The list is endless; the point is that far too frequently politicians and citizens alike ask the planner for professional answers to political questions. It is not surprising that planners, in those circumstances, ponder long and answer "wrong"—whatever they say.

Thus, the criticism of staff planners cannot be taken as criticism of their competence but only as evidence that neither they nor the politicians have been able to define a workable dividing line between their respective roles in the process. Tom Gill, a former politician with an abiding interest in planning, defined the problem and the typical result:

> Planners are unable, because of the nature of their job . . . , to make those kinds of political decisions. These are political decisions, and the politicians don't know enough to make them. As a result, you get a Mexican stand-off and nothing really happens, except another report.

If, however, the planners seek to break the logjam by offering answers based on their perception of the correct policy (or their perception of the prevailing policy), they can be expected to be attacked not as "do-nothing visionaries" but as "political pawns." That risk runs particularly high in the increasing number of cities where the staff is no longer the "city staff" but is rather the "mayor's staff" or the "council's staff."

As if more were needed to complicate the lives of staff planners, they frequently find that what they do try to do is frustrated because the implementation of their plans and programs is at the mercy of the people in the building and zoning department who have charge of administering and enforcing zoning ordinances. One former city planning director chronicled the frustrations involved:

> The Building Inspector, in effect, refused to enforce the zoning ordinance; and I, with some audacity, one time, assigned every planner on the staff to go out and find all the zoning violations we could find . . . and wrote a report on this. My boss had steam coming out of his ears because we were about to blow the lid off the top of City Hall. . . . And, you're perfectly right, the Building Inspector just took great pride in the value of the building permits from year to year, and I'm told when he knew of projects that were about to get off the ground, he would go around in the month of December soliciting them to come in and get the building permits so he could set another record. He really didn't give a damn about administering the zoning ordinance.

When zoning was an oddity that fit easily nowhere in the structure of city government, it must have seemed logical enough to put it in the building department with other plan-checking and code-enforcement functions. At the time, zoning was relatively straightforward, and neither special talents nor considerable time was required in its administration. Times have changed. Understanding and administering a modern zoning ordinance has become a full-time job. But in many cities it remains in, or a weak sister of, the old building department. City departments, including building departments, are, at least by their own definition, always understaffed. Zoning problems seem frequently to be at the bottom of the list of busy building inspectors. They seem either not to understand, or not to give much importance to, such esoteric things as the conditions imposed upon the grant of a variance or a special permit—and other stuff by which clever planners "fine tune" development patterns to assure everyone stays happy.

The historic pattern of zoning's adoption into the traditional structure has produced another frustration for the planners: when they complain that the other guys aren't paying any attention to them, no one pays any attention to them. The brutal facts of bureaucratic life were explained this way by one disgruntled planning director:

The planner is usually the new guy on the block and the building inspector tends to be an old timer. Survival seems to build prestige.

An elected official noted both the problem of the visionary in the planning department and the problem of the old construction foreman in the building department. He proposed to reorganize the city government to deal with both:

> Professional planners are new. We didn't know what a professional planner was in this county 10 years ago. Now, we're graduating a lot of planners. So we've got people with theory that came from somewhere, but not practical experience to relate that to. We're in a transition period of planning... where our planners aren't competent, basically because they don't have the experience of life.... We want to put professional planners in departmental areas.... We'll get divisions of the planning department lined up the same way as divisions of the other departments of the city.... So, for instance, there will be a public works division of the planning department.... Within that division we can take our theorist and our young graduates with very little experience and we can take some of our people who have been "programmers" in the various departments and put them together and let them knock heads. Let them teach each other.... We've never done that. We've always had the planners by themselves and somewhere down in the department level of government, you've got a division chief who says, "To hell with those guys. They can do whatever they want to, I'm going to run my business. I know how to lay streets; I know where they ought to be; I know where we need traffic lights. They don't know anything about that." But when you take that guy and put him in a division, a planning division with that theoretical guy, they can fight it out amongst themselves and when they get a solution, we're going to follow that solution. Right now, the planning staff is developing plans and nobody is following the plans.

Well, that sounds comforting until you realize that Honolulu, having for years tried to operate with a combined planning and zoning department, recently reorganized its government to put the planning function and the zoning function into separate departments so that the zoners can get on with the day-to-day business while the planners have some time to think about the long term, free of the pressures of that day-to-day business. We found a similar problem in other cities. Every effort to get the planners involved in the real world has been at the expense of their devotion to the long term. If, Pisces-like, you are about to decide that the last idea sounds like the best, be aware that at least some people in Honolulu are already concluding that reorganization has not helped the planning process, has resulted in a divorce of zoning from any consideration of long-term planning, and, in general, has resulted in little beyond the creation of two bureaucracies where before there was only one. The real question in all of this, of course, is whether, like the Keynesian economist, we ought once and for all to admit that in the long run we'll all be dead anyway.

Perhaps it is the frustration of being a professional in a political job that accounts for the high turnover in some city planning offices and the sometimes degrading and debilitating process of learning to roll with the political punches in others. One of the movers-on saw the steady climb of the hangers-on to positions of responsibility as one of the critical problems in city planning departments:

> The top brass of the Planning Department tends not to be professional. Not well-trained in planning. Not as well studied in the art and business of regulation. Probably not very articulate about the affairs of the city. I used to work with him. He's a nice person. He's a real gentleman, but I don't think he's mad about anything in the City. I used to be mad all the time. I still am. And I think it takes some of that to communicate the problems. I'm sure that [the new mayor] is trying to overcome some of this but he's got, boy, the weight of years to overcome. The people who might understand, who might care, who might be willing to raise a lot of hell, aren't going to be far enough up the ladder or in enough of a performing position that they can be spokesmen and I think that is a very profound part of the problem.

Before leaving this discussion of planners, one last thorn in their sides should be noted. With a uniformity that must suggest some conclusion (we wouldn't venture to say what), city planners laid a considerable amount of the blame for their problems at the office door of the city attorney:

> The city attorney had told them that they had to do zoning the way it had always been done because any kind of a change would jeopardize the zoning ordinance. I have a theory about why the city attorney's office said that. We have part-time city attorneys in there and they get a retainer or a salary paid by the city which is supposed to cover half their time. The other half, they practice law. And if they can draw half a salary and practice law nine-tenths of the time, they are going to be a lot better off economically and so it's, "Don't give me any work, baby!" When I was in City Hall and I needed to get legal advice, without exception, I couldn't get it....They would say, "Well, tell me how you want the question answered." So, as I posed the question to the City Attorney, I would set it up so that he could say, "Yes, it is possible that . . ." and then he would parrot the whole thing back to me. They didn't want to fool around with it.

A continent away, another planner's gripe sounded the same:

I'm concerned that we're not getting any direction out of our attorneys; we have no progressive attorneys; we have no one researching case law and saying, "Look, what the hell they did up here that you could get away with." As a matter of fact, it's the opposite way around, I broached some new ideas; the City Attorney reviewed it and put an "X" through it. He said we can't do anything like this. I talked to a person from the state Attorney General's office who cited me a case where this was done and I gave it back to the City Attorney.

In yet another city, we heard the same story:

Planner: The City Attorney is the one-man Rules Committee. He doesn't (don't quote me on this) give me legal opinions; he gives Attorney General opinions or judicial opinions. He doesn't give legal advice.

RFB: Oh, I see: "This you may do; this thou shalt not do."

Planner: Right, rather than saying, if this is what you want to do, here is the way to do it.

In light of all that, the following description by Norman Marcus of how the New York plan commission came to have its own legal adviser is remarkable:

Before I came to work here, which was 13 years ago, Corporation Counsel was responsible for all the legal affairs of the planning commission. The representation was quite dictatorial and quite uncreative. There were rules that were prescribed; you could do this, you couldn't do that. The rules for the most part, reflected case law and an attitude of the less trouble the better. Don't attempt things, then there won't be any cases to defend. When I came here, and I didn't come in with the title of Counsel, I came in as an assistant to the chairman, gradually we took things over from them. Now they were very overworked over there and they had more than enough to keep them busy. In fact they were always running after the volume because they couldn't catch up with it. So they acceded generally to an almost total relinquishment of what I would characterize as house counsel contract duties. The litigation remains handled over in the Corporation Counsel's Office. . . .

Perhaps—just perhaps—the zoning of our cities could become a vital tool again if the lawyers and the planners would show the type of mutual interest in each other's profession that is reflected in the following comments of Jonathan Barnett concerning his relation with Marcus:

Norman and I have a lot of rather amusing conflicts because Norman is always asking me what is good design, and I'm always asking him, what's the law. And I have a much more doctrinaire attitude towards legal matters than he does. He has a much more doctrinaire attitude towards design.

The ultimate elevation of staff's role is to give it decisionmaking power. In some places, the decisionmaking role of staff has been gradually increased without any considerable hoopla. In Rochester, New York, for example, the new zoning ordinance gives staff authority to grant variances of less than 10 percent from the ordinance requirements, authority to approve or reject site plans, and authority to make "use interpretations," which have the effect of allowing uses not specifically permitted by the ordinance. In Columbus, Ohio, the planning staff has authority to map floodplain overlay zones based upon city council adopted standards. In New York City's Greenwich Street Special District regulations, significant bonuses can be awarded to a development on the basis of satisfying staff that specified conditions have been met.

Provisions of the foregoing sort may be the first muffled shots of yet another "quiet revolution," but the issue of whether or not the revolution is a good idea is being debated more openly and more noisily in the context of the professional hearing examiner idea. In Indianapolis and Seattle, two large cities where the idea has, in somewhat different forms, been tried, nothing terribly earthshaking has resulted. Most people seem pleased with how the experiment is working. Despite that, however, the reaction of those who have not lived with the system is typically one of caution approaching paranoia. As noted in Chapter 11, politicians, developers, and neighbors all seem to take great comfort in having their friendly local elected official as the final arbitor of urban land use issues. The following reactions to the hearing examiner idea are predictable in light of that earlier discussion.

From a plan commissioner, the complaint is that staff decisionmakers will be insensitive to the real world:

> Staff may look at it from a total planning process and you know as well as I do that planners are pie-in-the-sky, dreamer-type people.... They are too tunnel vision.... Staff people ... are always buffering themselves against the community because the community will holler.

A city councilman and a zoning board chairman expressed fear of corruption:

> People say, well, you ought to have a hearing officer and get it all out of the council.... Boy, that is a dangerous situation. You know the only time I've ever been offered bribes in this city since I've been on the Council is on zoning matters....

> I just don't think it would be good. Put all that power in one person. It's

too much to ask of that person to remain honest. It's just not good to put
that much temptation in somebody's way.

A developer was afraid of bias:

> *Developer:* I wouldn't think much of that at all. It has been my observation
> through the years that these lay people, generally, are pretty good thinkers
> or they wouldn't be appointed in the first place. I don't mind a debate with
> that kind of person. On the other hand, this thing about a professional
> hearing officer . . . is totally wrong because that hearing officer is not
> objective. He hears only what he wants to hear and once he's heard it, no
> one else gets to hear it—he's heard it.

> *CLW:* Perhaps what you're saying is that frequently you get a body that is
> both decision maker and policy maker and its decisions are always imple-
> menting its policies rather than being based on the record before it.

> *Developer:* That's right! There you go. And that's what you'll get with the
> hearing officer, whomever he may be. And then, on the other hand, you've
> got the danger of this going the other way. You've got the danger of a
> hearing officer being totally against the policies. You know, who's going to
> appoint the hearing officer, the mayor or the planning board? You're going
> to get two different people.

David Curry, University of Chicago Law School professor and distinguished student of the federal court system and architect of the Illinois
Environmental Protection Act, has summarized the arguments for and
against the professional hearing examiner as well as anyone:

> While the exercise of quasi-judicial powers by administrators who do
> not enjoy the status of judges is a long-recognized phenomenon in this
> country, it remains a troubling one. . . . As Hamilton argued, the power to
> re-appoint and to alter salary are potent tools with which the executive or
> legislature can undermine that independence.
>   Given these reservations as to the continued independence of a quasi-
> judicial board, one might fairly ask why the [Illinois Environmental Protec-
> tion] Act established such a board instead of providing for a prosecution of
> violators exclusively in the courts. The arguments are well known: Arbi-
> tors who spend full-time on pollution matters will become more familiar
> with the complex and highly technical subject and thus will be less likely
> to reach mistaken results through misunderstanding; uniformity in apply-
> ing the law will be prompted by centralizing most enforcement in a single
> trial forum; crowded court dockets may be avoided and streamlined
> procedures instituted; the combination of rule making and adjudicatory
> power will promote consistent policy formulation; and, not least, the
> creation of a new tribunal permits selection of personnel sympathetic to
> the purposes of the program. There are countervailing considerations
> even if a specialized tribunal were given judicial status, which was not

thought a realistic alternative in Illinois: The loss of diverse views, the loss of the outsider's and generalist's perspective, and most importantly the danger of capture by the interest sought to be controlled. These considerations have led me elsewhere to oppose the creation of specialized federal courts and would lead me to argue against the establishment of a federal quasi-judicial tribunal to try pollution cases. But the alternative was not enforcement in the securely independent federal courts with their long tradition of excellence; rather it was enforcement by elected judges in the highly political tradition of Illinois. And although the history of other administrative agencies indicated a serious risk of progressive degeneration, the short-term advantages of enforcement by a new board appointed by a sympathetic governor seemed well worth having.[1]

The same sort of competing considerations are raised and debated every time the idea of a professional hearing officer is advanced. As in the case of the Illinois Pollution Control Board chronicled by Curry, there is no theoretically "right" answer: the poison you pick must depend on the evil that currently besets you. Sometimes the cure is worse than the disease; sometimes it is not. We conclude this discussion with a review of the hearing-examiner system as it has been implemented in Indianapolis and Seattle with the goal of demonstrating only that, where the idea has been tried, it has been neither cure-all nor catastrophe. (It is interesting to note that when hearing examiners have been used, the purpose has been almost entirely procedural reform rather than increased professionalization in the decisionmaking process. Thus, in both Indianapolis and Seattle, lawyers, rather than planners, have always held the post of hearing examiner.)

In Indianapolis, the hearing examiner's post is a part-time position clearly designed for the limited function of relieving the Metropolitan Development Commission of noncontroversial cases. The hearing examiner's jurisdiction is limited to making recommendations to the commission on applications for rezonings. The commission reserves .the right to bypass the hearing examiner; and, in practice, if both parties request a waiver, the hearing examiner generally waives the matter directly to the commission. If no one contests a recommendation of the examiner, then it bypasses the commission and goes directly to the city council for ordinance approval. However, if the petitioners, objectors, or staff take issue with the recommendation, the whole matter is heard de novo by the full commission. Perhaps the noncontroversial nature of the cases actually heard by the examiner is best evidenced by the fact that, based on the examiner's estimate, only 10 to 20 percent of his recommendations are appealed to the commission, and, of those, the recommendation is sustained approximately 80 percent of the time. Most of the cases that come before the examiner involve no expert testimony whatever. Although cross-examination is allowed, the right is seldom invoked.

The jurisdiction of the hearing examiner in Seattle is considerably broader and, to the apparent credit of the system, has been expanded regularly and considerably since the office was established in 1974. In addition to the original jurisdiction over zoning variances, conditional uses, zoning amendments, and licensing, the hearing examiner now hears appeals from decisions of the director of the Department of Community Development with respect to "short" (minor) subdivisions; appeals from decisions of the director of the Department of Community Development with respect to special districts; appeals from rulings and interpretations of the superintendent of buildings; appeals from city department decisions under the Washington State Environmental Policy Act; complaints of employment and housing discrimination; appeals from decisions of city agencies regarding relocation assistance matters; and matters relating to cable television.

With regard to zoning matters, the Seattle hearing examiner has jurisdiction to hold public hearings and make final decisions on variances, specified conditional uses, special exceptions, and sign variances. The decision of the hearing examiner in such matters is final unless appealed to the Zoning Board of Adjustment. The hearing examiner also conducts hearings and makes recommendations to the city council with respect to zoning map amendments and specified conditional uses. The city council retains final jurisdiction as to those matters.

The Seattle hearing-examiner system was developed largely in response to calls from both the Washington courts and zoning reformers for fairness and procedural reform in the zoning process. Given that origin, it is not surprising that the Seattle system appears carefully structured to promote procedural fairness. The city council appoints the hearing examiner, but the examiner is not part of the council staff. Originally, the office was, for organizational purposes, an arm of the municipal court system; now it is a totally separate and independent office. The examiner is appointed for a fixed four-year term and may be removed only for cause. An elaborate set of procedural rules governs the conduct of hearings and matters of ex parte communications.

All of the elaborate trappings notwithstanding, in practice, it appears that the true function and jurisdiction of the Seattle hearing examiner as to zoning matters is largely like that found in Indianapolis. The office is a way of eliminating noncontroversial cases from the docket of lay boards and politicians. No one is really willing to trust the professional process with the final decision of any matter thought to be controversial. William Snell, the current hearing examiner in Seattle, estimates that his typical agenda for the one day a week on which hearings are held consists of 13 or 14 cases, half of which are noncontroversial variance requests.

Saying that the hearing-examiner process has accomplished nothing but a weeding out of the cases that no one cared about anyway should not be construed as an indictment; in the minds of some, it is a valuable function. James Buck, an Indianapolis zoning lawyer, had high praise for the system's ability to do just that:

> The hearing examiner is certainly a step in the right direction. It weeds out a lot of cases that are either perfectly all right, perfectly legitimate or so gross that when the petitioner's attorney sees what he is up against, he backs off. The value of this is that it then gives the Commission more time to hear the more important cases. Rather than hearing 50 cases, 20 of which are non-controversial and 10 of which are very lightly controversial, they can hear the 20 cases to which they really ought to be giving their attention. Having a paid hearing examiner who is really doing his job has helped a lot.

Interestingly enough, according to attorney Jerry Hillis, the place where the hearing-examiner system has had its greatest influence is in those rezoning cases where the examiner's jurisdiction is limited to making a recommendation to city council. According to Hillis:

> The hearing examiner system . . . has made the predictability concept much more real. It's much easier to predict whether or not somebody can get zoning or cannot get zoning. It is going to be a much more professional type of decision and therefore the chances of being able to sway a hearing examiner are pretty nil.

The city council in Seattle has accepted the recommendations of the hearing officer in about 95 percent of such cases.

The story has been somewhat different in those cases where the hearing examiner, in theory, has final jurisdiction subject only to an appeal to the zoning board. Snell estimates that between 25 and 40 percent of his decisions in those cases are appealed to the zoning board of adjustment. Those who appeal have, based on experience to date, a 50-50 chance of securing a reversal of his decision.

Despite an ordinance that appears to provide that appeals to the board of adjustment from the hearing examiner are to be decided on the record, the practice has been that all appeals are heard de novo by the board. When the board of adjustment realized that the hearing-examiner idea was supposed to make it a purely appellate body, the members revolted. John Hendrickson, former deputy hearing examiner in Seattle and now examiner in neighboring Bellvue, described the Seattle board's protest as follows:

> They were, in essence, saying that they didn't like what the ordinance said, kind of two years after the fact, after it was changed, that the ordinance restricted them too much. They wanted to hear people; they didn't want to sit as an appellate body, reviewing the record in a very legal fashion and then rendering their decision, either affirming or reversing or remanding the hearing examiner's decision. They wanted to hear people. That was the essence of the thing. And once you hear one person, you have to hear the other side, and then somebody wants to rebut, so it turned into a situation where they were just opening up the record completely, allowing everyone to testify again. The Council just kind of dropped back and punted on the situation. They just let it go.

The difference in the percentage of reversals by the zoning board and the city council in Seattle may well be accounted for by the fact that the zoning board's informal practice of holding a de novo hearing means that, in cases appealable to that body, the hearing examiner's hearing becomes a little more than a practice run where, like the Indianapolis attorney quoted here, the smart petitioner will not show all of his or her cards:

> *Attorney:* I am always thinking tactics, I am a trial lawyer and so a couple of times where I have known that no matter who lost at the hearing examiner hearing, there would be an appeal, what I did was not give the hearing examiner all of my information. He came to me later and informally said, "What the hell happened. I don't understand how they could reverse me with the evidence I heard." I replied, "You didn't hear all of it. I didn't want the other side to be ready."
>
> *RFB:* In other words, it would be just like discovery.
>
> *Attorney:* Sure, and what I did in one case was to argue about surface water drainage and traffic and then come right back and talk about congestion of units and sewers and other things that I hadn't raised at the first hearing. It just totally flabergasted the other side. You couldn't do it in court.

So, in Seattle, the odd result of reform has been that one of the principal objects of the reform, the board of adjustment, has seen its power increase. In Bill Snell's words:

> It is such a backward system in many respects. . . . The Board of Adjustment originally, before the system was changed, heard the initial hearing and then the City Council heard the appeal. . . . The City Council was kind of a check on the Board. But now you have, even though a lot of the complaints were against what the Board of Adjustment was doing, they have now put them into the final decision making role.

And so it goes with the best laid plans of those who attempt to cut too deeply and quickly into the traditional fabric of the zoning process.

FOOTNOTE

1. David Curry, "Enforcement Under the Illinois Pollution Law," 70 *N.L.R.* 390, 444-45 (1976).

Chapter 14
Neighborhood Power:
The Suburbs Are
Alive and Well and
Living in Seattle

*We make an angry phone call to city
hall and then run down and answer it.*

—Neighborhood Leader

*Neighborhood groups are a pain in the
ass.*

—City Council Leader

Neighborhood power, during the past 10 years, has been "in." A report
prepared for the Boston Redevelopment Authority in 1972 made this
observation:

> Citywide advisory committees appointed by the Mayor have been par-
> ticularly short-lived and noticeably ineffective. The most recent city-wide
> effort, the Boston Urban Affairs Committee, had a life of little more than a
> year. Mayor Collins' 400 member Citizens Advisory Committee lasted
> longer but also had little influence.... In contrast, many neighborhood
> organizations have shown more staying power and have a growing role in
> the planning and development decisions. However, their sphere of influ-
> ence is limited to small areas of the City and there are frequent complaints
> of one group being played off by another.[1]

Throughout this book, the neighborhood and its citizen organizations
appear and re-appear for, more than any other single factor, it is what is
happening in urban zoning.

Milton Kotler, the executive director of the National Association of Neighborhoods and the country's foremost guru on neighborhood government, told a Chicago audience in early 1977: "Washington isn't going to save your neighborhood, nor is the State of Illinois, nor the City of Chicago—neighborhoods have to save themselves."[2] Other private interests see this phenomenon as a threat. Construction unions have opposed nonunion labor in housing renovation programs, police unions are suspicious of citizen patrols, and the retail clerks' union looks askance at neighborhood food co-ops.

The neighborhood has been analyzed, publicized, lionized, viewed as the only way cities shall rise from their ashes ("people-sized government"), and damned as the sure road to balkanization of our cities. It is not our intention to compete with the many social and political dissertations on this subject. It is our purpose in this chapter merely to describe the phenomenon of the emergence of the urban neighborhood in the zoning process and the consequences with respect to zoning and land development.

There is no doubt that zoning is the glue that holds most neighborhood organizations together. They seem frequently to have ancient roots in opposition to some expressway, as in Atlanta and Rochester, New York, but the eight-laned bogeyman frequently fades as a real threat and the neighborhood organization sprouts and grows in the more fertile soil provided by zoning controversies.

Several factors account for zoning's tendency to serve as a rallying point for neighborhood organizations. Zoning deals with highly visible neighborhood concerns. The threat of a high rise, a fast-food franchise, or another halfway house is ever-present to nurture neighborhood organization and vigilance. Zoning is an understandable function of government, in both how it works and what it does; it is not some mysterious technocrat decision made in the bowels of city hall. A zoning issue is that old-folks home proposed to come in next door. Zoning is also accessible to the common folk; it is the one aspect of municipal government where citizen participation has long been mandatory. Finally, zoning has been relatively effective in accomplishing neighborhood goals: in urban neighborhoods, change has most often been for the worse, and zoning's strong suit has always been the prevention of change. In short, zoning provides a forum where the frustrated and often fear-ridden citizen of the city can speak, not simply listen; where the citizen has at least a fighting chance to succeed; and where the results of citizen successes (and failures) are frequently both immediate and obvious. No wonder then that the urban citizen views zoning as a friend.

Whatever the reasons, there is no doubt that as large areas of our cities have slid downhill, neighborhood interest in, and influence over, zoning policy has steadily risen. As one zoning practitioner in Indianapolis said, perhaps with some license: ". . . neighborhood associations have taken over the whole damn zoning process." In St. Paul, neighborhood groups used zoning to try to close down an abortion clinic sponsored by Planned Parenthood, and the result was pretty ugly. Again, it is an example of zoning being used when all else had failed. The clinic was proposed to go into the Highland Park area, where it was a permitted use under the zoning ordinance. The reaction was violent, not just in the neighborhood but among anti-abortion groups throughout the city. The city council declared a moratorium on building permits for all abortion clinics, presumably on advice of counsel that facially such a technique would appear less as an attack on one project. So, in order "to study the problem," no permits for clinics for six months and, as a former planning staff member said, "the council will send it over to us and what the hell are we supposed to do about it?" In the meantime, the building, which, by the way, has a car wash on one side and a Burger King on the other, has the words "death" and "Dauchau" sprayed in white paint on the walls. Presumably, with the aid of the Civil Liberties Union, the case will end up in court. (A Massachusetts appellate court invalidated an attempt to zone out abortion clinics, saying in part: "The report of the Southborough planning board about public sentiment was thus an irrelevancy, and a dangerous one, for that way lies the extinction of many liberties which are, indeed, constitutionally guaranteed against invasion by a majority.")[3]

This growing neighborhood influence in zoning is, in part, a reaction to zoning practice as it had customarily been carried on for many years in the city. In many cities, land development policy had been a private game between city hall and the developers. One of the leading land development lawyers in Manhattan fairly described the old system:

> You know how it very frequently happens. You go to a social function and three or four of them are there. You grab this one. You grab another one—at a retirement party or a political dinner, or a fund raising, whatever the hell it happens to be—you put them together and say, "Hey, fellas, I got

this problem; it would take me a month to talk to all of you, you know—what do you say?"

Father Thomas Corrigan, a leader of Fair Share, a Boston-based, statewide coalition of neighborhood organizations, described how the neighborhoods wanted to change the process:

> It is important that the Boston zoning board of appeals, when they meet every week, make a decision based on the merits and not on the phone call they got the week before from a councilman or a developer.

From Atlanta to San Diego and Seattle to Boston, back of the emergence of the neighborhood as a force in zoning there was a history of local government that, more frequently than not, was identified with, if not part of, the land development industry:

> You've got to understand something about Atlanta.... Atlanta traditionally has always been a developers' town. There's been no interest in historic preservation; no interest in ecology; very little interest in saving the trees which are such an important part of the heritage of the city. Decisions were usually made behind closed doors by the business community in conjunction with the city administration where the mayor was either a member of that great elite community himself or was in fact controlled by that community and responsive only to the business community.... There was this sort of fraternity of men that made decisions, but they didn't include the entire population in any sense whatsoever... a tremendously long tradition of that.

Pete Wilson's election and re-election as mayor of San Diego was in large part due to a citizen reaction to years of coziness between city government and the building industry. Indeed, in Wilson's last campaign, his supporters treated the fact that his opponent was a very successful contractor as though it were a prima facie disqualification for public office.

The rise of the neighborhood may indicate that the old system is passing from the scene. However, it is also possible that the trauma of the cities has led us into an urban romantic age where we are tempted to grasp and glamorize any evidence, however fragile, that suggests a revival—a sort of grass roots grows in Brooklyn. Some say, like Murray Friedman of Atlanta, that the alleged power of community groups in zoning really is not all that pervasive, that it only appears so because of the remarkable contrast with the previous scene:

I don't think neighborhoods have as much power as they are given credit for. I think suddenly there's someone who can debate with the developer and make a lot of sense and can win a few times. In the old days all they had to do was say this is what I want and they didn't have to explain it. Now someone says to them, "Tell me why you think so and why your argument is better than someone else's."

In Jacksonville, Florida, it was put this way: the neighborhood just helps to balance off "the right law firm."

Nor should the sophistication and know-how of community organizations be exaggerated. While some are extraordinarily savvy, many are not. As one Minneapolis neighborhood newsletter confessed:

> Our contacts and support have grown so that we now know where to send all the carbons—although we still don't know sometimes where to send the letter.[4]

Some expect more from the process than it can give. This exchange took place in a large East Coast city:

> *XXX:* I'll never forget one of the first things that happened is that a bunch of ladies came in to see me, and they wanted an R-6 area downzoned to R-5. I tried to explain to them that the problem was that there wasn't any investment, that it wouldn't make any difference what the hell the zoning was, nobody's going to invest and build anyway. But they had heard, you know, that this was a good thing, this R-5, so we gave them some. . . . They had this idea that zoning has some role that it doesn't play. It's simply irrelevant.
>
> *RFB:* How it is perceived though is important.
>
> *XXX:* Is enormously important, that's right. And you have accomplished something by changing the designation of the map no one ever reads. But the people who have done it won a victory, and you know, sometimes it's hard to win victories over real enemies. . . . You've really got to try to meet these legitimate expectations, to come in and wave your magic wand and go away, but it is only going to work for a very brief time—it's a good thing to do during a campaign, but it's not too good for re-election.

Still, the neighbors cling to the zoning ordinance and zoning process because they frequently have no place else to turn. After a major round of hearings throughout the separate neighborhoods of his city, one plan commission member told us:

> There are times when I literally felt like crying because what those people were saying was true, that they were suffering, that the city had been terribly remiss and in fact there was nothing we could do because it

was totally out of our area. But yet the Plan Commission was the only body that they could come and appeal to, and we came at a time when they could be there, in the evening. . . . I've never forgotten the pathos and anger and frustrations that the communities felt.

Another point should be made at the threshold. There is no necessary correlation between economic status or homeownership and effective use of neighborhood influence on the zoning process. You don't have to be rich to know how to apply pressure on city hall. Of course, many of the most articulate neighborhood spokespersons are members of the white middle class who have rediscovered the city; Capitol Hill, an aggressive neighborhood in Seattle, is, in the words of one neighborhood leader, "a ghetto of lawyers." In contrast, however, one of the more aggressive neighborhoods in the country, when it comes to land use policy, is Ocean Beach in San Diego. It has a large transient population, 80 percent of the residents are renters, and it contains many young people who, as one city planner said, "are kind of counter-culture and they've beaten the system." The uptown area in San Diego, between Hillcrest and the central business district, has been vocal in zoning matters. The community consists of half-million-dollar homes and units that rent for $175 a month. The Clinton area on the west side of Midtown Manhattan, which compelled city hall to create the Special Clinton District, is made up of a mix of low- and moderate-income whites. The neighborhood in Minneapolis that drove out a porno theater is a racially mixed neighborhood of moderate means. The Little Italy Special Zoning District in New York was the child of an association of persons of Italian descent although Americans of Chinese descent outnumber those of Italian heritage. In Honolulu, however, the Chinese have thus far held back the chamber of commerce types who want to knock down the city's Chinatown area and build a nice "Oriental-American shopping center/cultural center." They used a favorite WASP tactic; in the words of a disgruntled Honolulu businessman, they "quietly got the whole doggone area put on the National Register of Historic Places."

The Back Bay Associations of this country may get a greater press, but the emergence of neighborhood power in zoning in our cities embraces most of the economic, ethnic, and racial spectrum.

The attitude of elected officials to all of this is, to put it gently, ambiguous. The professed enthusiasm of these officials for local community groups, reflected in their public statements ("mandatory water-ing holes for politicians"), may be more than balanced by the opinions they expressed in private conversations, such as: "The neighborhoods are run by the people who, instead of bowling on Monday night, go out and harass their elected officials and they don't care right from wrong; they enjoy the conflict." Even the public attitudes of city administra-tions vary widely—from Seattle where the current relationship be-tween city hall and the neighborhoods is so intimate that it is hard to make out who has pre-empted whom, to Jacksonville, Florida, where the ties are not so evident, and Hartford, Connecticut, where the relationship is tense. In Detroit, the city administration has gone out to help set up neighborhood organizations, apparently on the theory that things can't get worse.

In San Diego, Mayor Wilson's predecessor began to see the commu-nity planning committees as groups who were intervening in the poli-tical process and beginning to develop some clout. He was very close to killing them when *Look* magazine gave San Diego an All-American City Award and the Mayor concluded it would be awkward to kill what had gained San Diego national distinction. More recently, the San Diego City Council, under Wilson, appropriated $5,000 to hold an election in Ocean Beach to determine who should speak for the community. The resolution calling the election was, however, careful to make explicit that this was an experiment and would not necessarily be replicated.

In New York, the plan commission, when John Zuccotti was chair-man, instituted a zoning training program for communities, and, according to Norman Marcus, counsel to the commission, "the folks all became zoning freaks." Yet in New York some of the city council and the borough presidents have been nervous about the growing sophis-tication of the communities and the neighborhood review boards. A former member of the New York plan commission described the prob-lem as follows:

> We fought at length with Percy Sutton [Manhattan borough president], a very sophisticated political leader. For a long time Sutton would not let us make any mailings directly to community boards because he knew that was the arena in which these decisions were going to be made. . . . He finally changed because we had a couple of instances where the sending of our stuff by his people just broke down. The boards would come scream-ing to us and we'd piously say, well, gee, three weeks ago we sent all that stuff to the borough president's office.

Another New York opinion was more blunt:

> The elected officials are deathly afraid of community boards. I don't
> think they really understand them.... I mean our really higher elected
> officials. They see them as an impediment to their ideas, what the city
> should be, and how it should develop, and something they have to work
> around, not with. And it's even more pronounced with the passing of the
> charter which almost all public officials opposed.

Indianapolis, which received national attention with UniGov, the
consolidation (for some purposes) of the city and Marion County, also
was directed by the state legislature to divide the city-county into
"MiniGov" districts that would elect their own councils and have some
voice in their governance. The mandate for MiniGov remains the law,
but the council has not implemented the state's command and it is not
about to do so.

Much of the increased neighborhood participation in the zoning
process in the urban core takes the form of informal political pressure,
long accepted in suburbia, or of unstated administrative practices.
There may be no legal obligation for a developer to talk with the
neighbors, but such a practice may be urged on them by elected
officials. "When I was on the council," one Minneapolis lawyer told us,
"I'd say to the developer: Listen, you're the one's going to make money
on this—you go out, you knock on the doors, you go calm the neighborhood."

The techniques of informal pressure, so well honed in surburban
communities, are now practiced in the neighborhoods of the cities. The
following description of the process in Atlanta is typical of what we
found in most cities:

> *CLW:* When you oppose a rezoning or get a notice that somebody's filed
> an application, where are the pressure points in the system?
>
> *Citizen:* The Board of Directors in my neighborhood determines whether
> we should oppose it; if they determine that we should oppose, we im-
> mediately talk with the applicant and discuss with him what it is we're
> about—why we oppose it. Most of them don't even know there's any
> middle-class people that live there. They just don't understand it, and
> they're absolutely flabbergasted that anybody would care about convert-
> ing the house to a garage. After that discussion, they get shocked, then they
> start rethinking their position and they'll offer some conditions on the
> rezoning which would tend to address our concerns. That's happened
> twice.... After that, we go down and find out, talk with the City and see
> what their feelings are on it. Now, this is generally informal with City

Planning Staff. Then the other thing we try to determine, assess the possibility of the rezoning or special use permit being denied, and at that time there's a letter prepared to the chairman of the Zoning Review Board with a copy or a separate letter going to the Chairman of the City Council Development Committee identifying our position and for what reasons. I think we try to do it fairly systematically and we try to delineate the reasons. That's the procedure, and then, of course, mustering a lot of people at the hearing itself.

The informal pressure is evident in urban planning departments. As you enter the Indianapolis development and planning offices, you encounter a four- by five-foot map of the city with neighborhood boundaries delineated. Minneapolis, Seattle, and San Diego, to name only a few, have similar maps in the planning offices. Notice requirements to local groups beyond those required by statute or ordinance are a common administrative policy in planning departments. Seattle has published a series of pamphlets directed at neighborhoods telling it like it is about zoning; a sort of "Look Jane, look; see the spot zone; see the spot zone spread" series.

In Chicago, Alderman Dick Simpson, in the Lake View area, set up a Community Review Board on a purely voluntary, nonofficial basis. In *Neighborhood Zoning: Practices and Prospects,* a comprehensive review of the issue by Efraim Gil,[5] this operation is described as follows:

Although initially viewed with suspicion and recognized only as the alderman's advisers, the board slowly has gained respect and recognition in its own right.... So far, in every case, the Zoning Board of Appeals has accepted the recommendations of the Lake View Community Zoning Board.... Other points worth noting in regard to the Lake View experiment are:

- the board deals only with zoning matters;
- board members are elected by the Ward Assembly [another creation of Alderman Simpson's];
- the board has at its disposal the staff and office facilities of the alderman; no other finances are available to the board;
- the board has been dealing with minor zoning changes, appeals, and variances; the experience of the past two years has shown that, in order to deal successfully with major zoning issues, the board would have to function from a legal base.

Another Chicago alderman, perhaps to quell any suspicions by his constituents who have seen a predecessor go to jail for zoning bribery, has appointed a seven-man zoning committee. Each applicant for a zoning change must make a presentation before this group, and the alderman vows to follow its judgment.

Not all neighborhood zoning power is of the ad hoc, unofficial type; there are cases where community participation has been institutionalized. (Recall that from the earliest days of zoning, from the Model Standard Zoning Enabling Act of 1926, the law has required a supermajority vote of the city or town council to override a protest of neighboring owners.) In some instances, the creation of special zoning districts (discussed in Chapter 9) is no more than the laying on of hands by city hall of community control.

Nowhere is this institutional approach more dramatic than in the amendments to the charter of New York City that became law on November 4, 1975, a step shoved down Mayor Lindsay's throat by the late Governor Rockefeller. New York City is, by the charter, divided into communities, each with a local board. All requests for amendments to the zoning map and all requests for variances must be referred to the local board. If the community board holds a public hearing on a map amendment, no hearing is required to be held by the New York planning commission. If the New York Board of Standards and Appeals (the local term for the zoning board of appeals) approves a variance, a community board may take an appeal to the Board of Estimate, which has legislative jurisdiction over changes in land use regulations in New York City and may, after making quasi-judicial findings, reverse the decision of the Board of Standards and Appeals on variances. To Norman Marcus, this now is a "legitimization of many of the *de facto* powers enjoyed by these communities under the old charter."

In Minneapolis no proposal for any development of more than 10 multi-family units may be heard by the city council unless it has been approved by a neighborhood board. That provision was a result of a trade-off between developers and the neighborhood associations. Builders wanted the state legislature to enact a tax break for the construction of higher density units. The community groups told the builders they would oppose the legislation unless the builders agreed that neighborhoods would have a larger voice in the design and location of multiple family units. According to Norma Olson, a prominent neighborhood leader, "... we told them, we know you can't pass that legislation if we choose to oppose it." The bill passed the state legislature and the ordinance passed the city council. Seattle is experimenting, with less than total success, with local review boards.

Not all such efforts are received with enthusiasm by city hall. In Chicago, an ordinance to make official Alderman Simpson's community boards of zoning appeal in each ward died in a council committee, unmourned by the late Mayor Daley's organization. Nor are the neighbors always sure they like the idea of institutionalizing their right to rise up; they suspect subversion. As the president of a grass roots community group saw it, it was all right to let the city-chartered "official" neighborhood group prepare plans, but when it got down to the real issue—zoning—the grass roots group would, thank you kindly, handle that on its own:

> We had an argument, a strong discussion, with one or two council people as to whether the Neighborhood Planning Unit should have an opinion on zoning. It's my feeling they should have a plan that could be put up and say this is what the NPU says is the neighborhood plan. But a particular zoning case has to be much more contained to a neighborhood or street. . . . The guy who lives across the NPU, he doesn't really have the same interest in that zoning case.

If the relationship is wary and overlaid with suspicion on both sides, it is a fact that, both informally and on an institutional basis, the city neighborhood is becoming a force to be counted in zoning practice. As long as our city halls find it difficult to cope with neighborhood problems, as long as it remains economically difficult for persons of moderate means to migrate to housing in the suburbs, and as long as the rediscovery of the city by the rising young middle class continues, the institutionalization of a neighborhood voice in zoning policy will continue to spread.

This is not to say that this tendency is all cakes and ale. There are serious problems. One is the issue of who speaks for the neighborhood. Often this is used as a cop-out or excuse by city hall to fob off the locals, and its articulation should be taken in small doses. But there is at least a grain of truth in it, particularly when a neighborhood is a mix of commercial and residential, as in Capitol Hill in Seattle, or where, as in the Little Italy section in Lower Manhattan, an old power group retains control despite its dwindling numbers in the neighborhood population. Zoning policy in such cases may reflect the best organized but not necessarily either the most residents or the most significant investments in the neighborhood. The following are representative of the usual complaints of officials and developers:

Fifteen people can stop a project in New York.

and

You don't get a real direction from the organizations because maybe 10 or 12 people will show up out of an area of 1,000 homes. As a result, you're not getting a true picture—it's just this guy setting himself up as a leader. He's elected maybe by 15 people out of the whole area and he wants to become a political figure and tell you what to do in the area.

and

Decisions on how land should be used are placed in the hands of the whimsical: The neighborhood leader who enjoys a platform and who does not have to bear the responsibility for accuracy. They claim a constituency of one or two thousand homeowners, but when we examine it factually, we find they are speaking, generally, their own interest.

and

That particular movement [neighborhood power] presents a difficulty in that quite often those who have the leisure, the money and the freedom to attend meetings are people who have vested interests. The people out there in the community who should be attending are busy trying to survive. And so, very often, the views of the community become distorted.

Various neighborhood groups may assert jurisdiction over the same zoning dispute. The map of neighborhoods in Indianapolis reflects this overlapping, and one Indianapolis zoning attorney told us that representatives of as many as five different neighborhood organizations have shown up to protest a client's proposal.

As noted earlier the San Diego city council became so frustrated with the cacophony of conflicting voices over zoning in Ocean Beach that it paid for an election. As is customary in community elections, persons 18 years or older from three groups were permitted to vote: residents, landowners, and licensed operators of businesses. It was no surprise that when the ballots were counted on May 4, 1976, a majority of the local council were from the residents known as the Community Planning Group. In Capitol Hill, Seattle, the conflict on planning policy erupted in an election for a commmunity council, and, as one activist described the result, ". . . they tried one more time to stab us in the back by running an opposing slate of real estate men against us but we really bore down and beat them a thousand to a little over a hundred."

The conflict within neighborhoods between commercial interests and residents may sometimes appear more as a xenophobia against "outsiders" than as anti-business. In its campaign pamphlet for the

Ocean Beach election, the Community Planning Group in San Diego boasted that "... Seven-Eleven, a franchise of a giant corporation, has been stopped from coming into the neighborhood several times." In the Back Bay area of Boston, Dan Ahern was executive director of the Back Bay Federation as well as the executive director of the Back Bay Association. The former is an umbrella group that includes business-people in the area; the Association is composed of the residents. Few could always balance such potentially conflicting interests, and there have been fights. One of the biggest was over high rises and the residents beat back the businesspeople. According to Ahern, "most of the businessmen now realize that the restored townhouses represent a far better bet for housing and for the economy than knocking down for a highrise." Aston Glaves, chairman of Community Board No. 4 on Mid-Manhattan's west side, constantly faces this conflict:

> A very high percentage of the people who are in theater live in the Clinton area. A good percentage of the rest of the people walk to work to the commercial establishments around them. You are in very strong union country—the blue collars. When you put all that together you begin to realize that jobs have real meaning to the residents and therefore there has to be a close, harmonious relationship with the business and commercial interests if both are to survive. And one of the things my board has been trying to sell to the commercial people is that they do not have to maintain an irrational fear of my board.

Few, if any, commentators have focused on this intramural land use conflict between business and residents in the neighborhoods, but an equitable resolution of the neighborhood role in central city develop-ment policy cannot ignore it. Indeed, if fights between community chambers of commerce and community clubs persist, the sure result is that elected officials will play them off against each other or will ignore both parties.

A more serious impediment to formal neighborhood participation in the zoning process is the lack of staying power that is frequently directly related to the absence of money. (In New York City each of the 62 boards will get $15,000 a year from the city.) Few are lucky enough to be like Back Bay, where the association has more professional input from volunteers than most city governments will get from hired pro-fessionals, or Beacon Hill, which, as one developer described it, "is alive with attorneys that may not be active in their practice but they're terribly active in the neighborhood, and if you try to push something through you get an enormous outpouring of very good legal opinions and an ability to out-shout each other."

In New York, the planning commission rules for local boards require only 20 percent of the members to be present for a quorum, which speaks to the difficulty of maintaining a sustained interest when the neighborhood voice becomes institutionalized. A staff memo of the New York planning commission described the reaction of community leaders to the charter revisions that would vest greater power in each local board:

> In general, they endorsed the procedures, although their reservations were voiced on the difficulties some of its provisions will impose on the boards' hitherto informal operations. The boards are in various stages of readiness to implement the new procedures. Some boards are short of full membership. (All board members are volunteers.) Attendance at board meetings and hearings in some areas is sparse. And, among other concerns, the boards are already considering a wide variety of local matters which presently weigh heavily on them. The procedures thrust an additional burden on the boards.
>
> One item of major concern to the speakers was the provision of sufficient funds to implement the new regulations. . . .

In the end, the most serious problem surrounding this renaissance of the neighborhood in land use policy is the difficulty of balancing a consideration of the community's interests with an equitable and fair governance of the entire city. Even if we put aside the ongoing agony of debate over centralized or dispersed administration of our urban schools and the quixotic efforts of some neighborhoods to turn a sow's ear into a silk purse by way of special district status, there remains the real question of whether land development policy for a city of several hundred thousand, or four million, can be coherent when any one, two, or three subcommunities can influence or make the final decisions. The neighborhoods of our cities may cherish the sentiment that they are just a conglomerate of villages, but a century of consolidation in politics and infrastructure stands in the way of their claim that they are identical to their suburban cousins. The ascendance of the neighborhood may be romantic, but there is an easily perceived fear, even among those who were in the van of the effort to neighborize land use policy, that it may also be anti-city (which brings to mind the late Saul Alinsky's second thoughts about his success in mobilizing community action in Chicago's Back-of-the-Yards). The roots of this fear lie in a perception of an attitude that characterizes many neighborhood groups that have successfully organized around land use issues: they are against change; they are committed to the status quo ante even when the status is dismal and the ante is unlikely to persevere. These inner-city neighborhoods are opposed to change because they have observed change these last 20 years, and, to their minds, it has generally been bad. (Or for other reasons, such as: "If there's a vacant lot, they think there is a god-given right to have that lot vacant and the owner should still pay taxes because it's his duty as an American to pay taxes. That's know-nothing opposition.") Zoning represents an apparent barricade against change. They are wedded to the side-yard principle and the front-yard principle just as are their cousins in the suburbs.[6]

Occasionally, even the neighborhood leaders admit the weakness of their approach:

> For the most part the thing that's strong cement for most of these community groups has been resistence to change of land use, and I think that has on the whole worked out quite well, although I can't say that people look their best when they do that.

Another neighborhood sympathizer also admitted to a certain narrow-mindedness among the good citizens: "They are like early Christians in that everything is judged in terms of absolute 100 percent purity." That view was echoed by a Minneapolis resident:

> Each neighborhood group tends to be the most conservative group imaginable. They want no changes; all they really want is to have what they like preserved without regard to its relationship to the balance of the city. Everyone of them came in with their own proposals to keep the in-place residents happy. It's almost like what I read about these California towns.

Norman Marcus, with his sense of history and his remarkable balance, seemed to say it best:

> The rise of communities carries a problem. In a place which is as constricted and congested as New York, it is very difficult for anybody to do anything without impacting somebody else, and the more you raise the locals' expectations, the more difficult it is to do city-wide kinds of things. What's emerging is a sort of a non-answer to Robert Moses—and also an odd defense of Moses. The critics of this decentralization process point to Moses and say, well, he achieved things—assuming you value those things—because there was no process of the kind we are busily creating today and the city is the loser for that. It really becomes a kind of ideological tug of war as to which set of values you put first: the more modest and

process-oriented values, or the tangible, development-related activities. Certainly this shift may be creating the organisms that permit the city to survive at the same time it denies the more tangible evidences of the city's success.

It is difficult to say what the future of this urban phenomenon of the past 10 years will be. Will city hall, caught between the nether regions of the communities and the upper regions of state mandates, become an anachronism in land use policy? The only fair response is that no one knows. As one neighborhood leader said, it probably " ... can't go on. Everybody's too accommodating so far." Beyond that, it is difficult to see.

Perhaps the beginnings of the next phase of this development are to be seen in the fact that, at least in a few cities, neighborhood organizations are forming effective coalitions. In Hartford, Connecticut, a coalition of neighborhoods actively supported a bond issue for land for a small shopping center in a black community. The politicians gave the proposal little more than lip service. It passed in 30 of the 32 community districts, and that in a city often polarized along racial lines. The Council of Community Councils in Minneapolis represents about 24 neighborhood groups in Minneapolis, and its support is almost essential for a proposition to be approved. The Establishment leaders—business, labor, newspapers, elected officials—supported a new stadium near downtown, everyone except "the people," and it was badly defeated. If such coalitions may crack up on divisive issues, then they try to avoid them. In Boston, one coalition fighting for better housing and consumer protection on a broad front does not touch the busing issue because, one leader blandly says, "we have a membership who differ on that issue."

The coalitions provide new evidence that the neighborhood movement is growing in strength and influence. It is a force with which city leaders will have to deal for some time into the future. And yet, in the success of coalitions may be the beginning of the demise of the neighborhood revolution. They may topple the traditional political alliances and change the political faces, but revolutions do consume their own, and today's dissidents can become tomorrow's central bureaucrats. Neighborhoods may find, to paraphrase Pogo's aphorism, that "we have met the government and it is us." On that day, neighborhood leaders will have to face the facts that there is more to the city than their neighborhood and that the status quo is often just another name for the stagnation in which diseases of every kind find it easy to breed.

FOOTNOTES

1. *Urban Renewal and Planning in Boston* (Boston Redevelopment Authority, 1972), pp. 45-46.

2. *Chicago Tribune,* February 24, 1977, sec. 7, p. 1.

3. *Framingham Clinic, Inc.* v. *Board of Selectmen of Southborough,* 367 N.E.2d 606, 611 (Mass. 1977). See also *Fox Valley Reproductive Health Care Center, Inc.* v. *Arft,* 446 F.2d 1072 (1978); and *West Side Women's Services, Inc.* v. *City of Cleveland,* 454 F.2d. 796 (1978).

4. Metro Council, *Perspectives,* April-June 1976.

5. Efraim Gil, *Neighborhood Zoning: Practices and Prospects* (Chicago: American Society of Planning Officials, 1975).

Chapter 15
Regional Impacts:
The View from Upstairs

*We just have no problem as far as
zoning is concerned but we do have
this environmental thing....*

—Seattle developer

*The Development Framework concept
of guided growth needs to be revised in
order to achive the ...revitalization
objectives for the ...Fully Developed
Area.*

—1975 Report of Minneapolis-
St. Paul Metropolitan
Council Task Force

In the Spring of 1974, a group of Canadian investors, organized as the Polygon Corporation, proposed to construct a 13-story, 47-unit condominium on the south slope of Seattle's Queen Anne Hill. The area, close to downtown, had been zoned multiple-family for 20 years. In the words of the Seattle superintendent of buildings, the project was "in compliance with all [municipal] zoning, building, health, traffic codes and street use regulations." Nevertheless, the application for a building permit was denied. The project was, the superintendent said, "inconsistent with the intent of the State Environmental Policy Act [SEPA]." In reaching this decision, the official said that "the most significant impact on the community and the City as a whole appears to be visual."

During a pretrial deposition taken in the course of the ensuing lawsuit, then Seattle Mayor Wes Uhlman testifed that "I felt even though [the project] was legal, it was still my duty to try and save the neighborhood and do whatever I could to stop it." "That," one city official wryly observed, "occasionally happens." The Washington Supreme Court upheld the denial of the building permit on the ground that SEPA applied and the EIS showed the project would have adverse aesthetic and economic impacts on the neighborhood.[1]

The Polygon experience is a vignette of the growing entrance of the state into land use policy in the cities as well as the countryside. The latter has been thoroughly documented; the former has not received the attention it deserves.

During the first half-century of zoning and subdivision regulations, all power was vested in municipalities, so much so that many forgot that cities and towns were exercising this authority as agents; the power to regulate eminated from the state.

This long-cherished tradition of local authority is now being challenged, and the struggle between municipal and higher levels of authority will be with us for the remainder of this century. Most of the attention and comment on this contest has been directed to the suburbs or the scenic areas. Charges of exclusionary suburban zoning have been made from Massachusetts and New Jersey to Colorado and California. Attempts by states to preserve wilderness from tract housing and second homes, because "local governments were," in the words of San Diego Mayor Pete Wilson, "quickly giving away the store," have created bitter controversies such as the acrimony over the Adirondack State Park legislation in New York.

But now the question of who should exercise authority over land use is also being raised in our larger cities, and not all mayors are as eager to employ the state as was Mayor Uhlman in his fight with Polygon. Indeed, as city hall observes the clamor from the neighborhoods for a greater voice and notes the increasing intervention of supramunicipal agencies, the city must begin to ask whether, in land use policy, it will become a vestigal reminder of a bygone era.

Control over the use of private land in our urban cores is being challenged today by at least four varieties of supramunicipal meddling:

- Metropolitan agencies vested with authority by the state;

- Experiments with metropolitan government or what might be called "the expanded city";

- State pre-emption of authority on an ad hoc basis over specified uses of land; and

- State environmental legislation applicable to private development.

THE ROLE OF METRO

Metropolitan planning is *not* as American as apple pie. In most areas it is even a worse devil than state intervention, probably because it is, to our experience, exotic, or it appears as a cover for a big-city effort to subvert suburbs. For years—perhaps even until today—a group of women would gather at meetings of the Northeastern Illinois Planning Commission. They would sit and knit, a modern composite of Madame Lafarge, solemnly observing NIPC's decisions and duly reporting the nefarious commission schemes to turn the suburbs over to the socialists or, worse, to Mayor Daley.

Metro planning with teeth—as distinguished from the state or "the expanded city," has not found a fertile soil in this country. Minneapolis-St. Paul is the only extant example of this species. That, however, may be occasion less for dismissal and more for a recognition that Minnesota has often been at the forefront of reform in this country—or, as noted later, it may not.

Whatever its future, however, the metro idea may be irrelevant as far as the center city is concerned. For the most part, metro planning agencies have been created in response to, and have occupied themselves almost exclusively with, issues affecting suburban sprawl. They have dealt with the urban centers only indirectly, if at all. They focused on sewer extension policy, on open space, and on highways. If they were bold, they talked about housing policy, but the policy related to fair share in the suburbs, not rehab in the city.

The Metropolitan Council was established by the Minnesota legislature in 1967 and was delegated authority over major sewers, mass transit, solid waste disposal, highway routes, airport sites, and regional open space in a 3,000-square-mile, seven-county area embracing 135 municipalities, 60 townships, and 100 special districts. The council has performed a responsible job in those areas, tip-toeing with notable agility through the suburban mine fields.

But not until 1976—10 years after its creation—did the council create what is known as the Task Force on Fully Developed Areas; "Mature Areas" as one euphemism describes the assignment, making it sound as though it really belongs in the chapter on pornography, along with other things nice folks don't usually discuss. On June 21, 1976, a staff memo advised the task force: "The focus of regional policies has to become more directed toward the older communities." And the staff of the council, in an apparent effort to shame the council members, wrote an eloquent report on "Throw-Away Cities," suggesting that too often we regard our urban areas as akin to a refrigerator or a Buick that can be discarded and as quickly replaced.

This long indifference to the central cities on the part of the nation's most prestigious, if not only, example of a serious attempt to combine metropolitan planning with implementation is understandable. If the 1950s gave birth to sprawl, it is not surprising that it generated the response of the '60s—anti-sprawl. And that is what Metro focused on. Even though containment carried inevitable conflicts with some suburban interests, it struck a responsive chord in those who were already aboard. Perhaps a few Metro commissioners even believed that by containing sprawl through control over sewer extensions and the drawing of a Metropolitan Urban Services Area (MUSA), they would, in some way, stem the flight from the Twin Cities and, better yet, redirect the housing market inward to the older areas.

Concern and good works on containing sprawl did not have that result. The flight has continued and even leapfrogged. The Fully Developed Area Task Force staff concluded:

> Establishing a MUSA line around the urban and urbanizing portion of the Metropolitan Area that allows a 5 to 10 year average of developable land may or may not be of much assistance in the redevelopment, re-use, or private reinvestment in the Fully Developed Area. Should the MUSA be reduced or altered in some fashion?

That staff query may have been prompted by a rather blunt communication from a member of the St. Paul planning department:

> Most of the efforts by the Metropolitan Council to date have been directed to...the developing suburbs and urban-rural fringe areas. . . . In addition, it appears that the Metropolitan Council has assumed that by merely establishing an urban growth policy or line in the other suburbs, that this automatically will mean that future growth will be directed back to the central cities. The accuracy of this assumption is highly debatable, since the effect of establishing a growth line may be to encourage further leapfrog development in the counties beyond the 7-county metropolitan area. (There is evidence that this is currently taking place.)

The council staff should be retained by the City of San Diego, which considered a program to slow growth in the outer fringes with the belief this will result in development in the inner residential areas. That city has not yet produced any study that demonstrates the feasibility of such in-close development nor an answer to the leapfrog consequence of an urban services line. Indeed, San Diego has not yet recognized, as has the Metro Council, the contradiction in asserting that there is within the outer service line a substantial margin of vacant land for development and, at the same time, claiming that control over growth on the periphery will result in a redirection of growth to the inner core. With a candor that should be emulated by growth-management advocates, the Metro Council's Task Force on Fully Developed Areas reported in January 1977:

> [W]ithout programs and policies which give at least equal attention to the older developed areas and to existing development, even modest growth in the Fully Developed Areas is unattainable. *Unless the reinvestment and maintenance half of the guided growth concept can be made to work, metropolitan growth will go predominately into the developing communities....* The Fully Developed Area Task Force strongly believes that for the [Metro] Development Framework plan and its policy based forecasts to be achieved, current development incentives need to be changed.... Regional urban development policy for the Fully Developed Area is not being achieved. [Emphasis added]

In such candid recognition of the problem, there is, at least, a glimmer of hope. However, one has to be very careful about drawing conclusions from the Minneapolis-St. Paul experience. Any temptation to give over to ecstasy must be tempered with the reality that there are special circumstances in this area that prompt caution in using it as a prototype. Probably nowhere in this country does an urban area have such a combination of (1) twin urban cities, (2) major home-office industries, (3) minor racial confrontations, (4) a history of civic commitment, and (5) a diffusion of the power structure. Add to this that the outdoors is a great leveler and you have perhaps an explanation of why this special system appears to be acceptable in Minneapolis-St. Paul.

If, in that benign climate, Metro cannot cope with the problems of the urban core, no similiar efforts seem likely to work elsewhere. And difficulties are foreseen—apart from the obvious one that it is a lot easier to decide not to run a sewer across five miles of farm land than it is to persuade middle-income families to move back to a deteriorated neighborhood.

One difficulty relates to scale. For a metropolitan commission, most issues on the fringe are, as the planners like to say, macro. They are big regional parks, a metropolitan airport, a major highway. When it comes to the inner city, the issues are too often at the other end of the scale, rehab of 20 units, a tot lot, the closing of a street. Are those regional? A member of the Metropolitan Council said, "Regional up to this date has always meant big; and now we're saying regional can be small."

What is of "metropolitan significance," according to him, is not size alone but whether the development may disrupt or conflict with those major metropolitan systems the council is charged with controlling. But will not this inject the council into every proposal for rezoning when protesting neighbors invoke one of those metropolitan considerations? Again, the councilperson remarked:

> We usually have to go through a 15-minute analysis with the rest of the committee members to make sure they understand that all we're looking at is how does this impact metro systems. The fact that they may not like highrise buildings next to lakes or parks, unless that's a "regional" resource, then that's a local issue.

Minnesota elected not to go the route chosen by Florida—that is, to define "regional impact" in terms of scale. In Florida no regional agency is involved if a development is below a designated size. The problem with Florida's approach is that incremental growth may cause even more damage. Florida may not be trampled by elephants, but it may be stung to death by gnats; in Minnesota the council may restrain itself and choose the gnats it attacks, but it's going to be engaged in a lot of swatting. And, as it begins swatting at "regional" issues in the city, it will have no easy time in getting agreement as to where its jurisdiction begins and ends for, like the old joke, one man's gnat is often another man's trained flea.

Indeed, the contrast between the positive, if not aggressive, policies of Metro when dealing with the outlying areas is in stark contrast to the tentative, subjunctive, and often rhetorical approach of its Fully Developed Task Force when it deals with what needs to be done by Metro in the inner city:

> "The quality of life within the older developed areas must be turned around." "Strong consideration for the use of public funds *should* be given to these neighborhood priorities." " ... [S]olutions for the problems faced by older developed communities *should* be issue oriented. . . . " "From the equity standpoint there *should* be a preference within the [Metropolitan

Urban Service Area] for the already developed and well serviced areas."
[Emphasis added]

And on and on.

THE EXPANDED CITY

Metropolitan government in this country for the most part means a consolidation of a center city with an entire county, and it is unlikely to be otherwise because it takes the consent of two units to merge (in addition to the permission of the state legislature) and it is hard to conceive of a county consenting to allow a part of its territory to be merged into a new unit. For that reason, metro government will continue to follow established political boundaries in spite of the allegations of advocates of such systems that old boundaries are irrational and incapable of dealing with current metropolitan crises: thus Nashville and Davidson County, Tennessee; Indianapolis and Marion County, Indiana; and Jacksonville and Duval County, Florida.

We wanted to know what were the consequences to land use policy from such mergers. Coming as we do from a metropolitan area where the "suburban noose" is evident and is exemplified by zoning controls, we had romantic visions of a nirvana where regional policy was co-extensive with regional regulation. As with most such romances, the truth was less than expected, perhaps in some cases worse than before, but again better on occasion than most cynics would predict.

First, did land use policy play any part in the decision to consolidate in Indianapolis or Jacksonville?

Zoning played practically no part in the campaign for UniGov in Indianapolis. The effort in Marion County was a result of a merger of the interests of the good government types and the Republican Party. While UniGov brought a consolidation of housing and planning into a single Department of Metropolitan Development, Marion County had a long history of county-city planning and some centralized control of implementation. Efficiency in government—not concern over irresponsible private development—was the articulated reason for consolidation. The unarticulated reason was not, contrary to the typical fears of opponents of metro government, some dark scheme by inner-city folks to take over the upper income suburbs; rather, it was a scheme to strengthen the Republicans' hold on city government.

Consolidation was initiated by then Mayor (now U.S. Senator) Lugar, after his first election (before consolidation), which he won by about 9,000 votes in the old city. In the second election, after consolidation, he won by more than 50,000 votes but got no more in the old city. In the 1975 election, Lugar's successor lost in the old city by about 16,000 votes but won the election. QED. It was, as one Indianapolis attorney said, "a political vehicle to allow the Anglo-Saxon suburbanite to have voting rights in city elections." The political tactics that went into this are beyond the scope of this account, but it is a monument to the results that can be achieved by the union of politically savvy persons with reformers, an alliance not often evident in our society. (The opposition, as might be expected, came from that other alliance—the conservative suburbanite and some black leaders in the old city.)

In Jacksonville, zoning policy did provide a stimulus to consolidation, primarily because of alleged corruption in the process in the county. But this was only one spoken issue; certainly a concern that old Jacksonville would go black was unspoken but present. The idea of consolidation was not new; it had been talked about since the Civil War, when it was viewed as a necessary governmental response to the devastation of the Reconstruction era.

The change, insofar as it involves land use policy, is not easy to perceive in either city. Where it is, it may either be coincidental to consolidation or because consolidation was perceived as a civic reform and it brought into government reform types who managed the land use system with greater responsibility. Six years after consolidation, the Indianapolis-Marion County Zoning Board of Appeals was still merrily granting variances to developers for projects they could not get through the Development Commission or Council by way of zoning amendments. Reform in that area of zoning policy came after public jawboning of the Board by Mayor Lugar and the addition of fresh faces on the Board.

Bernard Landman, a housing and land use lawyer in Indianapolis, says: "Consolidation didn't have one iota to do with zoning, and it hasn't helped, it hasn't hurt. We would have the same zoning today if there hadn't been UniGov." This may be because Marion County had an earlier tradition of countywide planning policy for, as Landman pointed out: "Since the zoning authorities had county-wide jurisdiction, the fact that 100 people come down and remonstrate isn't that great a thing." In Jacksonville, one former plan commission member said, "the developers still put things right where they want to put them."

The expanded city may not only be ineffective in directing growth; it may have counterproductive effects within its jurisdiction. If government has a more widespread jurisdiction, a crisis in one neighborhood may seem less important. As one member of a close-in Jacksonville neighborhood organization said: "Consolidation has given more emphasis to the fact that we have the whole county so let's not worry about one little area. We can spread out over here and take care of it."

Perhaps the absence of tight control on sprawl within the expanded city limits is explained by the concern evident in both Jacksonville and Indianapolis, that by merging city and county, development is encouraged to go outside even the expanded city limits: in the automobile age a job seeker will drive 50 miles to work. In one report on growth in the Indianapolis metropolitan area, it is estimated that "the bulk of the present single-family homebuilders are building in the seven counties on the periphery of Marion County." The same report said that some "20 percent to 30 percent of total SMSA housing activity was occurring in adjoining counties." Bill Lemond, attorney for the Indianapolis Homebuilders, said that 75 percent of the single-family homes in 1975 in the Indianapolis metropolitan area were built outside Marion County. In Jacksonville, a massive planned unit development at the periphery of the expanded city was approved, perhaps not surprisingly because half of it was located in the sleepy county next door.

One interesting item on the debit side of control via the city-county merger is the loss of the leverage that comes from annexation. A city is not obliged to annex, and, especially if it controls sewer and water, it can use annexation as a bargaining tool: do as we say or no annexation and, therefore, goes the unstated grabber, no water or sewer. A Jacksonville planner noted the change in bargaining power that occurred when vast open areas were consolidated into the city: "Okay, you want to build outside the city limits, we're not going to provide city services, period. But if the land is in the city, well, hell, I'm in the city and I'm paying my taxes."

Even where consolidation appears to result in a more equitable housing policy, it may be less a consequence of the system than of the extra-legal techniques employed by reformers attracted to government because of an evident change in the system. Indianapolis has as good a record as any metropolitan area in the successful distribution of subsidized housing. Whether this climate is due to the governmental structure is dubious. Dr. Frank Lloyd, for many years chairman of the Indianapolis Metropolitan Development Commission, suggests another cause:

We tell the developers that if you want approval for some of your classy apartments, here are some things you have to do, such as build some subsidized housing.

Philosophy more than structure may determine the impact of the expanded city upon land use. Certainly the pro-growth policy so evident in Jacksonville has not been diminished by consolidation. One planning staff member in Jacksonville described the outlook in the following way:

We had a rezoning not too long ago, way in the hell out in the west part of the county, and we recommended a denial because it would result in development far removed from adequate public facilities and that this would not be in the interest of the taxpayers. Well, that was our staff statement and the application went right past the council, you know, pfft! If the guy wants to build a subdivision up there, why not!

The strong development-oriented attitude assumes that the Lord gave man property to use as he sees fit:

There's no way you can tell me if I own property out here I've got to wait for ten other people to develop their land before I can develop mine. That won't work in a capitalistic system.

Imagine how those sentiments would be greeted in Ramapo, New York, or San Diego! They are extreme, perhaps, but not far from the prevailing views in northern Florida. Consolidation in that climate is largely irrelevant to land use policy.

STATE AD HOC PRE-EMPTION

Some re-entries by the states into the land use regulatory business may have a greater impact upon suburban or rural areas than in the larger cities. The Florida Land and Water Management Act, with its provision for state review of proposals for specific uses—Developments of Regional Impact—probably will be felt more in developing communities than in the central cities.[2] In some instances, state or federal environmental laws that affect some development may indirectly benefit the urban cores by making more difficult the emergence of large-scale commercial or industrial competition in the outlying areas. But there are some instances where state pre-emption, on an ad hoc use-by-use basis, may operate more severely in the urban than in the suburban area. Often these are odd consequences, perhaps even unintended.

In Michigan, as in several other states, legislation authorizes the state to override local zoning when a state license is issued for an intermediate-care home (halfway house). The following provision of Michigan Act No. 396, Public Acts of 1976, is typical:

> In order to implement the policy of this State that persons in need of community residential care shall not be excluded by zoning from the benefits of normal residential surroundings, a state licensed residential facility providing supervision or care, or both, of six or less persons shall be considered a residential use of property for the purposes of zoning and a permitted use in all residential zones, including those zones for single family dwellings, and shall not be subject to a special use or a conditional use permit or procedure different from those required for other dwellings of similar density in the same zone.

While, in theory, such legislation applies uniformly to all areas and municipalities within a state, the practicalities are somewhat different:

> Well, shoot, that does away with our residential zoning. . . . Economically, nobody is going to go out and take a $150,000 home in Gross Pointe and put six people from the State hospital or the State prison in that home. But the same size home in the City of Detroit that's in a neighborhood that is 70 years old, they can do that because the home is worth $20,000. I don't know what our State legislature is thinking of, but they effectively emasculated all zoning in areas where the economics cannot exclude them.

The same disproportionate burden was alleged to be occurring in New York City, particularly in portions of Queens, under the New York licensing of nursing homes and foster parent group homes. One New Yorker explained the problem this way:

> Well, lo and behold, in 1971 or 1972 they began to build nursing homes. They loved the water, and we have a place that's right on the water, called the Rockaways, and one by one they got hunting licenses from the state without any direction saying where they could build nursing homes. No direction whatsoever. And 90% of them started buying up land in the Rockaways. Now the communities began to see these homes going up and began crying about it. The first reaction of the city was, you know, what are you complaining about—a nursing home, it's elderly, they need it, we need it in the city, we haven't got enough. What kind of problem are they? Who are they going to mug? And we didn't understand what was going on because the controls were in the hands of the state. We had no idea how many were coming in. We were never told.

In December 1976, the New York Supreme Court, Second Appellate division, held that municipal zoning could not exclude such uses because, by law, the state had pre-empted control.[3]

STATE ENVIRONMENTAL PROTECTION ACTS

Jerry Hillis, a prominent Seattle land use lawyer, says that five years ago 90 percent of his work was in zoning litigation; today 90 percent is, he asserts, in SEPA-type litigation. The promoter of a controversial project in downtown Boston did not complain of problems with zoning. His complaint lies elsewhere:

> We've got to get clearance so that the state is no longer legally involved. There's been one delay after another involving the environmental report. This one thing alone could nit-pick the development to death.

Hillis, who represents the residents of Queen Anne Hill in their fight with Polygon, and the developer, who has had repeated clashes over his project with one of Boston's well-organized community groups, know what is going on: When neighborhood organizations are frustrated by an inability or unwillingness on the part of city hall to block an unwanted project, they are turning to the state. Nowhere has this technique been raised to such a fine art as in Minneapolis, where, under state law, signatures of 500 Minnesota citizens can compel the state environmental agency to determine whether a project requires a state environmental approval:[4] not just a large project—any project. The signatures need not be of residents of an affected neighborhood or even of the same city; a resident of Duluth can validly sign a protest over a project in East Lowry Hill in Minneapolis. As one prominent Minneapolis neighborhood leader describes it, "It's not hard to get 500 signatures because you can go sit on a street corner and get them." Sometimes the technique is tried because the zoning is unacceptable to start with; sometimes it is used in response to a rezoning by the city that has been protested in vain by neighbors.

An operator of adult-film theaters took over a closed movie house in a small neighborhood business area at Chicago and 48th Streets in Minneapolis:

> We attempted [said a neighborhood leader] to hold up the granting of the license by working with city officials but there really was no legal

ground to do it on and so we went to the state. We got the city to make an environmental assessment of the situation and presented that all to the state people. Really, it was no more than a delaying action when you come right down to it. What we hoped to do was to involve this gentleman in sufficient legal expenditures and delays that he would kind of abandon the thing. The net result was that it was delayed for about six months.

In that case the State of Minnesota declined to conduct a full-fledged review. The neighbors then resorted to peaceful vigils outside the theater, which finally compelled the operator to give up.

In other instances, Minnesota has responded affirmatively to petitions by residents. The parcel known as 2900 Dean Boulevard is zoned industrial. On it is located an abandoned grain elevator adjacent to a railroad spur track. The immediate neighborhood has a mix of offices, apartments, and, closer to Cedar Lake, some single-family residences. The developer proposed to tear down the grain elevator and build 200 to 250 apartment units. The Minneapolis city council, more than three years ago in response to the developer's request, rezoned the property for multiple-family units. Then word spread that this was going to be a high-rise project, and residents of single-family homes became concerned that this would be just the first of many high rises around or near Cedar Lake. They obtained the required 500 signatures, and the State Environmental Quality Council suspended the development pending an investigation of the environmental consequences not of that single project but of the impact of many high rises in the area of the lake. The abandoned grain elevator still remains on the site.

A former staffer at the St. Paul planning department explained it this way:

> What has happened is there are many strange groups using environmental laws for reasons other than environmental concerns. As you know, there is a crisis of confidence between the public and the political leaders, not only at the national level but it filters all the way down to the local level, and because of this distrust of local elected officials, many of these neighborhood groups are now using environmental laws to stop or delay these projects.

The irony, of course, is that in an era when the conflict lines are being drawn between local and state or federal authority, those most local of all, the neighborhoods, are looking to the state and federal governments as allies. Ideology pales in the face of self-interest.

But one must be cautious about drawing too strongly on this as a widespread development. St. Paul is the state capital, Minneapolis is next door, and access to state government is easy for citizen groups. A similar phenomenon is observable in Boston and Honolulu, both state capitals.

In Boston, during a two-hour interview, State Representative Barney Frank received six phone calls, all dealing with problems that, had it been Chicago, would have been taken up with an alderman or ward committeeman. It is understandable: The Boston city council is elected at large; the state representatives are from designated districts.

In Hawaii, a consultant who described himself as "an advocate planner for the advantaged," told us:

> In Honolulu the state legislature is right across the street from city hall, and that's indicative of how close everybody is to the same concerns. You find, for instance, that people in the grass roots, if they have a little problem—paving the street, patching up a pot-hole, unstopping a storm drain—they won't stop at the administration or the city council, they'll just call everybody, including their state legislators, and the legislators will get involved in it.

The leader of another Honolulu neighborhood said that his group frequently must go to the state because city hall "gives you the hooma-lemale [To flatter or humor someone instead of giving one's problem serious consideration]; they 'talk store' with you forever."

The developers, even those who have come to welcome increased state involvement when the perceived enemies are suburban legislators, find that the injection of state policies into urban land use practice has special problems. The inevitable conflicts between city hall and the state house are exacerbated when one of the antagonists is not a village, but the largest city in the state. One lawyer in Honolulu, referring to the standoff between the city and state, observed:

> They're both standing there shouting at each other and meanwhile nothing gets done—which is good in some of these cases.

In Boston, the story was the same:

> In general the city and state are at war with each other so from the developer's point of view you have to deal with them sequentially. For example, for one project, the state required us to obtain a sewer extension permit from the city. Boston has not recognized the validity of the amendments to the water pollution control act that requires the issuance of such a permit. So the state used our project building as leverage to get the city to accept the amendments. They did it using us as the instrument.

For our financing we had to get all local approvals which meant we had to get a sewer permit. The city refused to give it to us because it did not want to come in under the state program. The state refused to sign off on the environmental impact statement until we got the permit. Around and around. It took four months of head banging.

Sometimes there are direct conflicts between state and city regulations, inconsistencies that might be ignored were the municipality small and not hung up on maintaining its status vis-á-vis the state. A land use lawyer in Manhattan asserts:

I have advised my clients in certain cases to make an application to the Board of Standards and Appeals to eliminate a required garage on the grounds that it violates the SEPA standards.

Even when conflicts in regulations and political confrontations are absent, the overlay of state regulations in a major city adds significant time to the process. Three thousand miles from Boston, in San Diego, a planner said:

All approvals seem to be sequential and you can trip up at any one of these hurdles. You can go through the first ten gates and then be shot down at the last meeting.

And in Minneapolis, a Metro memo confirmed this: "Favorable review at one level has no bearing on any further reviews." Because delay means added costs and costs mean the consumer will pay more, more customers will be cut out of the market.

The tendency, as here reported, of state or regional tinkering in local land use matters not to help, and frequently to compound, the problems facing our struggling cities leads us to question the wisdom of expanding such intrusions. In Chapter 17 we trace the history of the move toward regionalism to demonstrate that the results of the movement are barely responsive to the major issues that prompted it and conclude that neither the original problems nor the resulting structure of regionalism has much to do with cities and their problems.

FOOTNOTES

1. *Polygon Corp.* vs. *City of Seattle,* 578 P.2d 1309 (1978).

2. The Florida Environmental Land and Water Management Act of 1972, Ch. 380 Fla. Stat. (1978). Portions of the act have been held unconstitutional. See *Cross Key Waterways* v. *Askew,* 351 So.2d 1062 (fla. 1st DCA 1977) *aff'd, Askew et al.* v. *Cross Key Waterways et al.,* 312 So.2d 913 (Fla. 1978); *Postal Colony Co., Inc.* v. *Askew,* 348 So.2d 338 (Fla. 1st DCA 1977).

3. *Group House of Port Washington, Inc.* v. *Board of Zoning Appeals of North Hempstead,* 390 N.Y.S.2d 427 (1976).

4. Minnesota Stat. Ann., 116 D.04 (3).

Part III

A Preliminary Prescription for

What Might Be

Chapter 16
The Age of Experiment:
Academic and Otherwise

> *This shows how much easier it is to be*
> *critical than to be correct.*
>
> —Disraeli

At least one sage in every generation since the hey-day of the Greek city-states has made the point that those who can, do, while those who can't, become critics. That points up not only the perils of being a critic but also the difficulty of being original. Having, in the first two parts of this book, provided not only a description but also something of a criticism of the existing urban zoning scene, we feel some obligation to provide a few suggestions on how things might be done differently. However, before getting on to our own ideas for the brave new urban scene, we pause in this and the next chapter to comment briefly upon some of the currently popular prescriptions for reform, to see why they won't work in cities and to find what they suggest about what might.

THE NO-ZONING-IS-THE-BEST-ZONING SCHOOL OF REFORM

There is no better place to begin a review of current suggestions for zoning reform than with the idea, most persuasively (and incessantly) elaborated by Professor Bernard H. Siegan of the University of San Diego Law School, that abolition is the only effective zoning reform (Babcock and Bosselman have called it "the final solution" to the zoning problem.)[1] Professor Siegan summarized the no zoning arguments in his article "No Zoning Is The Best Zoning," which forms one chapter in the book *No Land Is An Island*,[2] a volume largely dedicated to the proposition that the biggest problem confronting land use regulation is land use regulation. The gist of Siegan's position is that Houston has survived very well without zoning and there is no reason that the rest of us couldn't do the same. Based on the Houston experience, Siegan concludes that "Market forces operate there efficiently and effectively and accomplish that which zoning is supposed to but has proven incapable of doing."[3] Of course, any zoning lawyer worth his or her salt can provide a host of arguments to rebut the position that our craft ought to be abolished.

To begin with, there is the "a rose by any other name" argument. As Siegan concedes, Houston is anything but a wide-open town when it comes to the regulation of land. The pattern of large land ownership in Houston has permitted the development of an extensive system of private covenants that are in many cases more restrictive than any zoning ordinance. It is difficult to see how anyone who objects to zoning can seriously suggest its abolition in favor of a Houston-like system of private covenants. The covenants are frequently more exclusionary, more restrictive, and more rigid than the most suburban of suburban zoning ordinances. In the most extreme cases, they control not only land use but also architecture, maintenance, and aesthetics. If you object to the government telling you where you can put your garage, you're likely not to be much more enthused about your neighbors telling you that you must keep its door closed.[4] Unlike zoning, which is subject to change in a variety of ways and for a variety of reasons, the goal of most systems of covenants is perpetual control. In any event, the practical possibilities of duplicating the Houston system of covenants in any other city are essentially nil. But even if you like private covenants, you should know that Houston's covenants aren't all that private. Since 1965, Houston has, by statute, had the right to enforce private covenants.[5]

Nor is Houston lacking in other forms of public regulation of land. As Siegan himself notes:

Houston has subdivision, building, traffic and housing regulations that do not appear to differ appreciably from those of cities in its region....

Houston has also adopted an off-street parking ordinance for residential development only. It also controls the size of single family lots.... There are some front yard and side yard requirements but not backyard requirements. The City also has regulations controlling the development of townhouses intended for individual ownership, and of mobile home parks.

There are no density restrictions for rental units except the indirect one of required off-street parking.[6]

Of course, in most zoning ordinances, it is the lot size and parking requirements, rather than density limitations, that provide the effective ceiling on development.

It also bears noting that Houston's lack of zoning has not prevented it from attempting to play the games that others play in the name of zoning:

During 1970 a number of 236 projects were built in "white areas" [of Houston] where the neighbors, to put it gently, became very upset.

Late in 1970 an attempt was made to establish additional controls over low- and moderate-income housing projects by the introduction of an ordinance based on the "paramount importance" of "environmental ecology" which required that sewer mains and treatment plants be protected from overload by denying building permits for any construction other than single-family housing if the utility and street system facilities were found inadequate to meet the proposed density of population. Although on its face neutral, it was clearly understood in the debates over this ordinance that its purpose was to deny permits for low- and moderate-income housing developments in areas where they were unpopular.

There was substantial doubt about the validity of this ordinance and it was not adopted. A substitute was worked out, however, in the form of a city council resolution requiring that each proposed 236 project site be reviewed [and approved] by a Neighborhood Analysis Committee, which is to file a report with the FHA and the City Council.[7]

Finally, even Houston has found it increasingly difficult to go on without zoning. Like other cities, its neighborhoods are being threatened by a variety of uses believed by most to be incompatible with a residential environment (despite what the "free market" might think about it). The intruders range from pornography shops in the gray areas to high rises in the stable areas. Late in 1978, the city requested proposals from consultants to develop a system of local ordinances to deal with such problems. The Request for Proposal emphasized that Houston did not want a document called a zoning ordinance, but it clearly wanted a police power regulation that would do what a garden variety zoning ordinance does. Among the tasks to be included in the work program were these:

● Develop legal and administrative framework for regulating those factors that contribute to residential deterioration in viable neighborhoods.

- Develop quantitative and qualitative performance standards for control of each of the individual and/or group of factors contributing to residential deterioration.

- Conduct feasibility study and recommend whether performance standards should be applied to all viable residential areas or should vary in accordance with specific areas.

Thus, in choosing Houston as his model for reform, Siegan has not picked a very persuasive example of "no zoning." But even if Houston can fairly be said to be unzoned, Siegan's prescription for reform must be rejected simply because it is so completely unrealistic for any other city. There is, we would suggest, little chance that the elected officials of any major city would attempt to abolish zoning and even less chance that they would remain elected officials if they did.

The ultimate answer to Siegan's proposition is, however, that it is bad policy. Professor Siegan's distaste for zoning when wedded to his acceptance of a trunk load of other governmental regulations and his enthusiasm for private covenants leads one to suspect that, before he was a teacher, Siegan must have been a developer. Most developers want to impose restrictions—so long as they may select them—and most developers rightfully regard zoning, not building and housing regulations, as the bette noire in their skirmishes with local officials. In a society that has concluded that the public welfare demands the regulation of everything from taxidermy to taxicabs, it is difficult for us to understand the suggestion that land should be exempt.

Siegan's position is bottomed upon a concept of a free market in land that is mythical. Land, as such, has little intrinsic value. It is valuable only for what you can take from it or what you can do with it. In an urban setting, the former has little significance and the latter is almost entirely dependent upon public investment. Without the public infrastructure that makes urban land usable, the land would have little value, and the value of land varies rather directly with the degree to which it is advantageously located in terms of that infrastructure. That being the case, the regulation of land can and should serve the valuable purpose of providing some equitable distribution of publicly created benefits and publicly imposed burdens. The fact that the public regulation of land has not always achieved, or even sought to achieve, that goal is not a persuasive reason for abolishing the system. We surmise that Mr. Siegan would not be persuaded that the free market system should be abolished simply because it has failed to work perfectly in practice. It would be no more difficult to construct a theoretical system of public land use regulation that would be completely rational and just (see the discussion of Professor Hagman's theory later in this chapter) than it is to construct a theoretically perfect free market system. The unhappy facts are that neither system can be made to work as well as theory suggests it might.

Even though we cannot accept the Professor's prescription, we can agree with his diagnosis of several troubling symptoms. There is, for example, something sick about a system that discourages development by throwing up needlessly complicated procedural roadblocks and by refusing to formulate, and then abide by, an intelligible set of substantive standards. Nor, as we have noted earlier, do we find anything of particular merit in a system that offers the Woodlawns and Harlems of this world the same protection against the "intrusion of incompatible uses" as it offers in Winnetka or Westchester. As Siegan aptly points out, it is doubtful that wealthy homeowners in Houston's estate area lie awake at night in fear that a slaughterhouse or glue factory will move in next door because there is no zoning. It would appear equally clear that, in the more congested and diverse (i.e., the more urban) areas of the city, no one is very upset by the introduction of a few convenience commercial establishments to serve the needs of the neighborhood. In fact, after one studies the Houston situation for a time, it appears that the most significant difference between it and other cities is not an absence of zoning but rather an absence of strict use districting. As Siegan points out, the absence of that strict districting has not generally proved devastating.

The market does, to an extent, provide a natural ordering and arrangement of uses in terms of their compatability with each other and with the man-made infrastructure that serves various areas of a city. We cannot agree with Mr. Siegan that this "natural" ordering is totally sufficient. In the early years of this century, that natural order resulted in the total obliteration of many of the most magnificent features of the natural environment in our cities. Nor can we agree with Siegan that there is anything natural about a shopping center or a gas station springing up on every corner of every major intersection; and a high-rise apartment building blooming in the fertile soil of a well-to-do subdivision may be nature run wild. To this extent, however, Siegan's point is well taken: zoning has frequently been overzealous in its attempt to control some aspects of land use compatability. But arguing that you should abolish urban zoning because you don't like sterile, "pure" use districting is about as rational as urging the abolition of planned parenthood because you don't like castration.

LAND BANKING

While the concept of public land banking as a means of development regulation has been kicked around since at least the 1930s,[8] the idea of using land banking as a method of regulating urban development in the United States first received serious attention in this country from the National Resources Planning Board in its 1941 report on public land acquisition. That report stated the case as follows:

> [N]o method of land use control can be as effective as outright owner-ship of the land involved. A landowner may resist the pressure of taxation or the lure of subsidy; the city fathers may grant too many exceptions to the zoning ordinance or master plan; the budget may not allow for enough inspectors to enforce the building and sanitary codes; all attempts at enforcement are subject to litigation and delay; but if the government itself owns the land, its control is absolute.[9]

Thus stated, the idea certainly has a compelling ring to it. Whether the concept can, however, have any useful role in solving the land use problems of a major city is doubtful.

First, it should be noted that, as commonly understood, the concept of land banking has no practical application to an already developed area. The Reporters of the American Law Institute's Model Land Development Code define land banking as:

> A system in which a governmental entity acquires a substantial fraction of the land in a region that is available for future development for the purpose of controlling the future growth of the region.[10]

By that rather traditional definition, land banking is primarily a tool to be used at the periphery of an urbanized area. It is a device to control sprawl and leapfrog development. With few exceptions, the cities of this country are no longer in a position to control the development at their peripheries. That development is occurring in suburban jurisdictions over which the core city has no control. Of course, there are a few scattered situations—San Diego, for example—in which the concept might find application, and more limited notions of land banking in the sense of "advance acquisition" of land in anticipation of specific future public needs have been suggested.[11] However, even in these situations, where the concept might find application in an urban setting, we doubt its efficacy as a significant tool for regulating land use within major cities.

One must question the return on the immediate and long-term costs of even a limited land banking program. Sylvan Kamm, perhaps the most articulate critic of large-scale public land banking, has pointed out the economic realities of any significant program to acquire and hold land for future development.[12] To the obvious problems of initial costs and long-term carrying costs of any such program must be added the special problems involved when the program is proposed for implementation in an urban area. If land in the core is to be acquired, the initial cost will be many times higher than the cost of acquiring undeveloped peripheral land. That means that the carrying costs due to the interest on capital and to taxes will be more burdensome. If the banked land were to be excused from local taxes, the end result is the same; the local government is subsidizing the carrying cost. Even the advocates of land banking are forced to admit that there will be a lengthy initial period during which the land bank's operations would not be self-sustaining and during which there would be a continuing need for additional capital investments with little, if any, offsetting revenues.[13] Asking a core city to sacrifice either its current revenues or its debt capacity to such long-range objectives is, we suggest, totally unrealistic in light of the pressing demands upon those limited resources. Nor do we believe that federal or state funds provide the easy answer. Such a solution would, in all likelihood, require a surrender of both local control and local benefits. Beyond that, however, every session of the state or national legislature makes cities painfully aware of the fact that the total amount of state and federal resources available to deal with their problems is both limited and inadequate. Diverting those funds is no more a solution than is diverting local funds.

Even if the practical problems could be solved, we would question some of the basic theory underlying land banking proposals. Fundamentally, the advocates of land banking base their case on the assumption that it is the lack of effective means to an end, rather than the lack of an agreed end, that accounts for much of the irrationality of urban land use patterns. That assumption is unfounded. While the tools and techniques of land use regulation now available may not be perfect, there is little doubt that they are not now being used to their full potential. Even were it conceded that land banking is a more effective tool for implementing land use policies than those currently available, there is no reason to believe it would do anything to help land use regulators with the knotty problems of deciding what goals, policies, and programs to implement in the long run and of figuring out how to survive the problems of the short run.

If anything, we expect that land banking would exacerbate the problems. If honest city officials now find it difficult to resist the promises of immediate public gain from the investment, jobs, and taxes that new development represents and if dishonest public officials now find it difficult to resist the potential for corruption and profit inherent in their power over the regulation of land, how much more difficult would it be for both honest and dishonest officials to resist the temptation of the much larger, and more immediate, gains inherent in a system involving the public purchase and sale of land?

We cite, as the final argument in support of our position, the barren lots, blocks, and acres that remain in cities across the country, the yet unhealed pock marks of perhaps our boldest venture into land banking of major urban land areas—the federal Urban Renewal program.

THE CITY AS DEVELOPER OR LANDLORD

We have attempted to restrict our observations in Parts I and II and our proposals in this Part to the regulatory process. Tax policies and eminent domain are crude devices that require comparatively little imagination to implement. To improve the lot of the city by regulation requires a more deft hand. This quality—adroitness—prompts us to note here a series of experiments in nonregulatory land use control taking place in and around a number of central city business districts. While the last word on their success is not in, they deserve close watch.

The technique discussed here builds on some of the same theoretical bases as land banking and urban renewal. The important distinguishing factor is the timing and purpose of public acquisition or participation. Urban renewal and land banking have cast the public in the role of land speculator and saddled it with all the risks and carrying costs inherent in a land acquisition program that tries to out-guess or out-wait the market. A few cities have come to realize that there are more secure and profitable roles to play in the real estate business.

Pasadena

Some savvy real estate entrepreneurs long ago figured out how to minimize the risks of land speculation while still reaping a good share of the profits that successful speculation brings. The most common example is the speculator who enters into "back-to-back" real estate contracts: the first is a contract to buy a residential lot contingent upon being able to get it rezoned for a gas station; the other is a contract to sell the same lot, at a greatly inflated price, to an oil company, also contingent upon rezoning. All the speculator risks is the cost of trying to get the rezoning. If he gets it, he closes both contracts on the same day; if he doesn't, he walks away from both deals.

Pasadena, California, has used a similar technique with some success in redeveloping its downtown area. The full story is told by Gerald Trimble, executive director of the Pasadena Redevelopment Agency in a recent *Urban Land* article.[14] In essence, Pasadena passed up federal Urban Renewal money and relied on tax increment financing in order to be able to move projects more swiftly. It made the most of its limited funds by first getting commitments from end users for specific sites and only then acquiring and clearing them. On its first project of this type, the redevelopment agency had a contract to acquire, clear, and prepare a three-acre site for a developer, who in turn had a contract to develop and lease the site to BankAmericard Corp. With these firm commitments, the agency was able to get interim bank financing to acquire and clear the site; the interim financing was then retired through the sale of tax increment bonds to be paid off out of the increased taxes generated, in part, by the new development. As in more traditional urban renewal programs, the agreement by which the redevelopment parcel was conveyed binds the purchaser to develop and use the parcel in a specified manner, thus permitting control well beyond that available through a standard zoning ordinance. The agency has since put together a number of similar back-to-back deals. In some of them, the agency has not disposed of the redevelopment parcel by sale but has rather entered into a long-term lease with a private sector user. The lease income provides security for the bonds that finance the acquisition and preparation of the site.

Boston

The concept of the city as landlord is gaining considerable popularity as a device to both promote and control development—while at the same time producing a handsome income for the public.

When the United States Navy decided to close down the South Boston Naval Annex, the city entered into a "Protection and Maintenance Agreement" with the Navy under which the Economic Development and Industrial Corporation (EDIC) of Boston could sublease out portions of the facility but could not realize any profit and had to return income in excess of protection and maintenance costs to the federal government. The two primary goals are the development of job-intensive industries and the growth of marine-oriented industries. The standard lease requires lessees, whenever possible, to hire and train unskilled and semi-skilled residents of Boston. It also requires the lessee to give the city notice of all job opportunities and prohibits the tenant from hiring any non-Boston resident during a two-week period in which the city has the right to supply qualified applicants for the job. The following is from a letter of intent between EDIC and Braswell Shipyards, Inc.:

> Braswell will sponsor training courses for Boston residents for 12 certified welders and 12 certified pipefitters. Courses will be 6 months in duration. Braswell will enter into pre-agreements with beginning trainees that they will be first-hired. Training will be subject to approval of Braswell. Braswell's participation in training costs will be covered by separate agreement.
>
> Braswell will strive for minimum average employment of 100 persons, and will give preference in hiring of Boston residents.

Indianapolis

Frank Lloyd is a doctor in Indianapolis and the former president of the American Society of Planning Officials. Charles Whistler is an Indianapolis attorney. Both men served on the Metropolitan Development Commission when the commission entered into negotiations for the lease of a one-block area between Washington, Illinois, and

Maryland streets and Capitol Avenue. There had been an old Shera-
ton Hotel on the verge of being closed and a series of badly deteriorated
buildings. The city acquired the property for approximately $2.5
million. Rather than sell the parcel, the city took bids on a lease and
ultimately entered into a 60-year lease with options for two 15-year
renewals. Section 6.02 of the 105-page lease provided that the redeveloper:

> ... shall include a combination business and commercial development
> consisting of a four-story base building to cover the entire Demised
> Premises, with a basement servicing area, and from which four-story base
> building will rise three tower structures to include a first class Hyatt
> Regency Hotel, or a first class hotel of another national hotel chain,
> containing approximately five hundred (500) rooms, such hotel to be of a
> quality comparable to the Hyatt Regency Hotels in Atlanta, Georgia, and
> O'Hare International Airport in Chicago, Illinois, and two office towers to
> contain an aggregate of approximately four hundred thousand (400,000)
> square feet of gross floor area. The four-story base building is to include
> retail space, parking facilities and an enclosed pedestrian mall. Prior to
> construction of the initial improvements, City shall examine the plans and
> specifications for such improvements and approve the same as being in
> conformity with the requirements of this Section 6.02.

The basic rent was $360,000 a year. In the seventh and each suc-
ceeding year, there was to be an additional percentage rent based on
the gross revenues of the development. The redeveloper was required
to acknowledge in the lease that the property would be taxable under
the applicable Indiana statutes and had to agree not to apply for a tax
exemption based on the city's ownership of the fee interest in the land.
The lease also provided that any statements and audits that the city
acquired from the developer would not be treated on a confidential
basis and required the developer to acknowledge the nonconfiden-
tiality of any financial information that found its way into the hands of
the city. The lease gave the redeveloper a credit against the rent for the
real property taxes he paid plus any other governmental charges. Thus,
the city's rental earnings on the project were net after deducting any
real property taxes. Nevertheless, Indianapolis had made a good bargain. As Charles Whistler said:

> ... we hired one of the best real estate finance lawyers in the country who
> also happened to practice law in this town.... We were in a position of
> having government functioning through people who had a knowledge far
> in excess of the average government employee.

Hartford

Hartford, Connecticut, invested $30 million in a civic center. Then it granted an air-rights lease over a portion of the site to Aetna Life and Casualty Company on which Aetna prepared to construct the Hartford Center, a complex of retail shops and office space. The lease for 50 years calls for a base rental of $104,000 and 1 percent of the gross rentals from its tenants. The taxes are to be paid by Aetna with a separate agreement that taxes would remain fixed for seven years. It is a "net lease." The Hartford Redevelopment Agency has also acquired and renovated a downtown office building and leased a substantial portion of it to American Airlines for the handling of airline reservations. The 33-page lease, a typical commercial lease in which the city assumes all the usual burdens of a landlord, provides for the rental of 58,000 square feet at $5.50 per square foot for 25 years with an option to lease an additional 12,000 square feet. Lessee will pay all taxes, and lessor agrees to spend $600,000 on improvements.

A member of Hartford's city council had this to say about this assertive policy:

> The realities of the economic condition led the City to enter the field of real estate, but with very distinct *public goals* to be accomplished. These goals in their most simplistic form relate to the creation of jobs, the stimulation of private investment, the stabilization of our tax base and the creation of a long-term income stream for the City of Hartford. Stated another way, the investment of public money in real estate must provide the public with adequate economic return, tax base stabilization and jobs to warrant the use of public dollars.
>
> . . . In addition to the project itself, the "spin off" effect must be analyzed. In this example, the relocation of American Airlines to Hartford prompted a development proposal for a 244-unit apartment bulding with additional retail development at an investment of over ten million dollars. . . .

Toledo

Perhaps the most intriguing of all the leasing arrangements is that entered into between the City of Toledo, Seaway Food Town, Inc., and River East Economic Revitalization Corporation, a nonprofit Ohio corporation.

Main Street was the usual story of an in-town commercial center that had succumbed to the suburban shopping centers. In 1950, after serving the city for 70 years, J. C. Penney moved to suburban Northwood. The Main Street shopping area was a six-block, one-half-mile-long strip.

Few retail stores were left in the area, most were service storefronts not serving the estimated 40,000 shoppers in the local market area.

In 1974 a combination of clergy, local business people, and city officials organized the River East Economic Development Corporation (REEC) to do something about the area. It employed a professional market analyst and sought to recruit a major tenant. That was not successful. Then it went to the city and proposed that the city acquire a four-acre block of land on the condition that it, the Economic Development Corporation, would obtain a contract with a developer before the city committed to spend any money. After numerous unsuccessful efforts, REEC obtained a commitment from Foodtown to take the major tenancy and be the developer. Foodtown agreed to construct a 22,000 to 27,000-square-foot food center; a hardware store committed for 10,000 square feet.

In August 1976, the city committed to spend $2 million to acquire the site and lease the land to Foodtown. According to one source: "Since the revitalization program began, eight new businesses have located in the River East area, six in existing stores and two in new facilities."[15]

The agreement to enter into a lease provided:

> Subject to all of the terms, covenants, and conditions of this Agreement, the City will lease the Project Property (comprising approximately 178,440 square feet) to the Redeveloper.... The Lease shall provide for five (5) renewal terms of five (5) years each on the same terms, conditions and rental as the Base Term. The annual rental, payable in equal monthly installments in advance to the City from the Redeveloper, shall be Fifteen Thousand ($15,000.00) dollars.... Further, this shall be a triple net lease approved by counsel for River East. Said Lease shall be in a form permitting the Redeveloper to obtain conventional mortgage financing or corporate lease financing of the cost of the Improvements. All expenses in connection with construction of the building, preparation of driveway, seeding, landscaping, and other miscellaneous charges shall be borne by the Redeveloper, excepting such terms as are set forth in this Agreement to be completed by the City. Under no circumstances shall River East have any responsibility to expend any monies whatsoever under this Agreement.

River East insisted upon some restrictions upon the type of uses:

> *Use Restrictions:* Both the Redeveloper and River East have had numerous negotiations pertaining to the types of tenants to be located in the area denoted as the "retail area" on the Site Plan. Attached as Exhibit C are those restrictions and they are incorporated herein by reference and they shall be incorporated into the Lease.

Among these limitations are the following:

(b) Service establishments, which are stores which derive more than ten (10%) percent of their income from providing services as opposed to selling retail products shall be prohibited in any of the retail area except as hereinafter excepted. Further, certain type stores which are hereinafter described are hereby prohibited.

(c) The purpose of this entire redevelopment is to bring retailers to Main Street in East Toledo, Ohio and both River East Economic Revitalization Corporation and Seaway Foodtown, Inc. shall be able to advertise leasing space and to attempt to solicit prospective tenants for the contemplated retail areas. In this respect though, it is agreed that River East, under no circumstances, shall be the agent of Seaway Foodtown, Inc. and all lease negotiations shall be handled exclusively by Seaway Foodtown, Inc. or an agent designated by it.

Finally, River East reserves significant powers and benefits:

(b) *River East Veto Power:* Notwithstanding anything else contained herein to the contrary, River East shall have authority to veto any substantial change in construction plans....

(g) *River East Benefits to City:* The City of Toledo recognizes that River East was essential to the negotiations and in bringing the Redeveloper to the City and that River East has performed substantial services and benefits to the City. Specifically, rentals under the Agreement that are received from the Redeveloper shall be payable to River East only for the first three (3) years upon receipt of same from the Redeveloper, provided River East continues to exist as a non-profit corporation. Thereafter, River East or its successor shall submit to the City of Toledo City Council an annual budget specifically showing how said monies shall be spent and the City Council of the City of Toledo shall have the right to approve or disapprove said budget. However, it is acknowledged that the intent of this agreement and the guideline established hereby is that said monies shall be used by River East for the purposes for which that organization was originally chartered.

While these nonregulatory approaches to big-city revitalization offer hope, a word of caution is in order. At bottom, public ownership of land, in whatever form and for whatever purpose, is nothing more than a technique for implementing public policy—it is not a substitute for rational policy. As in the case of zoning or land banking or any other implementation tool, the tool can be no better than the policies that back up its administration. Indeed, as the age of nuclear weapons has taught, the more effective the tool, the more are caution and wisdom necessary in deciding when and for what purposes to use it. The availability of nonregulatory implementation tools may make it easier to implement policies and decisions; it will not reduce the need to develop a rational and fair process for making the policies and decisions necessary to guide the use of the tool.

WINDFALLS FOR WIPEOUTS

Don Hagman, a UCLA law professor, has, in recent years, devoted considerable effort to studying and promoting the idea of compensating landowners for "wipeouts" (any decrease in the value of real estate other than one caused by the owner or by general deflation) and recapturing "windfalls" (any increase in the value of real estate other than that caused by the owner or by general inflation.)[16] With apologies to the 800-page text that Hagman, in collaboration with economist Dean J. Misczynski, has put together to explain the idea, what they propose, in essence, is to tax the increase in the value of land that occurs when rezoning or permission to develop is granted and to use the revenue thus secured to compensate other landowners whose land is devalued by similar governmental actions. They offer their proposals in two alternatives. The "omnibus proposal" attempts to encompass all windfalls and wipeouts however caused and would provide that any owner of property receiving a windfall would be taxed some percent of that windfall and any owner suffering a wipeout would be paid a similar percent of that wipeout. The "incremental proposal" focuses wipeout mitigation on losses arising from governmental land planning and regulatory activities coupled with a separate windfall recapture tax that would be, hopefully, sufficient to fund the wipeout mitigation obligations of government. Not even the authors find enough grains of reality in their omnibus proposal to seriously pursue it. They devote their efforts to building a theoretical, historical, legal, and economic structure in support of their more modest incremental approach. This is not the place to explore that work or the unhappy experience in England with a similar concept. A few general comments are sufficient for our purpose. As in the case of many of the other currently popular proposals for land use reform, it is difficult to disagree with the basic goals of the reformers. We all agree that the current system has problems and that we ought to be working on solving those problems. We also share the

Hagman-Misczynski belief that at least a fair share of the current problems are traceable to the system's current lack of concern for the real-world economics involved in land use regulation and development and that the system might be considerably improved if the planners and regulators had to worry more about the economic consequences of their actions and the property owners had to worry less about those economic consequences. Notwithstanding all of that, however, the Hagman-Misczynski vision of a "windfalls for wipeouts agency" as a solution can be rather summarily dismissed, at least as it relates to urban land use problems, for two reasons.

We doubt that even the authors expect to see their idea sweep the country in the next decade, or even the next half-century. Despite their comprehensive and engaging presentation, the idea is horribly complex. Beyond that, it challenges such a large and diverse group of basic social and economic beliefs that there is almost no one who would not be highly offended by some parts of it. At a minimum, it seems a couple of decades of educating and politicking will be necessary to get the idea out of the books and into practice. For cities facing immediate problems, the windfall for wipeout idea is one whose time is still too far off.

A second reason for rejecting the Hagman-Misczynski proposal as a solution for urban land use problems is that, except to a limited extent and in special circumstances, the two basic assumptions upon which it is bottomed are not found in older American cities. First, the concept of an in-city wipeout by governmental land use regulation is not very realistic. The real wipeouts are occurring mostly in the hinterland, to a lesser extent in the suburbs, and only to a minor extent in the cities. The real wipeouts, in short, occur when government seeks to prevent development or to limit it to unnaturally low densities. Not much of that goes on in cities. To be certain, there are some wipeout situations in cities, but they are rare and probably more easily dealt with in their own specific contexts. Even in those situations where city wipeouts exist, they are of a different genre than their country cousins. For the most part, when they occur, city wipeouts are not a result of government denying a private property owner the right to invest his or her own money in servicing a piece of raw land so as to maximize its development potential; rather, they result from the denial of permission to take full advantage of a development potential that is due in large part to public, not private, investment. We wonder whether it is really a wipeout to limit CBD development to an FAR of 10 rather than 20 when neither would be practical without a vast system of publicly provided urban infrastructure.*

The story is somewhat the same on the other side of the coin. The sort of massive, localized windfalls that accompany the opening up of virgin areas with public infrastructure and a zoning map based more upon a

---

*When we first put this question on paper, we knew of no particular support for the concept that a private owner's property right in urban land had to be somehow discounted for the value added by society. However, one of the happy circumstances of working in an area in such constant flux is that you can often write your brief and wait for the authority to develop. That was the case here; we can now cite no less a jurist than Chief Judge Charles Breitel of the New York Court of Appeals for the proposition that:

... it is the interaction of economic influences in the greatest megalopolis of the western hemisphere... that has made the property [Grand Central Terminal] so valuable.... Of primary significance, however, is that society as an organized entity, especially through its government, rather than as a mere conglomerate of individuals, has created much of the value of the terminal property.... Plaintiffs may not now frustrate legitimate and important social objectives by complaining, in essence, that government regulation deprives them of a return on so much of the investment made not by private interests but by the people of the city and state through their government. *Penn Central Trans. Co.* v. *City of New York,* 366 N.E.2d 1271, 1275 (1977).

The common thread connecting the *Penn Central* view of city land value with the *Just* v. *Marinette Co.* view of virgin land value (see p. 15, *supra*) is striking. The two cases suggest a radically new definition of private property and a sweeping expansion of government's regulatory power over it. By their teaching, private property no longer includes the right to exploit either nature or society for individual development gain, and government may regulate land to prevent such exploitation.

That is heady stuff; and, while we are confident that these faint rumblings of a new theoretical base for land use regulation will lead into new reaches in the next several decades, this is not the place to try to explore where the path is going. Certainly one of the problems to be faced along the way is that no one has priced land on the basis of these new rules and a wipeout is no less painful simply because you're told that, while it was a wipeout under yesterday's rules, today the rules are different. Given that and other difficulties, it is somewhat comforting to know that the common law system will, if left reasonably to its own devices, take us down this path one cautious step at a time. If there is a common problem with many academic proposals for land use reform, it is that they suggest sweeping legislative revision that would require us to plunge too fast into unknown areas.

figment of the planner's art than a recognition of existing reality are rare in urban settings. Again, this is not to deny that urban windfalls, as Hagman defines them, exist. However, the windfalls are more generalized. All property in the city enjoys the benefit and increased value associated with the urban setting and infrastructure. Some properties are, of course, more valuable because they are zoned for more intensive use, but that zoning typically was imposed after nature and economics had already created the basic fabric. While suburban zoning may create value, city zoning, viewed in broad perspective, has involved more the recognition than the creation of development value. In the final analysis, there are, of course, many specific parcels in any city that enjoy a unique windfall attributable more to governmental action than to natural potential. Some of those cases, like the parcel made unusually valuable by spot zoning, can and should be eliminated simply by better administration of the current zoning process. Others, like the parcel made more valuable thanks to some new public improvement, can be dealt with by a creative application and adaptation of some of the more traditional devices of value recapture, which Hagman and Misczynski discuss, such as special assessments, special taxing districts, and development exactions. Or the whole notion of a windfall can be avoided by requiring developers to bear the "public" costs occasioned by development. Schemes of conditional, incentive, and bonus zoning are becoming more and more common and are readily adaptable to a variety of circumstances. Whatever their particular application, however, they boil down to a way of "selling" development approval to a developer in return for his undertaking to privately finance some "public" benefit, whether it be the creation of a plaza in front of his office building, the construction of a pedestrian bridge linking his building into a pedestrian circulation system, or an agreement to, in effect, subsidize some socially desirable use, whether it be a theater on Broadway or a low-income apartment in the Clinton District.

Thus, the current system has several windfall-wipeout mechanisms already built into it. Getting far beyond those existing mechanisms is generally, we believe, not likely in the time frame dictated by current urban problems. One windfall-recapture/wipeout-compensation scheme does, however, offer some hope of early implementation in a city context—transferable development rights. It is to that subject that we now turn.

TRANSFER OF DEVELOPMENT RIGHTS (TDR)

Professor John Costonis, who experienced the real world as a lawyer with our firm before electing to take up residence in academia, has more recently become the principal architect and exponent of the theory of transferable development rights. His theory is founded upon the notion that there is no unalterable rule that says that the development potential of a given piece of property may be used only on that piece of property. In his words:

Development rights transfer breaks the linkage between particular land and its development potential by permitting the transfer of that potential, or "development right," to land where greater density will not be objectionable.[17]

Costonis has identified four variants of the basic TDR concept:

The simplest is represented by the New York City Plan, which seeks to protect landmarks by permitting their owners to transfer their unused development rights, typically office space, to adjacent sites, again typically for office-space use. The second, illustrated by the Chicago Plan, surges briskly ahead of the first: transfers are permitted on a district wide basis; the districts may circumscribe areas of landmark concentration or be located independently of them; the city may itself condemn and resell the development rights of threatened landmarks if their owners decline participation in the plan; and the municipality may pool the rights of publicly and privately owned landmarks in the development rights bank to meet overall preservation program costs. The third pattern, exemplified by the Puerto Rico and New Jersey initiatives, goes even further by enlarging TDR's objectives to include the protection of open space and agricultural and environmentally sensitive land: by expanding the sites of transfers to encompass non-urban areas; and by permitting transfers between non-fungible use areas, i.e., between rain forest and city or farm and residential subdivision. The final and most sweeping of the patterns appears to be the TDR proposals of Audrey Moore, a district supervisor in Fairfax County, Virginia, and William Goodman, a member of the Maryland Legislature. They urge that transferable development rights be assigned to all lands within the pertinent jurisdiction and that the private sector be empowered to disburse or concentrate these rights subject to general location and performance standards of adopted comprehensive plans.[18]

The fundamental problems yet to be resolved before the TDR idea could be implemented on any grand scale could easily fill a separate chapter.[19] However, being, as we are, keenly aware of John's ability and willingness to disembowel practically anything that seems inconsistent with, or critical of, his pet proposal—even if it happens to come from members of his former firm—we think it best to satisfy ourselves with a brief quote from Costonis as to the principal problems with immediate implementation of the Costonis theory:

> But let us be realistic. TDR's advantages come at a stiff price. Public officials should steer clear of TDR unless they are willing to shoulder expanded space management responsibilities, have the political gumption to underwrite the integrity of the TDR program, and are alert to the risks of impropriety and ineptitude that attend any discretionary land-use device. Again, TDR will not solve all land-use problems, nor is it in any way a substitute for sound planning or equitable police-power regulations. . . . TDR programs are largely restricted to resource-protection goals. Since TDR is only a tool or means, an independent planning process must be set in motion both to identify the goals to be served and to accommodate those goals with other worthy community interests. Also overlooked or played down by many of TDR's friends is the sticky-wicket of justifying zoning deliberately undertaken to create a market for development rights. Most analyses of TDR center instead on the far easier question of the legitimacy of protecting the resource in question, be it landmark, farm, or a major preserve. The omission is regrettable because, in my judgment, the former question is the most troublesome that TDR poses. It is only in wrestling with it, moreover, that a deeper appreciation of TDR's break with existing property conceptions begins to be grasped.[20]

In short, as anyone who has thought as deeply about TDR as Costonis has will freely admit, it cannot reasonably be expected to provide either an immediate or total solution to the problems inherent in our current systems of land use and land regulation. If anything, its full potential can be realized only gradually and only if, in the meantime, significant effort is devoted to making the traditional system function more closely to its own potential. With that reservation, however, we believe that the TDR technique, and the concepts and assumptions upon which it is bottomed, are likely to gain increasing influence in future systems of urban land use regulation. They strongly influence our own suggestions (set out in Chapter 19) for adapting traditional density controls to deal more effectively with the current land use problems confronting major cities.

In fact, in contrast to our reaction to most currently popular proposals for reform, we believe that TDR may have its most beneficial applications, and may be most realistic and defensible, in an urban, as opposed to suburban or virgin, setting. Costonis describes the urban underpinnings of his Chicago Plan as follows:

The Chicago Plan builds upon four characteristics shared by most urban landmark buildings and their environments. First, the typical landmark is undersized in relation to current zoning and building practices. Second, most of these buildings can be profitably managed. Their vulnerability in the market place is the product of the disproportionate value of their sites in relation to the diminutive landmark building on them. Third, these buildings are often found concentrated in one or more reasonably compact areas of the city, usually in its downtown section. Fourth, public services and facilities are typically most plentiful in downtown areas, enabling these districts to absorb large numbers of people with greater efficiency than the City's other areas.[21]

The interesting thing is that what Costonis finds typical about landmarks and their environs in big cities is also typical of much of the existing development in our older cities. The problem is that a disproportionate amount of value of existing development is represented by the value of the land rather than by the value of the structure upon it. As the structure becomes older, it becomes less economic to maintain, and, at the same time, there is a disincentive to maintaining it because maintenance of the structure in no way assists the owner in realizing the full development value of the property. If anything, maintaining the structure delays the day when the development potential can be realized through redevelopment of the property.

In a study undertaken some years ago by Professor Stanislow Czamanski for the Baltimore Urban Renewal and Housing Agency, it was concluded that accessibility to typical urban functions—such as government and private offices; cultural, amusement, and recreational facilities; research and institutional uses; specialized retail facilities; hotels and motels; and transportation centers—was, by far, the most determinative factor influencing the value of urban land. Even more significantly, it was concluded that, when all land use categories were considered together, blight and age of structures were positively correlated with land values; that is, the older and more deteriorated the present structure, the more valuable is the land upon which it is built, suggesting that, in general, the value of urban land may be largely a redevelopment, rather than a present use, value. In support of that conclusion, the study also found a positive correlation between land value and the existence of zoning permitting redevelopment of the parcel for more intense uses than those currently existing.[22]

Zoning ordinances have traditionally recognized this problem by increasing the density and intensity of use permitted on already developed property in recognition of its increased value and in the hope that, by recognizing the redevelopment potential, the city could encourage that redevelopment. Unfortunately, this has most frequently done nothing but exacerbate the situation by further increasing the disincentive to maintain property while at the same time making no significant contribution to the owner's ability to redevelop it.

What is needed, we believe, is a regulatory system that permits and encourages the maintenance of existing sound structures while at the same time permitting their owners to realize the development potential of the underlying ground. If that is the problem, then certainly the seeds of the solution lie in TDR theory and its underlying assumptions. We have a feeling, however, that if TDR is to become an effective tool of urban revitalization, it needs to be stood on its head. As thus far developed, TDR has been a tool to preserve something and it preserved that something—whether it was a landmark or a rain forest—by allowing an independent sale of its development potential. The idea has focused almost entirely on the transferor parcel; the transferee parcel has been viewed as little more than a necessary evil. What no one has paid much attention to is the fact that, in the typical TDR proposal, while the transferor parcel was being preserved, the transferee parcel was usually being redeveloped. In Chapter 19, we suggest a program in which the transferee parcels and the totality of the TDR district take on much greater importance than the transferor parcel.

NONLOCAL LAND USE CONTROLS

Perhaps no land use experiment has been pushed so far out of the laboratory and into practice as has the movement toward transferring local land use regulatory powers to a variety of federal, state, and regional governments and agencies. It is an experiment that demands more attention than the passing reference accorded to other new ideas by this chapter. We have already (in Chapter 15) described some of the current impacts of this movement on urban zoning practices. In the next chapter, we delve more deeply into the history and theory of the movement and draw some conclusions about its potential for success in solving the land use problems of major cities.

After the first draft of this book was completed, Chief Judge Charles Breitel delivered the opinion of the New York Court of Appeals in *Penn Central Trans. Co. v. City of New York*.[23] It is in many ways a remarkable opinion. It is, in addition, one of the first serious judicial evaluations of some of the new ideas discussed in this chapter. However, in reading it against the backdrop of our own work, we were most struck by its eloquent statement of a thought that has both troubled and comforted us as we have analyzed the proposals discussed in this chapter and formulated the proposals in the chapters that follow:

> In concluding the analysis, it is recognized that one does not pursue a path guided by ample precedent or wholly developed principles. The area is not merely difficult; it has at present viewing impenetrable densities. The last word has not only not been spoken; it has hardly been envisaged. For this case, and for cases that may follow in its wake, deference to the unknown must be accorded.[24]

FOOTNOTES

1. Richard F. Babcock and Fred P. Bosselman, *Exclusionary Zoning: Land Use Regulation and Housing in the 1970s* (New York City: Praeger Publishers, 1973), p. 87.

2. B. Siegan, "No Zoning Is the Best Zoning," in Benjamin F. Bobo et al., *No Land Is an Island* (San Francisco: Institute for Contemporary Studies, 1975).

3. *Id.* at 157.

4. For a report on how bad things can get, see "Conformity Is Made Law Under 'New Town' Codes," *New York Times*, August 25, 1975, p. 1.

5. Texas Rev. Stat., §974a-1 and §974a-2. The use of this technique was upheld by the Court of Civil Appeals, but the case did not raise all of the constitutional issues that commentators have suggested. *City of Houston v. Emmanuel United Pentecostal Church*, 429 S.W.2d 679 (1968). See comment in "Houston's Invention of Necessity—An Unconstitutional Substitute for Zoning?" 21 *Baylor L. Rev.* 307 (1969).

6. Siegan, *supra*, n. 2, at 157, 160.

7. Babcock and Bosselman, *supra*, n. 1, at 88.

8. See, for example, 2 James Ford, *Slums and Housing*, 841 (Cambridge, Mass.: Harvard University Press, 1936); Lewis Mumford, *The Culture of Cities*, 330 (New York: Harcourt, Brace and Company, 1938); Harold S. Buttenheim and Philip H. Cornick, "Land Reserves for American Cities," 14 *Journal of Land and Public Utility Economics* 254-65 (Chicago: Northwestern University School of Commerce, 1938).

9. U.S. National Resources Planning Board, *Public Land Acquisition, Part II: Urban Lands* (1941), p. 12.

10. *A Model Land Development Code, Proposed Official Draft* (Philadelphia: American Law Institute, 1975).

11. See Lyle C. Fitch and Ruth P. Mack, "Land Banking," in C. Lowell Harris (ed.), *The Good Earth of America* (Englewood Cliffs, N.J.: Prentice-Hall, 1974), p. 134.

12. Sylvan Kamm, "Land Banking: Public Policy Alternatives and Dilemmas," Urban Institute Paper No. 112-28 (12/31, 1970).

13. Richard P. Fishman, "Public Land Banking: Examination of a Management Technique," in *Management and Control of Growth* (Washington, D.C.: Urban Land Institute, 1975), vol. 3, p. 61.

14. Gerald Trimble, "Regrowth in Pasadena," *Urban Land*, January 1977, p. 4 *et seq.*

15. Stephen Serchuk, "Main Street is Revived on Toledo's Old East Side," *Planning*, December 1976, p. 18.

16. Don Hagman and Dean J. Misczynski, *Windfalls for Wipeouts?: Land Value Gains and Losses from Planning and a Catalogue of Methods for Redistributing Them* (Chicago: American Society of Planning Officials, 1978).

17. John J. Costonis, "Development Rights Transfer: Easing the Police-Power—Eminent-Domain Deadlock," *Zoning Digest* (1974).

18. John J. Costonis, "Whichever Way You Slice It, DRT Is Here to Stay," *Planning*, July 1974.

19. See, for example, Franklin J. James and Dennis E. Gale, *Zoning for Sale: A Critical Analysis of Transferable Development Rights Programs* (Washington, D.C.: Urban Institute, 1977).

20. Costonis, *supra*, n. 18.

21. John J. Costonis, "Space Adrift: A Synopsis," in *Management and Control of Growth* (Washington, D.C.: Urban Land Institute, 1975), vol. 3, pp. 106, 108.

22. Stanislow Czamanski, "Effects of Public Investments on Urban Land Values," *Journal of the American Institute of Planners,* July 1966, p. 204.

23. *Penn Central Transportation Co.* v. *City of New York,* 42 N.Y.2d 324, 397 N.Y.S.2d 914, 366 N.E.2d 1271 (1977) *aff'd,* 438 U.S. 104, 98 S. Ct. 2646 (1978).

24. *Id.* at 397 N.Y.S.2d 914, 922.

Chapter 17
The Locus of Power:
A Case for Local Control

*This country is in the midst of a
revolution in the way we regulate the
use of our land. . . .*

*The tools of the revolution are new
laws taking a wide variety of forms
but each sharing a common theme—
the need to provide some degree of
state or regional participation in the
major decisions that affect the use of
our increasingly limited supply of
land.*

—F. P. Bosselman
and D. L. Callies

*The federal government has been
carrying out an undeclared war on the
cities and the neighborhoods. . . . [T]he
ancient Goths or the marauding Huns
could not have devised a better method
of sacking and destroying neighborhoods and cities than our own federal
government has accomplished in the
last 40 years. It may be appropriate to
ask for reparations. . . . But in the
continued battle to save our cities, I'd
settle for at least a declaration of
neutrality.*

—Wes Uhlman

The big land use story in the mid-'60s and early '70s was the growing
pressure to curtail the traditional dominance of local government in the
control of the land use regulatory system. That pressure was the result
of two largely separate concerns, neither of which had much, if anything, to do with land use practices in cities. In part the movement was

born out of the rape of the countryside; in part, it was conceived as a mechanism to break down the "separate and unequal" societies being created and maintained by exclusionary suburban zoning practices. In those early days, the inherent conflict between the ultimate goals of the environmental movement and the open housing crusade was too far down the road to be of major concern. Whether your bible was *The Silent Spring* or *The Kerner Commission Report,* one of the devils was local control of land use, and the two armies marched arm-in-arm to the national and state capitals in search of a savior.

The success of the two factions has, however, been dramatically different, and the results are evident in the structure of federal and state control over local land use matters that emerged from the revolution. In analyzing that structure, one must begin by recognizing an important distinction between general planning policies and ad hoc particularized regulations. In the latter case we have witnessed a signficant, and apparently lasting, influence by the states and the federal government. The former saw a brief flowering followed by a notable retreat. We believe the explanation is simple: the injection of state and federal influence into generalized policymaking carried with it a threat to local governments' control over housing policy. Ad hoc regulations—especially all the baggage included in environmental legislation—did not appear to carry any social implications and did seem largely consistent with the parochial objectives of many suburban and ex-urban interest groups. They were not viewed as a significant threat. We will briefly trace each of these.

THE STATE AND FEDERAL ROLE IN COMPREHENSIVE PLANNING

At the beginning of this decade, Bosselman and Callies in *The Quiet Revolution in Land Use Control*[1] saw the states asserting an increased role in broad planning policy. There was persuasive evidence to support that view. Much attention was being given to the allegedly "exclusionary" practices of municipalities with respect to housing. The planning and law journals were drawing attention to the suburban municipalities, those "tight little islands," and their multitude of schemes for keeping out low-cost housing. Courts in a few states, most notably Pennsylvania, began to speak out, and it appeared that major state and federal legislative reforms would be adopted. Article 7 of the ALI Model Land Development Code was widely acclaimed and, indeed, copied in some jurisdictions. More than once Senator Jackson obtained overwhelming Senate endorsement of a national Land Use Bill. An effort was mounted in such Midwestern states as Michigan, Wisconsin, and Illinois to make major revisions in the state enabling legislation.

Suburban municipalities felt about as comfortable as a capitalist in the waning days of Romanov Russia as the reports of their land use excesses and the news of the "Quiet Revolution" spread at the same time. Along with other threatened interest groups, they determined to stand and fight. A significant counterattack was mounted in Congress and the state legislatures. The National Land Use Act was labeled a "federal zoning law" and repeatedly failed to get to the floor of the House. Senator Jackson finally refused to bring it onto the Senate. (As he purportedly observed: "Let Udall get it through the House first.") The attempts in Michigan failed; the Illinois effort fizzled out; Wisconsin came to nothing. What had not been noticed in the beginning of the legislative fervor became apparent: the states that had enacted significant new legislation were, for the most part, exotic. Such places as California, Florida, Hawaii, Vermont, and Maine were not New York, Pennsylvania, Michigan, and Illinois. New Jersey enacted a new set of planning legislation, but it did not dwell on the touchy issue of housing; the new statute concludes with a sickly section on voluntary regional cooperation. It had become apparent that if anything was to be done it would be through the courts rather than the legislatures; and in New York, New Jersey, and Pennsylvania, the courts have tried.[2] As a matter of declared policy, however, the move to inject the state and federal governments into local land use decisions on anything like a comprehensive basis has, despite some continuing calls for its revival, faded almost as quickly as it emerged.

THE EMERGENCE OF PARTICULARIZED REGULATION

If the successes in wholesale revision of planning legislation were few and far between, the same could hardly be said for legislation aimed at particular problems. The General Accounting Office summarized the federal situation as follows:

A 1973 study prepared by the Library of Congress showed that 23 federal departments and agencies were administering programs which impact on land-use policy and/or planning, including at least 112 federal land-oriented programs. The range of activity supported by these programs is very broad.[3]

At the state level, the movement has been equally pervasive. By the end of 1975, 13 states had adopted legislation requiring local governments to adopt land use plans, 10 had legislation mandating the adoption of local subdivision controls, and six also required the adoption of local zoning regulations. More than requiring local action, however, states have been pre-empting local action and taking over direct control of specific areas of land use regulation. Between 1969 and 1975, over 20 states adopted legislation giving a state regulatory agency power to approve or disapprove power plant and transmission line sites; six states had adopted controls over siting of developments of regional impact, and five states were directly regulating the siting of surface mines. Twenty-four states had adopted legislation giving the state control over areas of "critical concern."

Those statistics appear in one of the most complete studies of the accelerating shift of land use regulatory jurisdiction from local city halls to state capitols across the country, Nelson Rosenbaum's *Land Use in the Legislatures: The Politics of State Innovation.*[4] Rosenbaum lays a good deal of the responsibility for "the widespread consideration of innovative statutes" by state legislatures at the doorstep of *The Zoning Game.*[5] That may be so, but, in considering the results, we cannot say that the revolution has been terribly faithful to either the original Babcock prescription or to the movement's initial concern for opening up the suburbs to a diversity of racial and economic groups.

The thrust of *The Zoning Game* position was captured in the introductory paragraphs to Chapter 10:

> Under any politically acceptable system for resolving disputes over the use of privately owned land, the municipality will probably retain its role as initial decision-maker. The state will increasingly influence decisions on private land use where major public services are affected, and the federal government will insinuate itself into this arena by use of its traditional cash carrot. Nevertheless, there will remain thousands of disputes over the use of private land in which the exercise of judgment will be vested exclusively in municipal bodies.
>
> This is as it should be. Yet even if the decision-making remains local it is appropriate in those cases where the dispute may raise issues beyond that

of neighbor versus neighbor or may impose costs beyond the municipal boundaries, that the criteria for the decision should be consistent with the interests of the region. The error in zoning today is not that the decision-making is exclusively muncipal; the flaw is that the *criteria* for decision-making are exclusively local, even when the interests affected are far more comprehensive.

Reform in current land use policy will require a substantial change in our state enabling acts along three lines: (1) more detailed statutory prescription of the required administrative procedures at the local level; (2) a statutory restatement of the major substantive criteria by which the reasonableness of local decision-making is measured; (3) the creation of a state-wide administrative agency to review the decisions of local authorities in land-use matters, with final appeal to an appellate court. These reforms require that a distinction be made between procedural matters and those of substance; between control over the manner in which decisions on land use are made and the basis of the decisions themselves.[6]

In this field, where changes have been so rapid and so pervasive, the passage of a decade is more than enough justification to reconsider and recheck almost any bright idea conceived under the influence of times and conditions that bear little resemblance to those of today. Nevertheless, we cannot say that our views on the question of the proper division of the zoning power between local and nonlocal governments are any different than those set forth in *The Zoning Game* back in 1966. However, especially when discussing urban rather than suburban land use problems, we are troubled by the direction the revolution has taken since that time.

In essence, *The Zoning Game* proposal was that state legislation should set rather specific substantive standards to guide local zoning practice in those areas of legitimate state and regional concern and should require the establishment of local procedures to assure faithful application of those standards and basic fairness in the administrative process.

Those were, and are, reforms necessary to deal with the traditional suburban abuses of the zoning power. Their implementation would also serve to improve the administration of zoning in major cities and would, in addition, have positive benefits for major cities by forcing a break in the racial and economic walls suburban zoning has built around central cities. Those suggestions, however, have not been implemented. For the most part, local zoners continue to ignore their obligations to the region and to many segments of its population, and state legislators continue to look the other way.

In place of such reforms, we have seen (as described in Chapter 15) a number of largely ad hoc assaults upon the citadel of local land use control. In each case, the legislation adopted has been responsive to the environmental, slow-growth, stop-sprawl concerns of the early movement and has largely ignored the open housing issue. The result is a hodgepodge of legislation that fails to address the regional problems hampering the social and economic recovery of cities while at the same time creating new substantive and procedural roadblocks to all development with little or no recognition that such roadblocks may be at once less necessary and more overwhelming in the cities than in the suburbs and countryside.

REGIONAL AND STATE INTERVENTION IN LOCAL LAND USE DECISIONS

As noted at the beginning of this chapter, the push for direct federal, state, and regional involvement in the local land use process, which seemed so strong at the beginning of the '70s, had, as the decade closed, suffered a dramatic loss of momentum. The movement to wrest local control from local government has, however, left a few vestiges. As reported in Chapter 15, these have taken the form of transfers of part or all of the land use regulatory power to consolidated city-county governments, metropolitan planning agencies, or state land use agencies. As noted there, those experiments have produced no great success stories. That is not surprising. Reformers kid themselves if they believe that many of the problems plaguing the administration of land use controls can be solved by replacing a local official with a state or regional official. In that sense, calls for grand new approaches that completely scrap the existing system are cop-outs. Rather than facing and dealing with the real problems, that approach is based on the naive hope that, if we start all over, we may somehow avoid the reappearance of the same old problems. It is no more difficult to abuse or bungle regional powers than it is to abuse or bungle municipal powers.

On the big issues, race, ratables, and sprawl, regionalism has sometimes helped and sometimes not helped. The philosophy in Indianapolis and Minneapolis-St. Paul seems to be anti-racist, and regional controls have been used to break down barriers; the original motivation for regionalism in Jacksonville was quite the opposite. In Minneapolis-

St. Paul, without the total regionalization of government, some strides have been made to remove the incentive for fiscal zoning. In Jacksonville and Honolulu, total regional control has not resulted in a more rational approach to the location of commerce and industry throughout the region. Because those cities get the revenue no matter where the ratables locate, there seems less, not more, concern with careful planning for the location of such uses. In none of these "expanded cities" did we find much effective, hard-nosed control of sprawl; developers and land economics continued to dictate the location of new development.

Honolulu is a good example of what really happens. During the growth frenzy of the late '50s and early '60s, growth occurred wherever in the region developers wanted it; with the later rise of a slow-growth mentality, it became exceedingly difficult to develop anything anywhere in the region. So, as always, it is more the attitude than the jurisdictional area of the regulator that tells the story. To paraphrase Lord Acton, if local power tends to corrupt locally, then regional power tends to corrupt regionally.

To once again bring all of this back to our urban theme, the one thing that is clearest about the regionalization of either local government or local land use controls is that, where it has been tried, it has done absolutely nothing for the old city except to soften some of the adverse fiscal effects by expanding the municipal boundaries to recapture some of the fleeing middle-class households and businesses. The old downtowns of Jacksonville and Honolulu are as dead as if the new shopping centers were outside rather than inside the city; the old neighborhoods haven't become better places to live just because the new neighborhoods are now within the same political boundary. In a classic understatement, a staff memo to the Fully Developed Areas Task Force of the Metro Council pointed out that "Regional policies have considered the Fully Developed Areas in a rather indirect manner. . . ."

As discussed in Chapter 15, the other mode of regionalization, transfer of authority over specific types of development or development areas to state agencies, has frequently, as in the case of critical areas or power-plant siting legislation, been largely irrelevant both to what is going on in the cities and to those abuses of suburban zoning powers that tend to strangle cities; in other cases, however (halfway house and coastal zone legislation exemplify the range), such transfers have the potential either to promote or to hinder the recovery of cities, depending upon the sensitivity of state legislators and administrators to the need to differentiate between urban and non-urban areas in the application of such legislation. Urban leaders worry that such sensitivity may not develop. The experience with federal and state environmental legislation is enough to justify their concern.

ENVIRONMENTAL LEGISLATION

Local land use control has been more significantly eroded by the indirect intrusions of federal and state environmental laws than by any of the more direct attacks thus far discussed. The experience with nonlocal control in the complex environmental area has produced nothing to recommend further nonlocal intrusions into the complex area of urban land use regulation.

To date, federal and state environmental legislation has tended to declare that sweeping environmental goals shall be met while taking little note of legitimate competing goals. That legislative attitude presents special problems in an older city, where the competing goals are frequently compelling. A dramatic example of the extent to which national and state environmental programs can be insensitive to local needs is to be found in the United States Supreme Court decision in *Union Electric Company* v. *U.S. EPA.*[7] Union Electric is the utility that serves the St. Louis metropolitan area. The utility took the position that it was economically and technologically impossible for it to meet the criteria established by the Missouri implementation plan adopted pursuant to the Federal Clean Air Act. The court held that was no excuse. Justice Lewis F. Powell, with Chief Justice Warren E. Burger, concurred in the decision but added:

I join the opinion of the Court because the statutory scheme and the legislative history . . . demonstrate irrefutably that Congress did not intend to permit the Administrator of the Environmental Protection Agency to reject a proposed state implementation plan on the grounds of economic or technological infeasibility. Congress adopted this position despite its apparent awareness that in some cases existing sources that cannot meet the standard of the law must be closed down. . . .

Environmental concerns, long neglected, merit high priority, and Congress properly has made protection of the public health its paramount consideration. . . . But the shutdown of an urban area's electrical service could have an even more serious impact on the health of the public than that created by a decline in ambient air quality. The result apparently required by this legislation in its present form could sacrifice the well-being of a large metropolitan area through the imposition of inflexible demands that may be technologically impossible to meet and indeed may no longer even be necessary to the attainment of the goal of clean air.

I believe that Congress, if fully aware of this draconian possibility, would strike a different balance.[8]

While dramatic, that example is not atypical. After studying the problem, Bosselman, Feurer, and Callies summarized the situation as follows:

> ...the acts do not provide a mechanism for taking into consideration governmental laws and policies other than pollution control policies. For example, the policies of the Water Polution Control Act...may have substantial impact on efforts to revitalize city areas....[9]

The experience at the state level has been no better. Sam Wood, cofounder of California Tomorrow, has characterized that state's efforts as so much "stacking bits and pieces of plans on top of each other like pancakes...each largely without relation to the others and often in direct conflict."[10] In *The Permit Explosion*, Bosselman, Feurer, and Siemon amply demonstrate that Wood's comments could as easily have been made about any number of states in which the infusion of higher levels of government into the land use process has not resulted in any noticeable infusion of higher levels of rationality.[11]

Both in their substantive failure to differentiate between urban and non-urban areas and in their tendency to create, rather than eliminate, procedural barriers to getting anything whatever done, federal and state environmental laws have tended to compound the problems of major cities. Add to that the less-than-good-faith way in which environmental laws and agencies are sometimes invoked for motives having nothing to do with environmental concerns, and the good intentions behind such legislation start to look like so many cobblestones paving the road to hell.

Unfortunately, while the problem is easy to see, it is not easy to solve. Environmental problems are unavoidably regional in nature. The magnitude of the problem resulting from years of abuse and neglect now demands solutions that are, both technically and politically, beyond the capacity even of a large city to implement. Nonlocal control is mandated by the realities of the situation, but the resulting insensitivity to competing local goals and values poses a major threat to the old industrial cities of the nation.

As a practical matter, it is clear that, as a nation, we have neither the desire nor the ability to dismantle or substantially restructure the massive environmental machine we have already created. We do not, however, have to treat it as a model for reform in other areas of land use regulation. Having witnessed the attempts to solve the problems of the local land use system by sweeping programs that replace local decision-makers with regional or state decisionmakers, we become more, not less, convinced that the correct approach is state legislation to correct and perfect—not abolish—the local administration of land use regulations. None of the attempts to move authority up the ladder have miraculously produced either social justice, consistency and continuity, evenhanded administration, or procedural speed, accuracy, or fairness. If anything, the situation is sometimes a bit worse than it used to be. Worse, however, than this lack of success in curing many of the problems of the old system is the potential of nonlocal land use systems to introduce whole new sets of problems.

If the introduction of nonlocal decisionmakers is intended to cure the problem of local decisionmakers ignoring regional interests and impacts, it is a good bet it will succeed only at the expense of nonlocal decisionmakers ignoring local interests and impacts. That, however, is only the tip of the iceberg. With all its flaws and faults, one always suspects that when the local land use process ignores nonlocal concerns, it does so intentionally and with an understanding of the probable consequences. The frightening thing about moving the decision-making process away from the local level is that the decisionmakers frequently make decisions with very little knowledge or understanding of their consequences. When land use decisions are made primarily at the local level, we can usually recognize what is "wrong" with them and could, if it were politically acceptable, correct the errors. If the history of federal intervention into urban problems offers any guide, when decisions affecting complex local problems are made at the nonlocal level, it is frequently impossible even to know that something is wrong, much less to know what is wrong, before the situation reaches desperate proportions. By that time, it is all but impossible to figure out how to correct the situation without setting afoot even more distressing possibilities.

Our disinclination to see any further transfer of urban land use authority to regional, state, and federal governments proceeds, however, not merely from our conviction that such a transfer is at least as likely to exacerbate as alleviate the current problems plaguing the local administration of land use. We are equally motivated by the belief that the special problems facing major cities can be best solved at the local level.

The reassertion these last 10 years of state participation in land development policy in our rural and scenic areas may be necessary and appropriate when the competing social values are put on the scales. A cluster of second homes in the Vermont countryside may irreparably brutalize the landscape with little offsetting social gain. And it probably is true, as Mayor Pete Wilson suggested, that most small towns do not have the will or the way to respond to large-scale development. It is also indisputable that strong regional or state agencies are both essential and potentially effective when dealing with such peripheral issues as where *new* sewers will run and how a fair share of moderate-cost housing will be distributed among the suburbs. And there may be no cure for single-minded surburban parochialism other than the removal of significant decisionmaking power to more broadly based agencies.

We have serious reservations, however, whether on balance the same considerations are applicable in our cities; and we see the irony that supramunicipal policies may, given both the diversity and urgency of problems confronting our major cities, operate more severely and with less equity in the urban areas than in the suburban fiefdoms that have, by their excesses and eccentricities, produced the demand for such policies.

Especially in these distressed times, the issues facing cities are so complex, the competing influences bearing on the issues are so difficult to balance, and the immediate and future impacts of any land use decision are so difficult to predict and evaluate that the decisionmaking process ought to be kept as close as possible to the problem. The issues are not of the sort that can be resolved by the application of expertise. They are fundamentally political, frequently involving the balancing of conflicting, but equally valid and important, interests and objectives. They should be made by elected officials who are close enough to the situation to understand the ramifications of their decisions, who are advised by a staff that is close enough to the situation to define all the competing considerations, and who operate within a procedural framework that offers some hope of being able to give every side a fair hearing within a reasonable time.

The near universal preference among developers and neighbors alike (which we reported in Chapter 11) to see final zoning decisions in cities made by elected officials rather than by appointed lay boards or experts is, we believe, due in large part to a recognition that, at least in cities, local land use decisions are frequently more a matter of policy than of precision. Their republican heritage has imbued Americans with the belief that fundamental policy decisions affecting broad aspects of their lives should be made by those whom they elect and, at least indirectly, control. Despite its sometimes unsavory connotation, "political" is not a dirty word. The original concept of a political system was, in Webster's words, " . . . of, relating to, or concerned with the making, as distinguished from the administration of, government policy. . . . "[12] If there is a spark of genius in the local zoning system, it is that, when operating as it can and as it should, the system provides a sensitive political forum for the discussion and resolution of decisions that are essentially political. We doubt that any system of nonlocal land use control could duplicate that sensitivity to the broad range of issues that must be weighed in nearly every decision affecting the development of land in a major city. We believe, on the other hand, that, if the political will to do it exists at the state and federal levels, the local land use system can be forced to give responsible consideration to issues of regional concern.

Our conclusion, then, is that, at least in the context of cities, efforts to whittle away at local decisionmaking responsibility should be abandoned in favor of an effort to correct the specific deficiencies of the local decisionmaking process. Harold Jensen, the former president of the Urban Land Institute, captured the essence of our thought:

> . . . it is not some cataclysm which is destroying our cities, but the breakdown of everyday institutions. Consequently, instead of trying to reinvent the wheel, we should focus on those parts which have broken down. This process may not offer the excitement of a Marshall Plan for cities, but it is probably more productive.[13]

The reforms necessary to make the local land use control system work as it can and should in a major city are the subject of our next chapter.

FOOTNOTES

1. Fred P. Bosselman and David L. Callies, *The Quiet Revolution in Land Use Control* (Washington, D.C.: Council on Environmental Quality, 1971).

2. See, for example, *Township of Williston* v. *Chesterdale,* 341 A.2d 46 (Pa. 1975); *Berenson* v. *Town of Newcastle,* 38 N.Y.2d 102, 378 N.Y.S.2d 672, 341 N.E.2d 236 (1975); *Southern Burlington County NAACP* v. *Township of Mount Laurel,* 336 A.2d 713 (N.J. 1975).

3. U.S. General Accounting Office, "Land Use Planning, Management and Control: Issues and Problems" (Washington, D.C.: July 28, 1977).

4. Nelson Rosenbaum, *Land Use in the Legislatures: The Politics of State Innovation* (Washington, D.C.: Urban Institute, 1977).

5. *Id.* at 16.

6. Richard F. Babcock, *The Zoning Game* (Madison, Wis.: University of Wisconsin Press, 1966), pp. 153-154.

7. *Union Electric Company* v. *U.S. EPA,* 427 U.S. 246 (1976).

8. *Id.* at 269-72 (footnote omitted).

9. Fred P. Bosselman, Duane A. Feurer, and David L. Callies, *EPA Authority Affecting Land Use,* NTIS Report No. EPA 230/3-74-012 (1974), pp. 156-157.

10. Sam Wood, "State Planning and How It Grows," *Cry California,* fall-winter 1974, pp. 10-17.

11. Fred P. Bosselman, Duane A. Feurer, and Charles L. Siemon, *The Permit Explosion* (Washington, D.C.: Urban Land Institute, 1976), p. 20.

12. *Webster's Third New International Dictionary.*

13. Harold Jensen, "Some Reflections on Urban Revitalization," *Urban Land,* January 1977, p. 3.

Chapter 18
The Process:
The Control of Discretion

*I know no safe depository of the
ultimate powers of the society but the
people themselves; and if we think
them not enlightened enough to
exercise their control with a
wholesome discretion, the remedy is
not to take it from them, but to inform
their discretion.*

—Thomas Jefferson

*Equity is a roguish thing. For law we
have a measure, know what to trust to;
equity is according to the conscience of
him that is chancellor, and as that is
larger or narrower, so is equity. 'Tis all
one as if they should make the
standard for the measure we call a
"foot" a chancellor's foot; what an
uncertain measure this would be! One
chancellor has a long foot, another a
short foot, a third an indifferent foot.
'Tis the same thing in the chancellor's
conscience.*

—John Selden

Were we to choose two great lessons to be learned by urban zoners
from their suburban counterparts, they would be, first, that nothing is so
important to a successful scheme of land use regulation as discretion in
its administration and, second, that nothing is more subject to destructive abuse than that administrative discretion.

Discretion in the first zoning ordinances was all but nonexistent. The power to vary or amend specific regulations to avoid an unconstitutional application of the inflexible Euclidian regulations was the sum total of zoning discretion. The reason for, and the result of, the blossoming of ever more sophisticated discretionary devices in suburban municipalities is well enough stated in *The Zoning Game,* and we quote it here again:

> The elementary concept of districting (each pig in its own pen) could not provide the agility a welter weight must have to defeat or at least to discourage a Goliath. Unable, or more accurately, unwilling, to join together to battle the metropolitan explosion in the sophisticated developmental techniques of the land planners, the suburbs have seized upon each new device conceived by the planners to parry the blows of these formidable antagonists. Nowhere is this ingenuity more apparent than in the administrative devices which have been invented to provide the suburban communities with the discretion necessary to meet each new proposal of those who would challenge their security....
>
> It was the enthusiastic and unprincipled use of this special permit device that led Detroit planner-lawyer Walter Blucher to exclaim: "The question must be asked seriously whether zoning, as it is currently being practiced, is endangering our democratic institutions...? Is zoning increasingly becoming the rule of man rather than the rule of law? I would be inclined to answer both questions affirmatively." The municipalities could not care less about the protests of the professionals.[1]

The growth of discretion in suburban zoning was, then, attributable to the need to respond to complex proposals and situations and to the desire to preserve the right to say no. The situation in today's cities is only slightly different. The complexities of redeveloping and rehabilitating large areas of a major city make the problems created by the suburban boom look like child's play. The only real difference is that cities need discretion to say yes more than they want discretion to say no. That difference is, however, critical. It means that cities must find a way to preserve discretion in the zoning process while at the same time eliminating the red tape, delay, and arbitrariness that has characterized the coming of zoning discretion to suburbia.

As we noted earlier, so far as developers are concerned, the elimination of delay and uncertainty are the two principal incentives and attractions to developing in a particular community. Developers generally like the sort of flexibility inherent in the myriad of discretionary zoning devices developed to control suburban development. They like the chance to sell their wares, and they believe flexibility in the rules will ultimately result in better developments. However, when the price of that flexibility is uncertainty, inconsistency, and endless delay, the developers to whom we talked were in agreement that they would prefer rigid take-it-or-leave-it standards. It is not just the obvious, direct costs of carrying a project through endless administrative delay that bothers developers and increases costs for buyers and renters. Probably more important is the risk involved. Development always has been a high-risk business; long delays greatly increase the risk of encountering adverse changes in market conditions; unbridled discretion greatly increases the risk of adverse regulatory action. If the risks are perceived to be high enough, the developer will abandon the market; at very least, the developer will demand a higher return on equity to compensate for the risk.

While a return to rigid, pre-ordained regulations would eliminate much of this delay and uncertainty, it is not a realistic solution to the problems of today's cities. As one major Atlanta-based developer put it:

Rigid zoning guidelines are consistent; I can depend on them. I will either play or pass. But the cities are in dire straits today. If they take that position, then developers are going to pass more than they are going to play. They are going to choose not to develop because of the heavy-handedness of the regulations involved.

Thus, as Jefferson said, the remedy is not to take the discretion away from the zoners but to so inform and control it as to make it a positive tool for redevelopment.

Most suggestions for eliminating the abuse of discretion in the zoning process have involved some variation on a limited number of themes: professionalizing the process, reforming its procedures, or tying specific decisions more firmly to predetermined plans and policies. Each theme has something to recommend itself, and any effective solution will include elements of them all. However, it appears to us that most proposals for zoning reform have been ineffective because they have been grounded in essentially erroneous assumptions about the fundamental nature of the system.

In considering how a system of local land use control should be structured, we think it necessary to begin by frankly recognizing a couple of obvious facts about the system and the tools available to control it.

First, the urban land use process is essentially political in nature. In Oregon, of all places, home of *Fasano* v. *Washington Co. Comm.,*[2] an appellate court was bold enough to note the reality of the situation:

> Aside from petitioner's choice of pejorative terms, we see nothing improper with a decision on a conditional use being based in part on the feelings of the neighbors who will have to live with that use, if approved. *Fasano* used the term "quasi-judicial" to describe the procedures to be followed by local governments and the scope of judicial review in a case like this. *Fasano* cannot, however, negate the reality that land-use administration at the local level is fundamentally a political process. The *Fasano* rules open that process to more participation and more overt and reasoned decision-making, but do not abolish its political character. In our system and tradition, political process means democratic process. Just as it is permissible and proper for local governments to consider public sentiment in establishing a legislative land-use plan, it is permissible and proper for local governments to give such public sentiment such consideration as may be relevant under the circumstances in considering quasi-judicial changes in that plan.[3]

Second, long-term, comprehensive land use planning is a virtual impossibility and land-use regulation is most basically a system designed to allow orderly change in response to specific proposals:

> A zoning code is unlike other legislation affecting the use of property.... The expectancy that particular changes consistent with the basic zoning plan will be allowed frequently and on their merits is a normal incident of property ownership. When the governing body offers the owner the opportunity to seek such a change—whether that opportunity is denominated a privilege or a right—it is affording protection to the owner's interest in making legitimate use of his property.[4]

Third, change implies discretion and discretion can be, and has been, abused.

In light of these facts, the goal of reform should be not a vain attempt to predict change and eliminate discretion but an attempt to assure that, when the private sector proposes a change, the discretion to grant or deny it will be exercised openly, honestly, and on the basis of as thorough an inquiry and as full a participation as possible.

THE PLAN AND PLANNING

Perhaps the single most advocated solution to the problem of arbitrary zoning decisions is an insistence that such decisions be made "in accord with a comprehensive plan." The idea, of course, is not new. Those words appeared in the first Standard Zoning Enabling Act, promulgated in 1926. However, it is only in the last few years that the requirement has been given the sort of legislative and judicial backing that has been necessary to bring it to the forefront as a device to control discretion.

Legislation and court decisions mandating local planning in advance of zoning seek to force a degree of rationality into the exercise of the zoning power. That philosophy makes sense. Unfortunately, in attempting to implement that philosophy, most of the mandatory planning legislation fails to direct itself at the specific problems that have plagued the local land use system. Lack of consistency between a local zoning ordinance and a previously developed comprehensive plan has little to do with the problems of local zoning. The problems have to do almost entirely with the parochial desires of local governments to maximize the local fisc while excluding a variety of people and uses thought to have a negative impact upon the "character" of the community. The list of unwanted uses range from low-income housing to land fills, with the former being by far the most troublesome. If the goal is to make local governments act more responsibly, then states should find the courage to specifically address the real problems—as Minnesota has done with its Metropolitan Revenue Distribution[5] legislation in the Twin Cities area and Massachusetts has done with Anti-Snob Zoning Law[6]—and should give up efforts to force localities to go through a more round-about path to the same anti-social goals.

At the very least, however, if this placebo is to be administered in place of real medicine, cities should be exempted from the treatment. Mandatory planning as it relates to cities is an unnecessary interference with the urban land use process. The abuses such legislation is supposed to cure are largely suburban in origin. Cities have been among the victims, not the perpetrators, of exclusionary and fiscal zoning practices. Even if mandatory planning were a remedy for those evils, which we doubt, its not a cure the cities need. Nor is it a cure adapted to the problems that cities do have. The complex problems of maintaining and redeveloping a major city are not likely to be much helped by the development of long-range goals, broad policies, or detailed future land use maps, which is what most mandatory planning legislation mandates. City planning for a city demands a rather different orientation.

The rise of "The Plan" as a device to eliminate the abuse of zoning discretion is reminiscent of a pendulum swung too far and reveals a fundamental misconception about the essential nature of zoning and the zoning process—especially in the context of a developed city. Much of the current clamor for plans and for consistency between plans and zoning appears to proceed from the assumptions that change in land use regulations is an evil and that it is possible to eliminate the need for change by developing accurate, long-term plans for future development. Instead of being advocated as a device to control and direct discretion, the plan is promoted as a device to eliminate it. Those are unrealistic assumptions and goals. Especially in a major urban center, there are too many problems, too many uncontrollable variables, and too many unpredictable factors to permit any hope that long-range planning will provide an ultimate cure-all for land use problems and abuses. One need do little more than review the history of zoning administration in Hawaii since the *Dalton* decision[7] to see how both planning and zoning can be destroyed by unrealistic demands for consistency between plan and ordinance. Since the Hawaiian Supreme Court's pronouncement in *Dalton* that there could be no change in zoning unless there was a corresponding change in the master plan supported by studies as comprehensive as those preceding adoption of the original plan, the plan has ceased to be an effective policy tool and has become little more than another zoning ordinance, the revision of which complicates and delays the zoning process to no real purpose.*

If the plan is to become a tool to guide discretion, then, especially in cities, a fundamental redirection of the planning process is essential. As it has been practiced in the past, planning has been general, long-term,

---

*For those of us who believe that plans, like people, can be promoted to their level of incompetence, it was satisfying to see the Oregon Supreme Court, in the case of *Green* v. *Hayward,* 552 P.2d 815 (Or. 1976), awake with a shudder as the *Fasano* dream showed signs of becoming a nightmare. In *Fasano,* the court, in addition to mandating procedural reforms, established the principal that a specific zoning change could be sustained only upon proof that it was "in conformance with the comprehensive plan." *Fasano* v. *Board of County Commissioners,* 507 P2d 23, 28 (1973). In *Green,* the plaintiffs tried to push the court's pronouncement in *Fasano* to its illogical extreme. They argued that, because the general land use map adopted as part of the comprehensive plan showed the subject property classified for agricultural use, the proposed use for expansion of an adjoining industrial concern was not consistent with the plan. Happily, the court did not take the bait. It adopted a more flexible approach to the concept of "consistency" between plan and ordinance:

If the opinion of the Court of Appeals reflects or creates an understanding that our decision . . . was intended to hold that a local government's zoning map must coincide in detail with the map portion of the comprehensive plan, that misunderstanding should be corrected. . . . [T]here is as yet no agreement within the planning

and almost exclusively physical. It is now generally recognized that
there is something wrong with the old end-state, Year 2000 master plan
approach to planning. The more recent fashion is "policy planning":
Maps are out; policy statements are in. In most quarters, however, the
new jargon hasn't done much to make planning more relevant or
effective.

Honolulu is a good example. It has made as valiant an effort as any
city to introduce policy planning. The failure of that effort is well-
known and has been amply chronicled elsewhere.[8] The causes for the
failure are many and complex, but the principal reason that policy
planning worked no better than land use planning is that the shift from
maps to policies was accompanied by no fundamental change either
in the approach to plan development or in the attitude toward the
purpose of the plan. Whether through the fault of Honolulu's Charter
Commission, city council, mayor, or planning department (they all
point the finger at each other), the "policy plan" and the process
leading to it were characterized by all the problems of a Year 2000
"pretty picture" plan. The planners wanted to be politicians, and the
politicians wanted to be planners. The plan was drawn at a grand scale
and "comprehensively"; it was more a picture (albeit a word picture)
of what Honolulu should someday be than a prescription for dealing
with the problems of what Honolulu now was. Because of its grand
scale and far-off focus, effective citizen participation was all but
impossible.

Robert Rider, who was project director for the Honolulu plan revi-

---

profession as to the form which a good comprehensive plan should
take.... In light of the freedom given local governments, both in the past and for
the future, to design the form of their comprehensive plans, we refrain from
statements of general application about how such plans are to be read or inter-
preted. The relationship between the text and the maps within a particular plan
must be determined from the plan document itself, considered as a whole.

In the present case, the Plan itself tells us that neither the text nor the illustrative
diagram was intended to provide advance answers to the kinds of questions
involved in this case. We conclude that in the 1990 Plan, the plan map or diagram
was intended to illustrate what the text calls the "broad allocation" of land within
the area shown, but not to put a limit on the permissible uses of each and every
tract within that area. In order to determine whether a particular zoning decision
is in compliance with the Plan, we must look to other portions of the Plan in
addition to the diagram." 552 P2d at 517-19.

The Court then went on to review the plan in detail and concluded that, despite the
apparent inconsistency, the rezoning was in conformity with the overall goals and
objectives of the plan.

sion, draws these conclusions from the failure of Honolulu's experiment:

> Unfortunately, the charter commission was following a long history of city planning in which a general or master plan is a necessary prescription. But the commission and all the professional planners who testified before it failed to realize that the general plan was incompatible with the objective to promote policy analysis.
>
> Policy cannot fit into the formula of the general plan. It is as specific or as general as the problem warrants. Policies cannot be neatly programmed or divided into nine subject areas or, as required by the charter, reviewed at least every five years. They tended to be made in a piecemeal manner and limited to specific issues. . . .[9]

The fact is that cities cannot hope to plan and dictate development with anything like the same assurance that characterizes their suburban counterparts, who write on a much cleaner slate. City planning for a city must have resiliency and a capacity to react to opportunity when and where it emerges out of the existing reality. The idea of a long-term plan, or of a zoning ordinance to implement it, is, for a major city, both unreasonable and unrealistic. Rather than beginning with a generalized picture—whether in maps or words—of where a city should be in five or 10 or 20 years and attempting to deduce from that picture what actions the city should take tomorrow, we suggest that planning for major cities be reoriented so that it begins by answering the questions:

> What *must* we do today to deal with currently perceived problems?
>
> What, given our current resources and the present demands on them, can we expect to do tomorrow to deal with the problems and concerns we now foresee?
>
> If nothing unexpected happens, what might we want to do in the immediate future to avoid problems that a continuation of current trends is likely to produce?

Having answered all of those questions, the planners should finally ask themselves:

> Given our answers to all of the previous questions, where will the city be in five or 10 years, and how acceptable will that be?

If the answer is that it appears that where you will be is unacceptable, then the planners must go back and re-evaluate their answers to the initial questions in an effort to devise answers that, while meeting immediate needs, also lead to more acceptable end positions.

We do not mean to suggest that planning should become simply a synonym for coping with crises, although even now the staffs of many cities sometimes find it difficult to serve any other function. Planning that merely reacts to problems, even planning that merely solves problems, is not planning. But planning that does not contribute to the solution of immediate problems is not useful. Planning that focuses on development of specific programs to solve individual, immediate problems in a way that contributes to the long-term realization of broader goals and objectives is, we believe, planning of a sort that may be able to achieve a significant role in the governance and development of our cities.

Planners must realize that there is more than one way to build a jigsaw puzzle. If someone is good enough to give you all of the pieces at the beginning and the leisure time to sort them out and think about what you're doing, you can plan your attack, starting with those pieces most easily identifiable with relation to the whole picture and putting off for later the more difficult, monochromatic areas of the picture where individual pieces give little hint of their place in the ultimate solution. Unfortunately, that scheme of puzzle planning and building does not jibe with the realities of city planning and building.

At best, city planners and decisionmakers have a general notion of what the picture ought to look like when it's done and some general knowledge of what pieces have to be put together to make the picture. But no one provides either all of the pieces in advance or the leisure time to sort them out. The pieces come by fits and starts at the whim of people and forces over which cities and their officials have little control. Worse yet, in the real world, the hard pieces can't be set aside for later, more leisurely examination: They usually come first. No doubt, it is more difficult to build a puzzle under those conditions, but it is not impossible.

One thing is certain. If planners continue to insist that they will not start putting the picture together until they have collected all of the pieces and have had time to think out the best approach, those responsible for keeping cities running are going to quit giving planners the pieces. As Peter Blake has pointed out, there were no guarantees that space exploration would be successful before it was tried:

> To achieve that ambitious goal, much planning at Cape Kennedy had to be based on educated guesswork . . . before the facts were in. As a result, a great deal of time was saved—the kind of time that is often wasted in attacks on urban problems because no one is willing to take a chance until every theory has been tested over and over again.[10]

The switch from land use and policy planning to the type of problem and program planning we are suggesting requires planning to focus not only on a shorter term but also on narrower geographic and social areas and on specific implementation programs.

Great cities are more than a sum of their parts, and city planning and land use regulation must not lose sight of that fact. We do not advocate neighborhood self-determination in matters of zoning and land use regulation. The suburban mode of walled subdivisions within walled villages is not one to be emulated. Government by homeowners' association is not one of mankind's more marvelous inventions. It is the molding of diversity into a single entity that makes a city a city. At the point that zoning and land use regulations become totally subservient to any single interest group within a city, whether it be developers, downtown business people or neighborhood block clubs, urban zoning becomes simply a caricature of suburban zoning and subject to many of the same evils.

Nevertheless, a planning process that ignores the fact that every city contains within itself numerous distinct residential neighborhoods and economic sectors cannot possibly be responsive to the real and immediate problems of a city. To the residents and business people upon whom city survival depends, the big problems are most often those small problems that impact directly on their confined area of the city. They are, furthermore, frequently problems of manageable proportion. Their perceived importance and their manageability make them good places to start the development of a relevant and realistic plan for a city.

The possible approaches to the specifics of neighborhood planning are as diverse as the cities that might consider such programs, but no such program should stray far from the basic concepts outlined in a short section of an ordinance we drafted for Memphis, Tennessee:

> In determining the appropriateness of a proposed neighborhood plan and the advisability of its approval and adoption, the Office of Planning and Development and the legislative body shall take into consideration:
>
> a. The consistency of the proposed neighborhood plan with policies and capital improvement programs established by the legislative body, and with the interests of the City or County as a whole; provided, however, that any inconsistency between the proposed plan and existing zoning in the neighborhood shall not necessarily be a basis for a rejection of the plan.
>
> b. The extent to which the policies in the plan are set forth with clarity and are in a form to be usable in guiding future decisions by appropriate public agencies.

c. The extent to which the proposed plan does, in the opinion of the Office of Planning and Development and the legislative body, represent a substantial consensus of opinion in the neighborhood.

Implicit in those standards is, of course, the concept that problem and program planning is going on at the citywide level as well. But even there, the focus of planning should be on specific, immediate problems rather than on ultimate "goals and objectives." If the focus on the present is lost, it is all but impossible to avoid sliding back into the old style of irrelevant planning and plans. The future is too difficult to see and too far off to worry about. Unless the focus is on what people and politicians are worried about today, the people and the politicians can be expected to pay but little attention to planners and their plans. Without the challenge and discipline that comes from close scrutiny, planners are all too likely to lapse into daydreams about what might be if planners, rather than people and politicians, shaped the urban environment.

Once the planning process has identified immediate problems, it should move on to development of realistic, specific programs to solve those problems. Programs that can't be funded and commenced within a year or two are hardly worth thinking about unless you've already done everything you can to solve today's problems.

To the greatest extent possible, public programs should be devised to focus limited public funds where they will leverage private investment. In part that means that the capital improvements program should become a positive tool for the implementation of planning goals. Public infrastructure, much more than any planner's predictions or prognostications, provides the catalyst for, and the ultimate limits upon, private development. At a time when suburban communities, following the lead of Ramapo, New York, are using infrastructure and the capital improvements program as a way of slowing growth, cities should be using the same tools as a way both to encourage and to direct redevelopment. Developers who cannot find water, sewer, roads, and transportation in the suburbs, or are asked to contribute an unrealistically large share of the cost of providing such improvements, may be expected to respond favorably to the availability of such facilities upon reasonable terms in the cities.

In Tucson, the city government and the Southern Arizona Homebuilders Association have joined forces on a development that could ultimately provide over 150 new single-family homes within a healthy walk of downtown Tucson. The city is providing all on-site engineering and installing all of the necessary off-site improvements. Four hundred thousand dollars in HUD allocations plus an additional $35,000 in city funds have also been committed to the project. The city has agreed to waive a couple of troublesome provisions of its codes. The private developers are supplying the land and building the homes. Both initial and buyer financing have been arranged through a group of Arizona banks.

But programs to implement the plan should go further than the upgrading of public infrastructure in key areas. What is needed are programs that identify and promote the implementation of major public and private developments as anchors and catalysts for further private redevelopment. Cities must actively program public investments to promote private spin-off development. That will frequently mean entering into active partnerships with both developers and neighborhood groups to combine public and private resources to implement the plan. The efforts of half a dozen cities reported in Chapter 16 begin to show the way.

We started out to talk about the plan as a tool to control discretion in the urban land use process. We have taken some time to suggest how the practice of urban planning might be reformed because we are convinced that it is only through rather drastic reform that planning can become an effective tool for guiding a discretionary land use system. That objective will not be achieved by the currently popular pastime of passing laws to mandate consistency between zoning and planning.

The plan should be a flexible guide, not a straightjacket. Plans should serve a function that zoning ordinances, by their nature, cannot. Zoning ordinances are static and, for that reason, unrealistic. They do not, although perhaps it is time they did, reflect the reality that much of what is mapped on the zoning map can and will be changed upon receipt of an appropriate application satisfying specific goals and concerns of the city. By demanding the sort of consistency between plan and zoning ordinance found in a growing number of "mandatory planning" statutes and court decisions, the plan is deprived of its flexibility and its ability to look out of the present into the future. It becomes, like the zoning ordinance, simply an imperfect reflection of the present that serves to inhibit, rather than direct, movement into the future.

That sort of legal effect forces careful consideration of the plan only when there is a proposal to change it. That is backward and only a little better than the old system in which no one paid any attention to the plan until there was a proposal to implement it. Even worse, that approach does little to make it more difficult for decisionmakers to ignore the plan; it only makes it more time-consuming. A system that really values planning should force consideration of the plan when it is adopted, not when it is proposed to be implemented or changed. Furthermore, a system that values planning should recognize that developing practical political support for the plan, rather than mandating legal effect for the plan, is the surest way to guarantee its continuing effectiveness.

Our suggestions for reforming urban planning would, we believe, result not only in plans that mean something but also in plans that have real—as opposed to "legal"—effect. As we envision it, the plan would be more than pablum and pretty pictures. It would relate to immediate problems and near-term programs, not to a planner's vision of Utopia, U.S.A. Public participation in the planning process would begin at the neighborhood level, would be active, and would be directed to plan formulation and implementation rather than to "review and comment." Formal public hearings before the governing body would be required, and the governing body, rather than the planning department or commission, would have the final responsibility for adopting or rejecting the plan. Because of the plan's greater specificity and immediacy, it can be expected that elected officials, property owners, and citizens would all have a more active interest in the plan's contents than is now the case. The result of such active participation and serious consideration at the adoption stage is a plan that has a ready-made body of defenders and protectors. People seem by nature to be more dedicated to preserving their own ideas than to preserving the ideas of others. If the planning process demands the active participation of decisionmakers, property owners, and residents in the formulation of the plan, the plan becomes their idea and acquires a natural defense mechanism against destructive change or avoidance. At that point planning will have become not only a significant guide to the exercise of discretion but also a significant check against its abuse.

PROFESSIONALIZATION AND PROCEDURAL REFORM

In 1960 Babcock said administration was "the running, ugly sore of zoning...."[11] In 1966, Babcock said administration was "the Sargasso Sea of zoning."[12] Both comments remain largely accurate today.

(Weaver does occasionally wonder why Babcock can never seem to get anything done about this problem.)

We wrote—and then scrapped—yet another detailed prescription for reform. We scrapped it because the necessary reforms are, by now, well-known. The need for them cannot be seriously questioned. Why doesn't it happen? In part, it is because the local politicians involved in zoning know that procedural reform is the most potent of all zoning reforms and because local administrators prefer to muddle along doing things the way they've always done them. The following comment is characteristic of the prevailing attitude:

> They have made a conscious effort not to have any rules and their attorney says "we don't want rules because they can trip you up."

Another part of the reason is that zoning administration is perceived as dull stuff. Zoning scholars and zoning consultants don't consider it glamorous enough to merit their serious attention. In drafting zoning ordinances, as in all legislative drafting, there is a tendency to stop thinking and writing as soon as the policy is defined. But, especially in land use regulation, the implementation of policy is as challenging as its formulation, and unless both challenges are met, the system will not work the way it should.

Yet another difficulty in achieving effective reform of zoning procedures is that courts and reformers have simply refused to attack the problem head-on. It is, we believe, a sad commentary upon the state of zoning reform in this country that most people view the substitution of one artificial label, "administrative," for another artificial label, "legislative," as one of the major reforms of this decade. We have had 50 years of zoning grief because the United States Supreme Court looked at zoning and reasoned: if it is decided by a legislative body, it must be a legislative decision and, therefore, a zoning decision must be made and reviewed according to the same set of rules that apply to the legislative decisions of Congress or a state legislature. We are likely to have another 50 years of grief if we all now conclude that it is very clever to reason: zoning decisions are "administrative decisions"; therefore, we will treat them according to the set of rules that the legal system has developed for dealing with decisions of federal and state administrative agencies and officials. At some point, one would hope that those involved in, and those responsible for reviewing, the zoning process would give up trying to label it in favor of trying to deal with it. When they do, it will be immediately evident to them that local zoning issues and decisions are a sui generis combination of policy, politics, fact, and emotion. No attempt to bring the system under control is likely to succeed if it fails to address that fact, and yet few of the currently popular proposals for reform do so. Rather, they proceed from the essentially incorrect notion that zoning decisions are more a question of fact than of policy. This misconception is especially prevalent among those who see all the answers lying in a "professionalization" of the local land use system. If their major premise were accurate, the ultimate and most logical reform would be the institution of a hearing-examiner process. We happen to believe that that idea has much to commend itself. Its success in King County, Washington, Indianapolis, and Montgomery County, Maryland, is a tribute to what it can accomplish, but it is also a testimonial to its limits. Many zoning questions do, indeed, have a large factual component and only minimal policy implications; many others involve only relatively unimportant issues of either fact or policy. For those breeds of zoning questions, the professional hearing examiner may be the ideal solution. However, many zoning issues, even those pertaining only to a single parcel of property, involve major issues of community policy and direction.

We submit that is especially so in the case of urban zoning issues. The patchwork, largely unplanned patterns of urban development; the diversity of urban life-styles and interest groups; and the desperate intensity of urban problems are frequently reflected in, and invariably tend to complicate, urban land use questions. Having all the facts may be helpful to guide policy, but it cannot make policy. Two hearing examiners told us that they have on occasion sent zoning matters back to the local legislature with the statement that they could not resolve the dispute because the legislature had not formulated a policy on the issue in dispute. It is simply a mistake to assume that such issues can be decided on the basis of an impartial weighing of factual information. They are political questions, and the politicians rightfully claim jurisdiction over them.

The same erroneous premise about the nature of zoning decisions infuses much of the current thought on procedural reform. At the root of the reform movement, which began in earnest with the Oregon Supreme Court's decision in *Fasano* v. *Washington Co. Comm.*,[13] is the notion that "correct" zoning decisions depend merely upon a disinterested assessment of objective facts. Beyond that, however, the

Fasano movement is grounded on the unrealistic premise that procedural reform can guarantee that "illegitimate" considerations will not find their way into the decisionmaking process.

We would be the last to denigrate the overwhelming importance of *Fasano*-type procedural reform, but we think it important to keep clear what the true goals of such reform should be. Such reforms should not be structured and pursued as though their pricipal purpose was either to limit the role of the decisionmaker or to eliminate "politics" from the process or even to eliminate illegitimate and illegal influence from the process. None of those is fully possible. Such reform will, we believe, be more effective if it is directed at the goal of maximizing the opportunity for legitimate, informed participation in the process rather than at eliminating specific illegitimate influences. Specific devices to eliminate illegitimate influence can always be circumvented, but when the record fully documents the legitimate considerations bearing on a decision, it becomes much easier to identify those cases in which the decision must have been based on some other consideration. Thus, we are not very impressed with the type of "sunshine act" reform that tries to prevent cocktail party discussion of zoning or that is, as it was in at least one Florida case, carried to the point of criminal prosecution of two plan commissioners for discussing a zoning case as they drove together to a public hearing. We prefer reforms that concentrate on giving actual notice to parties with a potential interest, that make information available in advance of hearings, that provide opportunity for all sides to present a logical case at a well-run hearing, and that compel the decisionmakers to enunciate reasons for their decisions.

We have hope that, if significant reform in this area is ever to come, it may come first in major cities. The combined need to retain discretion while eliminating red tape and providing certainty is beginning to force urban officials to accept procedural reform as a way of assuring the development community that the city is prepared to deal quickly and fairly with any legitimate proposal. The acceptance of such reforms also serves to quiet the neighborhoods, which want assurance that zoning discretion is not just a cover for zoning abuse. In large part as a result of such pressures, we have drafted and succeeded in having adopted in a number of medium and large cities zoning ordinances in which the sections establishing procedural regulations and safeguards outweighed the sections establishing substantive rules.

There is nothing glamorous or exciting about drafting 150 pages of zoning ordinance provisions designed to assure that discretion is exercised openly, honestly, fairly, and in a way that allows both applicant and objector to influence and understand the ultimate decision. We are convinced, however, that the conscientious implementation of such mundane procedural reforms will do more to rationalize local land use regulation than a book full of revolutionary ideas or a shelf full of multi-colored master plans.

In discussing systems to control discretion in the *city* zoning process, it is also important to bear in mind, again, one of the fundamental differences between the suburbs that have dominated the zoning stage in the past 50 years and the cities upon which we have been focusing. Where, as in many suburban communities, a homogeneous majority holds absolute sway, preordained plans and rules become essential to protect the rights and interests of the minority—whether the minority is an excluded black family or a wealthy property owner denied the economic use of his property. In the context of such suburbs, the growth of zoning flexibility and discretion has frequently provided little more than a vehicle for the exercise of the arbitrary will of a parochial majority. The control of such arbitrariness has been, in our opinion, a principal goal of courts and state legislators in imposing planning and procedural requirements as a check upon the zoning power. The tendency toward greater and greater nonlocal control of land use authority can be traced directly to the abuse of such authority by suburban communities that place their parochial social and fiscal goals above all other considerations, including the newly important national goals of environmental protection and open housing.

The situation in practically any city of significant size is quite different. In most cities the seat of power is not so easy to find as it would have been even five or 10 years ago. Jerry Hillis' response to the issue in Seattle gives a fair characterization of our own reaction to the situation in many cities:

RFB: Who runs the city? Who really makes the big decisions in Seattle?

JH: I think the answer is that nobody runs the city. The reason I say that is I could just as easily say everyone of those groups are involved.... Neighborhood groups are very powerful.... The citizen groups certainly feel that they have power; on the other hand, they may say that the bankers are involved. Now if you go and talk to the bankers they'll say, "Yeh, we've got some power but we don't make the decisions, the citizen groups do." You talk to the technocrats and they'll say, "Nobody listens to us, they mistrust us, actually who makes the decisions are the downtown businessmen." In other words, what I am saying is that every group perceives the other group as having more power, which to me is an indication that probably nobody has real power in the sense of being able to dictate what happens.

That is a bit overromantic as a description of some cities; but, as recent events in Chicago politics demonstrate, it is more and more true in more and more cities. With the rise of neighborhood groups, with the increasing professionalization of city administrations, with the widening split between executive power and legislative power, with the growing instability of urban industrial and commercial bases, and with the pressing need of everyone to pull together in the face of mounting problems has come a diversity of interest and power in many cities that has made the old power brokers rethink their position. An Atlanta businessman described the situation in this way:

> We have done a lot of gear shifting in terms of the business community,...recognizing that the political environment and institutional environment is such that it is a slightly different ball game than it was in the 50's and 60's and before. In the days when the mayor came out of the business community and the mayor and the business community kind of made those momentous decisions on the golf course. It is now very much of a triumvirate of neighborhoods and city government and business and we have taken steps from this perspective to become part of that process.

While the old guard may bemoan the situation and while there are dangers in it, that diversity of power groups and interests may hold some hope for making zoning administration a fairer, less-abused process than it has been in the past in either city or suburb.

Where no single, monolithic constituency constitutes an effective majority, political power depends upon compromise and cooperation among a great diversity of interest groups. Control of destructive arbitrariness is inherent in the need for such compromise and cooperation.

Adam Smith built his remarkable theory of economics upon the belief in "... a certain propensity in human nature ... the propensity to truck, barter and exchange one thing for another."[14] What Smith said 200 years ago about the mainspring of a workable economic system can be said today with respect to the foundation of a modern urban zoning system:

> ... man has almost constant occasion for the help of his brethern, and it is in vain for him to expect it from their benevolence only. He will be more likely to prevail if he can interest their self-love in his favor, and shows

them that it is for their own advantage to do for him what he requires of them. Whoever offers to another a bargain of any kind, proposes to do this. Give me that which I want, and you shall have this which you want, is the meaning of every such offer; and it is in this manner that we obtain from one another the far greater part of those offices which we stand in need of. It is not from the benevolence of the butcher, the brewer or the baker that we expect our dinner, but from their regard to their own self-interest. We address ourselves, not to their humanity, but to their self-love and we never talk to them of our own necessities but of their advantages. Nobody but a beggar chooses to depend chiefly upon the benevolence of his fellow-citizens.[15]

Smith's system, of course, breaks down when someone is in a position to take what he or she wants without the need for barter. Where one can take by force of power—be it economic, political, or physical power—there is no reason to compromise. That has been the story of suburban zoning. The diverse interests that characterize most cities ensure, however, that if the zoning ordinance provides procedures to give each interest group an effective voice in the process, no invariable majority will be able to simply impose its will in matters of land use regulation. Deals will have to be made.

When deals must be made by relatively co-equal parties, each intent on protecting its own interest to the greatest extent possible, the result should be a solution that gives each side what is most important to it in return for the surrender of what is less important. No one gets everything, but, by definition, each party gets what it thought to be the best it could get under all of the circumstances. Absent that, the deal would not have been struck.

For Smith, the sum of the compromises made in a free economic system was, by nature and necessity, the common good of the society:

Every individual is continually extending himself to find out the most advantageous employment for whatever capital he can command. It is his own advantage, indeed, and not that of the society, which he has in view. But the study of his own advantage naturally, or rather necessarily leads him to prefer that employment which is the most advantageous to the society....

He generally, indeed, neither intends to promote the public interest, nor knows how much he is promoting it.... [H]e intends only his own security; and by directing that industry in such a manner as its produce may be of the greatest value, he intends only his own gain, and he is in this, as in many other cases, led by an invisible hand to promote an end which was no part of his intention. Nor is it always the worse for society that it was no part of it. By pursuing his own interest he frequently promotes that of the society more effectually than when he really intends to promote it. I have never known much good done by those who affected to trade for the public good. It is an affectation, indeed, not very common among merchants, and very few words need be employed in dissuading them from it.[16]

We share Smith's confidence and are persuaded that the most effective way to guide and regulate a system of land use controls to achieve the much-sought "public interest" is to assure that all the segments of the public having an interest in land use decisions have an opportunity to influence those decisions. Where, as in a large and diverse city, the "public" is composed of sufficiently numerous, informed, and influential interest groups to make regulation by compromise a possibility, the principal goal of land use regulations should be to provide and protect mechanisms to promote the free working of the political process, mechanisms to assure that deals are made on, not under, the table and are made on the basis of relevant competing public interests, not irrelevant, illegal, or purely private interests. If the system can assure the free interplay of the diverse interests and can encourage compromise and accommodation among those diverse interests, then there is much less need to be concerned with plans, regulations, and procedures that seek to limit artificially the discretion of those entrusted with the zoning power.

FOOTNOTES

1. Richard F. Babcock, *The Zoning Game* (Madison, Wis.: University of Wisconsin Press, 1966), pp. 6, 8.

2. *Fasano* v. *Washington Co. Comm.*, 264 Or. 574, 507 P.2d 23 (1973).

3. *Andersen* v. *Peden*, 569 P.2d 633, 640 (1977). In affirming the appellate court's decision, the Oregon Supreme Court set the rhetoric straight—local zoners, it said, are not supposed to pay attention to local opposition. *Andersen* v. *Peden*, 587 P.2d 59 (1978).

4. *City of East Lake* v. *Forest City Enterprises, Inc.*, 426 U.S. 668, 682 (1976; Stevens, J., dissenting).

5. Minn. Stat. Ann. 473 F.01 *et seq.*

6. Mass. Gen. Laws Ann. C. 40B, §§20-23 (Supp. 1969).

7. *Dalton* v. *City and County of Honolulu,* 51 Ha. 400, 462 P.2d 199 (1969).

8. Robert W. Rider, "Transition from Land Use to Policy Planning: Lessons Learned," *Journal of the American Institute of Planners,* January 1978, p. 25.

9. *Id.* at 32.

10. Peter Blake, "Cape Kennedy," *Architectural Forum,* January-February 1967, p. 59.

11. Richard F. Babcock, "The Chaos of Zoning Administration: One Solution," *Zoning Digest,* January 1960.

12. Babcock, *supra,* n. 1, at 154.

13. *Fasano, supra,* n.2.

14. Adam Smith, *An Inquiry into the Nature and Causes of the Wealth of Nations* (New York City: Random House, 1937), p. 13.

15. *Id.* at 14.

16. *Id.* at 421-23.

Chapter 19
The Residential Areas:
The Control of
Density and Diversity

*Towns should be built so as to protect
their inhabitants and at the same time
make them happy.*

—Aristotle

*What, one wonders, are the wise and
simple laws that would have saved the
situation if only they had been made
soon enough?*

—Edward C. Banfield

As we noted in Chapter 4, residential zoning in urban areas must
consider that the typical city has three distinct types of residential areas:
slums, stable areas, and gray areas. The zoning issues in the first two are
comparatively simple. To be sure, the simplicity derives from different
sources. Stable areas are simple because there are no real zoning
questions; slums are simple because there are no real zoning answers.

STABLE AREAS

Stable areas are easy. Preserving an economically viable status quo is
what zoning has always been best at doing. Where social and economic
factors are conducive to the preservation of an attractive residential
environment, zoning's only job is to prevent the intrusion of undesir-

able uses. That is a comparatively easy task in any area where the current owner-residents agree that the status quo is desirable and that change is not. The only significant problem faced by stable city neighborhoods is at their peripheries, where, because of the patchwork development patterns of many large cities, they frequently abut inconsistent uses. Apart from the political problems noted in Chapter 5, on industrial areas, even these problems of transition at the periphery are far from overwhelming. To the extent that the periphery represents prezoning development patterns, it is a fixed fact of life that the market created and now, in one fashion or another, recognizes. To the extent that new development is proposed at the residential boundary, ample site design and buffering techniques are available for inclusion in the zoning ordinance. They are not difficult to conceive, to understand, or to implement; they are also not worth talking about here.

SLUMS

Any realistic assessment of the zoning power must recognize its severe limitations as a device for promoting rehabilitation of existing slums. As suggested in Chapter 4, however, the treatment of existing slums and deteriorated areas by most urban zoning ordinances would be substantially improved by a greater sensitivity to the obvious fact that many zoning ordinance provisions that make perfect sense in a stable city neighborhood make no sense in a neighborhood that has bottomed out. In many cases, a more liberal treatment of permitted uses, home occupations, and occupancy provisions will be warranted. At the same time, the zoning ordinance should not, as many do, totally ignore the existing pattern of physical development in the hope that a huge increase in the permitted intensity of use will prompt the private sector to knock the slum down. In short, if city zoners succeed in adopting an ordinance that does not aggrevate the problems of existing slum neighborhoods and does not contribute to the creation of new slums, they have probably gone as far as is realistically possible.

The real answer to such areas, to the extent that government can offer an answer, lies in the promulgation and administration of codes other than the zoning ordinance and in the implementation of programs capable of dealing with the full spectrum of the causes and effects of slums.

Housing and other city codes tend, like the zoning ordinance, to ignore the realities of the slum. They ignore the fact that very low income households, as much as they might like them, simply cannot afford all of the niceties that the middle class has come to define as "minimum standard." Saying that the poor can, or must, settle for less is difficult to do without sounding harsh and unfeeling. However, if the only housing within the means of a low-income family is "substandard" by middle-class standards, tearing it down or boarding it up without providing a more "standard" environment is hardly a humane solution. That, however is what has gone on in many cities. The realities of the situation demand a more sensitive evaluation of those elements of community and structural amenity that should be encompassed within the concept of "minimum standard."[1]

This is not the place to discuss the sort of total approach to slums that is likely to have some effect. We have studied and reported on the problem elsewhere.[2] We are convinced that the only real hope lies at the point where the neighborhood is sufficiently organized, and sufficiently self-confident, to approach city government and the private sector as an active, contributing partner in the business of neighborhood revitalization and not as either an adversary or a charity case. Bill Whiteside's Neighborhood Housing Services Program, which grew out of pioneering efforts of the Allegheny Conference in Pittsburgh's Central Northside area, and which has now gained official status as the Urban Reinvestment Task Force under the auspices of HUD and the Federal Home Loan Bank Board, is undoubtedly the best model for success currently available.

GRAY AREAS

The real residential zoning issues in major cities occur in those gray areas that are neither stable nor slum but on their way from being one to being the other. Some gray areas exist in neighborhoods that are declining or threatened with decline, and the issues are how to stop the process before it is hopeless. Others are found in those rediscovered neighborhoods on their way up from the bottom where the issue is how to keep the momentum going without allowing the sort of runaway situation in which an overeager or speculative market destroys the underlying conditions that led to the revitalization in the first place.

These are the exciting neighborhoods for urban zoners and planners; they are the neighborhoods where challenge and the hope of success co-exist. Nevertheless, realizing the hope by responding successfully to the challenge is perhaps the most difficult of all urban zoning issues.

There are several realities about cities and about neighborhoods on the way up and neighborhoods on the way down that must be recognized in any zoning scheme intended to deal with these neighborhoods in transition. Perhaps the most important is that the process of transition, be it up or be it down, starts slowly. In a reviving neighborhood, there must be an initial pioneer or two capable of seeing and capitalizing upon the potential of the neighborhood and one or two specific pieces of property in it. In a declining neighborhood, there will inevitably be a handful of properties that will start the downward cycle—sometimes for no apparent or explicable reason. In each case, the zoning ordinance must be structured to create a market demand for those first pieces of property. As detailed in Chapter 4, the typical zoning response to both of these situations has been to increase either or both the intensity and variety of uses allowed throughout the entire neighborhood.

Because of a number of the other realities about cities and their residential gray areas, that approach offers little hope. In the first place, most of our cities are experiencing a decline of population; in that context, it is a pathetic anachronism to try to encourage development by offering to allow more than anyone wanted in the first place. The fact that Detroit's R-2 District allows everything from single-family residential through multiple-family with up to eight units in a building has not prevented its neighborhoods from being peppered with vacant lots. In addition to the lack of sufficient demand to justify a great intensification of land use in older cities, simplistic notions of increased density do not respond to the realities of the market. The suburban market with which in-fill development must compete is the market for people who want some kind of single-family dwelling unit, whether that be suburban detached or urban row house. City development at greatly increased densities is not going to compete effectively in that market.

Furthermore, the sort of liberal zoning allowances that might be necessary and justifiable to promote a revival or stop a slide will, if permitted everywhere in the neighborhood, both overtax the existing infrastructure and destroy the fundamental characteristics of the neighborhood, both of which are, without any help from regulatory blight, probably beginning to show signs of deterioration due to the natural aging process. Typically, attempts to revive an area by rezoning it are accompanied by total neglect of the physical infrastructure that must support the hoped-for revitalization; in the worst cases services are reduced rather than augmented. More important than the lack of regard for the infrastructure is the disregard of the neighborhood's physical character and social structure that often accompanies zoning revisions in graying neighborhoods. As Jim Golia, assistant to the president of the Borough of Queens in New York City, noted, "In-fill provisions that made perfect sense in Brooklyn's row house neighborhoods were unacceptable in Queens, because in this Borough, people like their sideyards." As noted by Brian Paul in San Diego, not only the physical character but also the social character of the neighborhood demands attention:

> We've torn out a lot of nice old houses and small apartment buildings and put in the San Diego equivalent of the 4 plus 1. And at that scale there is a noticeable change, and the units become smaller and they cater to a whole different lifestyle, and that's another part of the problem. If we replace family units with more family units at an increased density it's one thing, but if we replace it with singles units then it's another kind of problem entirely.

San Diego's recent efforts to provide more effective and less destructive encouragements to central city redevelopment merit a brief digression here because they give us a chance to talk about an obviously important subject—the need to attract not only residents but also developers. The approach proposed by San Diego's Growth Management Plan was, in essence, a proposal to artificially increase the disincentives to outlying development as a means to encourage redevelopment and in-filling. "Densification" of existing urban areas was to be fostered by prohibiting or discouraging development in the outlying areas.

The problem with relying on disincentives in the outlying areas to encourage development in inner-city areas is that, no matter how effectively you prohibit a mass merchandiser type builder from putting up 150 $75,000 homes on Farmer Brown's back forty, you are not going to overcome the organizational and market factors that prevent that same builder from putting up $75,000 homes on 40 or 50 scraps of land scattered through a variety of inner-city neighborhoods. Those builders simply are not equipped to handle small, scattered projects; if they could be made to try it, the chances are their product would cost even more than $75,000. Even at $75,000, the market for face brick and aluminum tri-levels in rundown city neighborhoods is limited.

However, just as there are housing consumers who are ready to come back to the city if it will accommodate their needs, so there are developers ready to develop in the cities if offered a bit of encouragement. From many reports it would appear that there are plenty of small developers and builders looking for markets in which they can continue to make a living despite the corporate giants out in the cornfields.[3] Just as the facts of suburban life have created a potential pool of housing consumers for cities to tap, so have the ample difficulties and disenchantments surrounding outlying, clear-cut development created a pool of potential housing suppliers ready to give the city a try. Cities will do better to concentrate less on adding to the woes of the suburban developer and more on doing something positive in the cities to take advantage of the existing pool of small developers looking for new markets.

More density is not the answer on the consumer side, and it also is not the answer on the supply side. Developers cannot get density in outlying areas, and yet they develop. It is not the lack of density that suburban developers, especially small suburban developers, are complaining about; it is the lack of public infrastructure and, even more, the abundance of red tape that delays every project for two or three years. No developer likes to spend money either on providing what he sees as "public" infrastructure or on bureaucratic delay, but for the small builder significant costs in those areas are simply out of the question.

Indianapolis has had considerable success in using capital improvements programming to encourage in-fill development. However, it has done so not simply by refusing to sewer outlying areas but by taking positive steps to upgrade its inner-city sewers at public expense. In the words of Dr. Frank Lloyd:

> Politics of sewers? If the sewers go south, you will have a township right south of here that will be one of the fastest growing places in this country. If it does that, you have ruined an opportunity to rebuild the inner city. Because you've taken a lot of pressure off; you've given them a place to rent. Lugar understood that quite well ... and under his administration those sewers were not built. What he did was upgrade the inner city sewers. They spent the money doing that.

If Ramapo could program infrastructure to slow down growth, it is possible that central cities can program it to encourage growth.

Of course, providing streets and sewers costs money, but eliminating needless red tape does not. Staff people in San Diego admitted that, while they were talking about encouraging in-fill development, their codes and ordinances in fact made it much more difficult and time-consuming to develop in an already built-up area than on virgin soil. The in-fill development process is fraught with its own set of unavoidable delays and difficulties. But so is suburban development; and, if cities will move aggressively to eliminate the *needless* delays, they will have taken a major step toward encouraging a resurgence of small-scale development in cities.

With that nod to the development community, we return to the principal problem of exploring ways in which cities can, through their zoning ordinances, create, or at least encourage, a private market demand for those first few parcels that become the beginning of neighborhood transition. We have said that the usual approach of wholesale rezoning for more intense uses is not likely to work. An across-the-boards liberalization of zoning in a reviving or declining neighborhood is almost certain to delay the revival or speed the decline. In both cases, the reason is the same, and understanding it may lead toward a better answer.

An overall liberalization of zoning simply increases the raw land value in relation to the value of the existing structure, thereby increasing the incentive to abandon the existing improvements. The point is perhaps best made by example. Assume that a typical city lot is worth $10,000 and that, on customary ratios, such a lot should support a $40,000 home. Thus, assuming a stable situation, the house and lot together would be worth $50,000. Now assume that the structure, over time, deteriorates to the point where it is worth only $30,000 but that the neighborhood remains basically sound leaving the lot value at $10,000. Noticing the decline in the neighborhood, city officials rezone the entire area to permit four units per lot in the hope of encouraging revitalization. Let us assume that multiple-family land is bringing $5,000 per unit. The value of the lot, if cleared, is now $20,000; the value of the structure on it remains $30,000. But, in this case, 20 and 30 do not make 50. To the person interested in buying a home, the value is still, at most, $40,000, perhaps less because now the single-family house is in an area where multiple-family is permitted. To the speculator or developer, the property is worth, at most, $20,000, but probably something less because the existing structure detracts from the raw land value. The result is that the rezoning has, at one fell swoop, both decreased the value of the property and eliminated the incentive to maintain it. In the long run, the property is probably more valuable without the structure than with it, but in the short run, the chance of anyone buying it for either multiple-family redevelopment or continued single-family use is diminished. Economically, the *sensible,* not evil or pernicious, thing to do is to maximize the current use value of the existing structure by converting it to two or three apartments, taking the cash flow and deferring maintenance on the structure, which is, in any event, a long-term liability. At some point in time, the value of the structure, and the added expense of removing it, will have been amortized down to zero. About the same time, the accumulation of deferred maintenance will have made the structure ready for the bulldozer.

Multiply that example times a neighborhood and you have a zoning-induced slum.

The difficulties of the scenario are compounded by the fact that rezoning the entire neighborhood for increased density simply increases the supply of lots available for redevelopment against what is, to begin with, a limited demand for housing in the neighborhood. By creating a buyer's market, the rezoning tends to defeat its own purpose by lowering the value of the land for redevelopment. That, in turn, suggests that even higher densities will be necessary to offset the cost of acquiring and demolishing the structure and adds further impetus to the market's tendency to amortize the value of the structure through a program of deferred maintenance.

In the meantime, the quality of life in the neighborhood declines at an accelerating rate as the zoning-encouraged conversion of existing structures to higher densities overtaxes the city's infrastructure at the very time the city is probably reluctant to put money into its maintenance or improvement; creates parking problems (or "solves" them by requiring the conversion of lawns into parking lots); and reduces usable open space while at the same time increasing the population.

But the question remains: what else can a city do? Once it has removed procedural impediments, increased intensity is about the only incentive that a city has to give, unless it is willing and able to spend significant public dollars to encourage private development. Clearly enough, then, density is the tool that cities must use, and the problem is to find a better way to use it.

What is needed is a system by which a few lots in a neighborhood can be given the right to monopolize all of the limited increase in residential density that the neighborhood as a whole can absorb—in terms of market demand, of neighborhood character, and of infrastructure capacity. The system should encourage the location of the increased density on larger parcels created by the assemblage of small lots. The system should make density increases available on a basis that encourages, rather than discourages, the preservation and maintenance of sound structures in the neighborhood. The system should encourage redevelopment that tends to solve, rather than compound, parking and open space problems. The system should encourage redevelopment that contributes to the solution of existing infrastructure problems. The system should encourage redevelopment plans and designs sensitive to, and compatible with, the existing fabric of the neighborhood. All of that is a tall order.

We believe it might all be possible if there were an effective way to solve the first problem of permitting a few lots in the neighborhood to monopolize the entire increase in density that might otherwise be spread across the entire neighborhood. Simple approaches obviously will not work. Decreeing that the four corner lots or every third odd-numbered lot in every square block should be allowed 10 times the density of any other lot in the block would concentrate the allowable density but would, in every regard, be a disaster. So far as the law is concerned, such a simplistic approach would be almost certainly invalid. So far as planning is concerned, it would be monumentally ineffective. As to equity, it isn't necessary to study the Hagman-Misczynski treatise to know that the owners of favored lots would receive a windfall, and everyone else would be wiped out. In terms of the desired objective, it is doubtful that the rezoning would produce any immediate redevelopment on the favored lots, and it would certainly contribute to the decline of the rest of the neighborhood. If and when the economic situation finally warranted redevelopment of the favored lots, the rest of the neighborhood probably would have declined enough to discourage any thought of new development. If the favored lots were redeveloped at higher densities, it is inconceivable that the owners of the rest of the lots in the neighborhood would not then cite the high-density development in support of their petition for rezoning to similar densities.

While hope does not lie in simple solutions, an answer may be found in the thoughtful combination of a few relatively common and accepted zoning techniques. This is not the place to draft a zoning ordinance to solve the problems of a diverse assortment of neighborhoods located in a host of individually unique cities across the country. But we can sketch the elements of an approach we believe offers a starting place.

Take as an example what might be a typical square city block containing 24 lots of 6,250 square feet each. Including its associated rights-of-way, the block would contain five acres of land. Presently, the block contains 24 units, one single-family dwelling on each lot. The neighborhood developed before the marked increase in the popularity of automobiles and is not well suited to them. There is no public open space on the block and only a minimal amount within easy reach, and that has to suffice for an entire neighborhood. The underground infrastructure remains essentially sound and is probably sufficient in size for some increase in density on the block, especially if the increase comes in the form of smaller units that would not accommodate the large families for which this neighborhood was originally built. Some of the public infrastructure, like sidewalks, curbs, streetlights, and parkways could be improved. Many of the homes are large enough to be converted into two, three, or even four smaller apartments if permitted by the zoning. A number of the homes already show signs of age and owner neglect. Property values have begun to decline.

Our idea begins by combining elements of the transferable development rights concept with the incentive and overlay zoning techniques in a "Redevelopment Overlay District." The advantages of the overlay would be available only in connection with redevelopment activity that met the standards of the ordinance. Absent such redevelopment activity, the existing zoning would remain in effect by virtue of the underlying district regulations. The overlay regulations would provide a scheme of variable densities depending upon the type of redevelopment being proposed. They would also provide for transfers of density from one lot to another, whether contiguous or not. The right to make the transfer could be secured either by acquiring the fee to the lot or by acquiring the development rights under conditions authorized by the ordinance.

Unlike the usual TDR application, our idea focuses on urban areas that have nothing particularly "special" about them. Rather than being concerned mainly with preserving a "special" transferor parcel, we are here concerned with the selective redevelopment of a limited number of transferee parcels in a fashion that will not overwhelm the existing character of the TDR district. Where the customary TDR program identifies a transferor parcel to be spared from market forces, our concern is to develop a program that lets the market identify those parcels that should be redeveloped and to make market redevelopment possible at an earlier stage in the neighborhood economic cycle. Finally, unlike most TDR proposals, which assign fixed development rights to each transferor parcel and fixed maximum development densities to potential transferee parcels, we seek a program that varies both the TDR's and the development potential assigned to each parcel in a way that gives the market a range of redevelopment choices but rewards those choices determined to be most in the public interest.

To return to our example, we have assumed that our block has 24 single-family dwellings on separate 6,250-square-foot lots. Let us further assume that, after studying the existing infrastructure serving the block and the character and location of the neighborhood, the city determines that the block would, if appropriately redeveloped, have a total carrying capacity of approximately four times its existing density, or 96 units. Rather than rezoning each lot for four units and inviting disaster, this is how the overlay regulations would assign density values to each lot:

1. Density absent any redevelopment—1 unit as permitted in the underlying district.

2. Density for conversion or redevelopment involving a single lot—2 units, subject to site and structure performance standards.

3. Density available for transfer to a noncontiguous lot—1.5 units with the right to maintain one unit on the transferor lot subject to the underlying district regulations or 3 units if the tranferor lot is to be maintained as neighborhood open space or parking.

4. Density for transfer to a contiguous lot where the contiguous lots will be redeveloped as a unified whole—3 units.

5. Density for development as a transferee lot in connection with a density transfer from any contiguous or noncontiguous lot—sum of (a) total units being transferred plus (b) equivalent to total units, up to a maximum of 3 units, being transferred.

6. Maximum density of development permitted on any parcel—1 unit per thousand square feet of land area in a single contiguous parcel.

In addition to the variable densities assigned to each individual lot, density bonuses or incentives might be established as follows:

1. Density bonus for specified infrastructure improvements—0.1 unit per 1,250 square feet for providing proportionate share of designated improvements or cash contribution to fund established to provide such improvements.

2. Density bonus for consolidation of separate lots—0.1 unit per 1,250 square feet of contiguous lot area in excess of 25,000 square feet where the development provides common open spaces and parking meeting the ordinance requirements.

3. Density bonus for design excellence—0.02 unit per 1,250 square feet of contiguous lot area in excess of 25,000 square feet for development design judged excellent in integrating new development into existing development pattern.

The foregoing density allocations and bonuses are fixed so that if a developer succeeded in putting together all 24 lots and achieving all available bonuses, he would be entitled to 96 units, the assumed maximum density of the block. The densities might logically be set slightly higher on the assumption that the maximum bonus situation would never be achieved. The basic transfer densities might be set lower to encourage the use of the bonus density incentives.

This system would also lend itself to density bonuses to achieve a city's social objectives. Thus, for example, the types of density allocations and bonuses thus far discussed might be fixed at a level somewhat under the maximum carrying capacity of the block so that additional density bonuses could be awarded for including some percentage of low- and moderate-income units in the redevelopment project. In effect, the system could provide a zero land cost for low- and moderate-income units by providing a density bonus of 1 unit per lot for each low- or moderate-income unit included in the development up to a specified maximum number of units. If the objective were housing for the elderly, the ordinance might even provide density bonuses in excess of the calculated maximum carrying capacity in light of the lesser impact of elderly developments on most infrastructure components.

The foregoing provides a crude outline of how we would begin to approach the treatment of density in residential gray areas. The possible refinements and variations are limitless and would have to be worked out in light of the specific problems being faced. The rather imprecise units per acre density control might be replaced or supplemented by more sophisticated controls that take account of unit type, size, and configuration. Regulations pertaining to bulk, yards, open spaces, light and air, parking, and other development factors would have to be added. Screening, buffering, and transition controls would have to be provided. Questions relating to the possibility of vacating existing alleys or other public rights-of-way would have to be addressed. Urban design elements of the type typically considered in special districts should also be considered. Thought should be given to the controls that would be applicable to lots that did not get redeveloped. In the underlying district, allowing the rental of one or two rooms without separate kitchen facilities as a home occupation by an owner-occupant might make the maintenance of a large old home economically feasible for an owner-occupant. Where redevelopment would consist only of the conversion of an existing structure to more units, regulations should be provided to control the possible adverse effects of such redevelopment. Such regulations might include control over exterior alterations, the amount and location of off-street parking spaces, minimum green area, and unit size and design standards. Changes in the subdivision regulations might also be appropriate to allow the development of additional detached single-family units on the back or side lots of existing units.

All of those sorts of regulations become, we believe, more effective and workable once a basic mechanism is in palce to permit the market to capitalize on the raw land values of an urban neighborhood without totally abandoning the existing structures.

By allowing density transfers from both contiguous and noncontiguous lots, but providing a greater transfer for contiguous lots, the system would encourage a developer to assemble large contiguous tracts and would tend to discourage any individual owner from holding out for an unreasonable price by offering the carrot of a higher transfer on sale to a developer in the process of assembling a large tract and the stick of knowing that, even without the lot, the developer could buy up sufficient transfer rights to make the development feasible. It is hoped that the system would work well enough to eliminate the need for consideration of more radical proposals like the use of the eminent domain power to aid a developer in assembling a tract large enough to support redevelopment.

A requirement of each density transfer would be that the developer make appropriate provision for the future use and development of the transferor lot. At a minimum, of course, that would involve covenants and planned-unit-development-type regulations prohibiting future development of the transferor lots at a density greater than that remaining following the transfer. Other regulations would depend upon the specific proposal. If a transfer was sought on the basis that the transferor lot would be maintained as open space or public parking, regulations providing for the development and maintenance of such uses would be necessary. If the transfer were made on the basis that the lot would continue to be used for a single-family dwelling, provision for necessary repair or rehabilitation of the existing unit as part of the development program would be appropriate.

The treatment of density is but one of two critical issues in city neighborhoods. The other is the allowance and control of use diversity. Of the two, we find diversity to be the easier issue, at least in terms of planning. Legally, it may be the more difficult. As suggested in Chapter 4, many city neighborhoods are already characterized by a diversity of uses, and most city residents display a tolerance for diversity that far exceeds that found in suburban neighborhoods. We do not believe that eliminating that diversity is a particularly sensible goal for an urban zoning ordinance. What is essential, however, is that the zoning ordinance limit and control the diversity at a level where it enhances, rather than destroys, the residential environment. Again, it is a matter of singling out a few lots for special treatment. But here we believe the planning problems are less severe because existing land use patterns and market considerations tend to permit city planners to distinguish among lots in terms of their appropriateness for accommodating various uses.

Take, as an example, the problem of transitional care facilities discussed in Chapter 8. Planners can predict, in advance, something about the type of neighborhood and the type of structure that is adaptable to such a use. The zoning ordinance can limit the use to appropriate neighborhoods and can establish minimum standards for the type of structure that may be converted to such a use. Other standards relevant to the particular type of use can also be established. They might, for example, relate to minimum yard areas, parking requirements, and relation to necessary supporting public and private infrastructure. To be certain, such pre-ordained standards could not, either realistically or wisely, be developed to the point of designating individual lots within a neighborhood available for such use. But that degree of specificity is not required. Once the minimum standards are established, the ordinance can rely upon the market to make the specific selection so long as it provides that, once the market selects a specific location within a neighborhood, it may not select another location within a specified area around the initial site. The combination of minimum requirements and spacing limitations ensures that each site selected for the facility in question will be appropriate and that the neighborhood will not be overwhelmed by an undue concentration of such facilities. With variations in the specific standards and requirements, we believe that essentially the same approach can be applied to most nonresidential and quasi-residential uses that are socially desirable or necessary but that, while requiring a residential location, tend to threaten the residential environment.

If the issue is the location of limited commercial facilities to serve a residential area, the planners can usually pick the most appropriate areas for mapping of limited commercial zones. Frequently, of course, that will involve simply recognizing and attempting to bolster an existing commercial development. Where that development is an old strip that no longer has either the amenities or population to support it, its consolidation into discreet "nodes" might be encouraged by a combination of infrastructure improvements and modifications, special tax status, and special zoning incentives to use part of the strip as transferee lots for residential development within the context of the Redevelopment Overlay District concept just discussed.

Developing an ordinance to permit, or even bolster, one commercial area at the expense of another presents in an acute fashion the troublesome legal issue raised by any zoning ordinance that attempts to allow, but control, a diversity of uses. Zoning for limited commercial uses involves the creation of a somewhat artificial zoning island. On one side of the line, commercial is permitted; on the other side, it is not. Unfortunately, there is frequently little to distinguish one side of the line from the other, apart from the designation on the zoning map. In the most aggravated situations, there may even be existing commercial uses on both sides of the line, as in the case just mentioned where planners attempt to salvage something out of a decaying commercial strip by rezoning large portions of the strip for noncommercial uses, leaving a limited number of commercial nodes in the hope that the limited demand for commercial space will gradually be concentrated in the nodes.

Such situations raise all of the old bugaboos. The neighbors who don't want the different use cry "spot zoning." The neighbors who see economic advantage in having their properties zoned for a similar use argue that the rezoning has established the "character of the area" justifying a rezoning of their own properties. Would-be competitors assert that the limited rezoning has created a monopoly in violation of the supposed rule that zoning may not be used to control competition.

Those are all arguments from the dark ages of zoning theory and practice. They make even a modicum of sense only when the zoning process is completely uncontrolled by either rational standards or pre-ordained policies. In suburban zoning, they have been circumvented by the planned development device which recognizes that there is such a thing as an optimum mix of uses within any development or neighborhood. In urban zoning, the same concept must be recognized by the repudiation of a whole variety of legal and planning theories that boil down to the position that permission to establish one of any kind of use is a confession that the neighborhood ought logically to be overrun by a half-dozen more of the same thing. If the planners do their job, we are convinced that the courts can be persuaded to abandon the decrepit legal principles that have forced the creation of monotonous, "pure" zoning districts out of fear that any allowance for diversity would open the floodgates.[4]

FOOTNOTES

1. See Georgina B. Landman, "Flexible Housing Codes—The Mystique of the Single Standard," 18 *Har. L.J.* 251 (1974); and Richard E. Starr, "The Housing Code: Sensitive Enforcement Is Necessary for Neighborhood Preservation," *The Building Official and Code Administrator,* January 1977, p. 16.

2. Richard F. Babcock, "Case of Corporate Myopia," *Chicago Sun Times,* January 26, 1975, "Viewpoint" section.

3. See *New Opportunities for Residential Development in Central Cities* (Washington, D.C.: Urban Land Institute, 1976), p. 15 *et seq.; House & Home,* December 1976, p. 12; *House & Home,* October 1977, p. 50; *Housing,* February 1978; *Housing,* February 1979, p. 60.

4. For more on the strategy of the legal assault, see Clifford L. Weaver and Christopher J. Duerksen, "Central Business District Planning and the Control of Outlying Shopping Centers," 14 *Urban Law Annual* (1977), p. 57; but see also Chapter 5, footnote 19, concerning the latest bugaboo—the federal anti-trust law.

Chapter 20
The Central
Business District:
The Control of Design

*Zoning has been a colossal flop
because it is supposed to do things it
cannot do.*

—Bernard Siegan

*The initial impetus behind most of the
creations of the Chicago School was
the commercial spirit. Hugh D.
Duncan writes, in a prefatory note to*
Chicago's Famous Buildings: *"The
greatest clients of Chicago architects
were businessmen and their wives."*

Professor Siegan's postulate is nonsense if applied to the total city but
merits some consideration with respect to zoning in the commercial
areas of major cities. In Chapter 5 we noted that zoning has played, at
best, a minor role in those areas. The explanation lies, we believe, not in
any inherent inability to control those areas through zoning but rather
in an implicit policy decision that in these areas the market should have
freer reign. That policy is, in large part, a result of three factors: a
municipal disinclination to offend the golden goose of major downtown development; a lingering uneasiness about zoning regulations
that restrict commercial competition; and an awareness that, especially
in the central business district, zoning is a matter of indifference to the
city residents who elect the city politicians. Those givens must shape
any discussion of proposals for revision of commercial zoning practices
in the cities.

In Chapter 5, we outlined the existing situation in the CBD and along the commercial strips. As to the latter, we have little more to add here. There are two major problems: protecting nearby residential areas from the offensive types of use that frequently crawl into a declining strip and promoting the revitalization of those declining strips. The first is an easy matter of adopting restrictions to exclude or limit those uses that are so marginal and offensive as to be an unacceptable alternative even to vacancy or abandonment. The problem of promoting revitalization of such strips is not easy. Several of the better attempts are discussed in Chapter 5; we described an idea of our own in discussing residential zoning in the last chapter. Those approaches, and others like them, which build on the basic theme of consolidating and upgrading what is left and providing an alternative use for what is already lost, offer hope of salvaging something from this difficult situation. The hope is greater or less depending upon the willingness of city officials to abide the charges of being "anti-competition" long enough to adopt and defend an ordinance limiting the areas available for new commercial development.

In the remainder of this chapter, we concentrate on the CBD, where, historically, public regulation of land has been of less practical significance than in any other area of the city. "Downtown" in Houston, with no zoning, is no more or less elusive or without engaging ambience than is downtown in Los Angeles, Phoenix, or San Diego, each of which has an elaborate set of zoning regulations for the CBD. The lack of character to downtown in these cities is not attributable to the presence or absence of land use controls any more than zoning deserves credit for the existence of a special identity that is evident in Philadelphia, Chicago, or Boston. (Zoning must, however, take responsibility for the ziggurats of older high rises in Midtown Manhattan.) The sunbelt cities, with or without zoning, suffer because they emerged from an obscure adolescence in the age of the automobile and in an era when elegance in design was less important than adequate air conditioning. That they were peopled by those who were concerned mainly with climate did not help.

One cannot avoid speculating on whether Chicago's tacky Loop and its Magnificent Mile would have been any different without zoning. Perhaps the condominium tower on top of the Water Tower Place would have been of greater bulk; possibly the First National building would have been built out to the sidewalk instead of offering one of the best examples of plaza design we know. But this assumes that zoning acts as a restraint on market forces in the CBD, a dubious premise at best. It also assumes that good contemporary design, when it does occur, is attributable to public regulation, a preposterous proposition, to put it most gently.

Given the obvious fiscal benefits of major downtown development, the huge investment it represents for the private sector and the absence of any significant impact on the quality of life in the residential areas of most cities, we cannot say that the public regulators have any great call or justification to increase their general control over the scope and direction of downtown development.

Having said that, we must pause to note an exception. Where new development is proposed at the expense of historic structures, one would hope for an increased public role to ensure the preservation of at least that modicum of our heritage that has managed thus far to escape the wrecker's ball. Cities are the repositories of most of the structural glories of our nation's history; to a great extent it is such structures that give definition, identity, and stability to the CBD's of our older cities. The rapidity of their demolition has been the occasion for a multiplicity of efforts to save them—short, naturally, of spending public funds to acquire them. These efforts have ranged from landmarks-preservation laws through such devices as transfer of development rights to inducements in the federal Tax Reform Act of 1976. Given the atomic effect of the latter, further discussion of police power incentives and regulations may be like including peashooters on the SALT agenda. Nevertheless, while taxes are always with us, one can never, in these days of tax revolt and egalitarianism, be so sure about tax breaks, and so we take some comfort in seeing the recent success of initial regulatory efforts to deal with this problem. Reading the opinions in the *Penn Central* case[1] and Norman Marcus' excellent article "Villard Preserv'd: Or, Zoning for Landmarks in the Central Business District"[2] is ample education in this field, and we need not extend this digression further to rehearse what is said there.

Returning then to our major theme, we expect that traditional use and bulk controls will continue to appear in CBD zoning regulations but that, for the most part, they will continue to have little practical relevance except in rather special situations. A height limit may mean something in San Francisco or Washington, D.C., but not in New York, Chicago, Atlanta, or Detroit. Maximum FAR will, in most cities, be important only in terms of defining the point at which FAR bonus and incentive systems come into play. Except in unusual cases like pornography shops at the ragtag end of downtown or ticket offices along Fifth Avenue or Michigan Avenue, the market, more than the permitted use list, will continue to control the mix of uses downtown.

There is, however, one area, in addition to historic preservation, where we believe the police power will, and should, continue to attempt to influence development in the CBD. If, as we believe, a city should have an identifiable focal point and if, as we also believe, the CBD remains the best candidate to fill that role, then the CBD ought to be so designed as to be an attractive and workable place for the great masses of people—from within and without the city—who visit it, who work in it, and who consider it to be "the city." We remain intrigued by the possibility of constructing police power regulations to promote excellence in the design of these great urban centers. What is needed in the CBD is some public device that will get the developer to the bargaining table for a single goal—the encouragement of superior new design and the preservation of superior old design—and that will reward the developer for achieving the goal.

Our prescriptions elsewhere have demanded forethought and certainty in public regulation. In the discussion that follows we should be taken as assuming that pre-ordained, fixed, nondiscretionary standards will be provided *wherever possible* in the CBD regulations. However, what we wish to emphasize now is that in some matters mathematical precision, or even definitive policy guidance, is simply not possible in advance of a specific proposal. In such cases, and design regulation is among such cases, urban zoners will have to find another way to achieve their goals.

Before trying to figure out a better way to regulate the design of the CBD, we should concede that a legitimate case can be made for the proposition that no attempt should be made to inject public judgments into control over design or taste. Stephen A. Williams, in a perceptive article "Subjectivity, Expression, and Privacy: Problems of Aesthetic Regulation,"[3] puts it in this fashion:

> ... aesthetic judgments often present the type of problem that Professor Fuller described as "polycentric." Polycentric problems arise when three

factors coincide: (1) a multiplicity of possible solutions; (2) an interdependency of relevant factors so that the outcome as to one feature of the problem will affect the outcome as to other features; and (3) a multiplicity of relevant factors that makes it difficult to trace one solution's superiority to any particular attribute or combination of attributes.

The problem of articulating aesthetic standards represents perhaps the extreme case of polycentricity. The number of potential designs is infinite; the choice as to any single factor, say materials, has an impact on all other factors; and one cannot identify any non-aesthetic features that will even begin to consistently justify the application of any aesthetic concept. At least in other instances of polycentricity one can usually say that certain characteristics will invariably be assets. In attempting to articulate aesthetic standards, however, one cannot say even that much, for the use of stone, or rectilinearity, or inclusion of windows, or any other nonaesthetic feature, is not invariably a "plus." . . .

It has been suggested that the problems of polycentricity in an aesthetic context can be alleviated if an impact on "property values," rather than "mere" beauty, is shown. The claim suggests that the market is available as an objective *deus ex machina* to define beauty. The suggestion is deceptive, for the market speaks in Delphic terms. When a house is sold, the contract ordinarily does not say, "Two thousand dollars has been marked off because the house next door is painted fuschia." Nor does it even say, "Two thousand dollars has been marked off because the house next door is grotesque." Conceivably, advanced techniques of statistical analysis such as multiple regressions could identify dollar penalities suffered by houses adjacent to particular visual features. But the multitude of factors relevant to perceptions of beauty and the complexity of their relationships makes one distinctly skeptical. The same polycentric character that prevents a legislature from articulating a rule of "beauty" will also prevent real estate agents from articulating rules for computing an "ugliness" discount.

Looked at another way, bonuses for amenities and grace in design are either redundant—if the amenity is desired it should be mandatory—or are a scheme to impose upon one segment of the taxpayers—the tenants—the costs of an embellishment that will nourish a far larger class.

We believe it is past hope that design will be left to the private market, and exactions as a condition of development permission are a way of life, increasingly sanctioned by the courts. So long as these conditions prevail, arguments over the theoretical merits of public regulation of design are academic, and the more fruitful inquiry centers around how to regulate it in light of the legitimate concerns expressed by Williams.

As we noted in Chapters 5 and 9, New York City has been in the van of those cities using trade-offs in the zoning ordinance to stimulate developers to provide amenities and quality of design in downtown development. Developers can obtain more rentable floor space if they select from a number of options that provide public amenities. The results have been mixed, and they suggest that pre-ordained formulas may not be compatible with such an evanescent concept as good design.

Ada Louise Huxtable, the acerbic *New York Times* urban design critic, has pointed out that the idea worked superbly with The Market at Citicorp Center and failed with the Galleria and Olympic Tower. Her review of the three buildings opens with high praise for the Citicorp effort: "To New Yorkers crowding into The Market at Citicorp Center, this delightful potpourri of shops, restaurants and pedestrian space is a lively and useful enrichment of Manhattan's East Side. It is clear that what could have been just one more forbiddingly elegant corporate tower is, instead, a new and very vital part of New York."

Galleria failed, according to Ms. Huxtable, not because the architect skimped on design features, but because of a minor flaw or two and because of the building's financial difficulties:

> As at Citicorp, the architect went well beyond minimum specifications. He created a theatrical interior space—a 90-foot atrium rising to a skylit roof, instead of the city's required 30-foot minimum ceiling. This baroque-brutalist passage was meant to be a lively conduit for shoppers, strollers, cafe-goers, people on their way to offices, apartments and a club, or just passing through from 57th to 58th Streets. A large, stepped platform was supposed to function night and day as a cafe-discotheque, and store displays were to line the entrance. There was even talk of a strolling violinist.
>
> Today, the place is dead. Few people stroll through, with or without violins. That this is a public pedestrian passage may be one of the city's best-kept secrets; its function is quite obscure from the outside.
>
> Inside, the cafe space is walled off with solid rows of stock planters, emphasized with a rope. The windowed offices that form the court's tiered walls and were meant to supply light and life, have their curtains uniformly drawn. The stores are empty, the showcases dark.[4]

Olympic Tower received substantial bonuses, enough to provide a FAR of 21.6. It is a whacking financial success but, according to Huxtable, a miserable design failure:

If the Galleria is an aborted effort, Olympic Tower is a near cop-out. This building probably got the most impressive set of bonuses going; it covers 50 percent of its 40,000-square-foot Fifth Avenue plot with a massive F.A.R. of 21.6, stacking up 51 stories of some of the most expensive apartments and offices in the world. . . . Olympic Tower has given the city the back of its hand.

These three buildings seem to define the possibilities under current attempts at zoning-induced design excellence: a developer may comply with the letter of the law, earn bonuses, and produce a design failure (Olympic Tower); a developer may go well beyond the minimum necessary to obtain the bonus and produce a smashing design success (Citicorp); or a developer may go well beyond the minimum necessary to obtain the bonus and *nevertheless* produce a design failure (Galleria). The fourth possibility, design success based upon compliance with the legal minimum standard, while theoretically possible, seems never to have been documented outside the planners' laboratory. All of this suggests the folly of continuing to pursue design excellence via escalations in the stringency and complexity of design regulations. As Huxtable's review of the Galleria evidences, it is nearly as easy to produce a design failure with higher standards as with lower standards.

Huxtable attributes part of the problem to developers' bad faith: "New York builders are notoriously adept at formulating a package that satisfied the letter of the law and does the least to fulfill what city planners had in mind." That is part of it, but the root of the problem lies in the ineffable nature of the goal. How is success measured? It seems not to be measured by the market; as the three New York projects evidence, financial and market success may or may not follow design success. Here is Huxtable describing what she likes about Citicorp's layout:

It is particularly pleasant to be able to buy a fresh-baked brioche and a newspaper and to sit in the middle of it all, watching the passing scene on all levels. . . .

Here is her description of the problem:

The problem with law and the design of amenities and any attempt to deal with the quality of the design involved is that such judgments cannot be quantified—they are unavoidably subjective, although responsibile judgment rests on a very specific set of standards and their interpretations. . . . A textbook could be written, . . . but there seems to be no way to translate such language into the measurable specifics required by law.[5]

Paul Goldberger, another *New York Times* architectural commentator, puts it this way:

> Architecture has never been a question of formulas—like all kinds of design, the making of a great, or even a good building involves something special, something magical if you will, that cannot be put into words.[6]

When a design incentive system succeeds, we expect it does so because it forces a creative private planner or architect to sit down with a creative public planner or architect (each supported by a willing "client") to discuss how their respective goals may be accomplished in a single creative design. When such a system fails, we suspect the failure can be traced to an attempt to quantify matters and processes that are essentially qualitative. It may also result in part from the temptation of one age of planners and architects to put into law those amenities it perceives as appealing. Witness the plaza generation of CBD regulations discussed in Chapter 5.

What is needed is an incentive scheme that (1) will encourage the developer to offer amenities and good design, (2) will discourage "letter of the law" compliance, and (3) will not enshrine one currently "popular" idea into the law.

This is not an easy task, either conceptually or legally. If our suggestion outrages architects, dumbfounds developers, and perplexes municipal attorneys, it may not be all bad; in any event, it would be fun to try, and the results could be no more unpredictable than under current regulations aimed at the same goals.

First, to bring the developer to the table, all development and redevelopment in the CBD over a specified size and scale should be a conditional use, not a use permitted as of right. Second, FAR bonuses, at least above some specified limit, should not be related to specified amenities, each of which is worth so many additional square feet of floor space. The allowance of such FAR bonuses should be based on qualitative judgments by those who have a demonstrated capacity to judge what is good design. An independent commission of three qualified persons should review the design of the building and its site to determine and recommend to the city council whether the FAR bonus proposed by the developer is justified on the basis of design excellence. (We will return to the question of standards shortly.) To meet our third criterion—this commission *must not* be the plan commission, a standing fine arts commission, or any segment of the professional staff. One judge should be selected by the city, one by the developer, and a third by them or, in the event they cannot agree, by the president of the local chapter of the American Institute of Architects. The ordinance should set out the types of person who are qualified to serve: architects, planners, landscape architects, and recognized critics or historians in architecture and related disciplines (ah, there, Ms. Huxtable!). The law should also provide that only one member may be a citizen of the state in which the development is to take place. No person should be allowed to serve on successive commissions in the same city. The costs and fees of the commission would be shared by the developer and the city. The commission may or may not hold public hearings, depending upon local preference for that form of civic flagellation, but its deliberations should be open and it should invite written comments from interested persons. Its decision should be in writing and in detail. It should have the authority to negotiate design changes with the developer. The consensus of all three commission members in a recommendation should be necessary to grant a bonus unless a super-majority of the city council agreed to grant a bonus based on the vote of two members.

A somewhat similar concept was used by the City of Chicago Department of Urban Renewal in the mid-'60s in connection with the disposition of sites. A group of architects were retained to review proposals for acquisition and to evaluate them. (According to Lewis Hill, former commissioner of the Department of Planning and Urban Development, the initial findings of the architectural review committee that a particular project was "unacceptable" was abandoned because the unsuccessful bidders then sued their architects to recover the fees!) The architects were selected by the American Institute of Architects with some emphasis upon obtaining objective judges without personal or professional axes to grind.

The invitation to bidders included the following objectives:

A primary concern of the Department of Urban Renewal is the quality of design in its renewal projects.

One of the major objectives is to secure a high quality of architectural design, site planning, and landscape design in treatment of open spaces, buildings, use of material, scale, functional utility, and harmonious relation to existing development or proposed development now under review.

Design objectives relate to two phases of development. The first deals with land use relationships, and the second with architectural and site plan relationships and design details which greatly influence the quality of the ultimate development.

The space around the buildings is as important as the buildings them-selves. Landscaping, walls, fences, etc., should be used to relate buildings to one another, emphasize important architectural features, confine spaces, and to screen service areas from view. Special attention should be given to the treatment of roof decks where a building is often seen from above....

The intent [is] to encourage residential development with a variety of structural types. For instance a portion of the dwelling units might be in elevator apartment structures, and the remainder in walk-up apartment and rowhouse structures. This variety of accommodations would provide units for rent and/or sale for families of moderate income. Variation in structural height and size will promote visual interest and structural grouping will result in the variation between small spaces enclosed by structures and the larger public open spaces.

As was previously noted in this statement residential use of these proj-ects is intended to form a coordinated neighborhood development. Com-plete community facilities to include neighborhood shopping, schools and playground, a community park, and churches will be provided in the neighborhood.

One such project put out for bid was a 30-acre site, located on the east side of Michigan Avenue between 26th Street and 31st Street. Four bids were received. A panel of five members of the American Institute of Architects was hired by the Department of Urban Renewal to review the proposals and examine the site. They were Charles Goodman, Washington; Ralph Rapson, Mineapolis; and Winston Elting, George Danforth, and Edward Dart, Chicago. Each judge was asked to and did sign the following statement:

In consideration of my employment by the City of Chicago to give architectural advice in connection with the judging of offers to purchase Slum and Blighted Area Redevelopment Project No. 6, I do hereby certify that I have no interest in any offeror, nor any other business or professional relationship which would inhibit my ability to give unbiased advice.

The panel evaluated all four proposals and then concluded, with some reservations, with a recommendation that "South Commons" by Central South Development Company be chosen. Here is the review committee's comments on South Commons:

Since this proposal realizes the objectives to a greater degree, the panel felt it necessary to comment more fully on this submission than on others. Consequently, the statements which follow (particularly in the nega-tive) are more numerous and in much greater detail than that which have been stated regarding the other submissions. Though the negative comments are strong the aggregate negatives of this proposal are not as detrimental as the aggregate negatives of other solutions.

General:

Due to the incorporation of a wide variety of dwelling unit types along with a well-integrated community and shopping facility focus, this proposal offers the promise and potentiality of a stable, balanced, coordinated urban community.

Though the variety of choice of dwelling unit and building types was felt commendable the panel expressed concern over the excessive variety of archtectural form and detail shown and specified. The panel feels most strongly that definite and considerable restraint be employed in the architecture so that the above promise and potentiality will not be negated through irrelevant and over-abundance of texture, material and form indicated.

Specific Comments:

Pro—General land planning, sequence of spaces good.

Play areas well handled.

Shopping community focus excellent.

Screening of utilities at community-shopping facility roof good.

Village quality of scheme good.

Mixture of dwelling unit types closely approaches the meeting of program objectives.

Variety of dwelling unit and structural types good—For this reason there is no need for architectural gymnastics in facade and detail.

Cost related to rent scale appears feasible.

Con—Staging of construction poor. . . .

Question complete cleavage of areas—expensive units to south and moderate income to north.

Vast parking lot creating this division unfortunate.

Suggest the recession of parking 1/2 level—More islands of planting.

Allowing 29th Street as a through street dangerous and unnecessary.

Exposed out-of-door corridors give scheme a CHA project look— Will this not discourage integration of occupancy?

The axis of Indiana Avenue should be visually terminated by landscape or buildings—uninterrupted view through and past fountain dull.

Unrestrainted use of so varied a palette of textures, colors, materials, forms unnecessary and most detrimental to the scheme.

Barracks-like quality of inner courts of five-story units poor.

Due to overabundance of architectural variety project lacks the dignity it must have.

Actual facilities and functions in community center building somewhat vague.

Security—long alley-like entrances between walls of low-rise units dangerous. Suggest good lighting here.

In another project, 570,000 square feet located at 37th Street and Cottage Grove, a different panel, consisting of William Deknatal, Daniel Brenner, and Gertrude Kerbis, all AIA of Chicago, was selected. Here is the jury's negative evaluation of a proposal by the Antioch Foundation:

General Comments:

This proposal by the Antioch Foundation shows an attempt to achieve architectural variety and interests through unusual landscaping amenities and architectural forms which were not sufficiently realized. By specific comparison with Service Development Associates' proposal, of the various elements such as parking, circulation, this proposal was inferior.

Specific Comments:

Pro—Variety of landscaping amenities: Sand River, Mall, Pool, Children's Lots.

Opportunity to provide social contribution through strongly guided community center.

Duplex apartment development in high rise a desirable objective.

Con—Although direct auto access may not be required in row house development, the panel felt auto access to high rise apartment building was required. There was inadequate definition of ground floor access, either vehicular or pedestrian in this proposal for all building types.

Fragmentation of town house rows left arbitrary unusable spaces.

High rise apartment dwelling unit planning: Though duplex planning in high rise desirable, undefined and waste space found on bedroom level could not be justified. The panel felt there was a possible building code violation in need for additional exit from bedroom level.

High rise apartment house plan: Oppressively long corridors ranging to 150 feet. Inadequate number of elevators. Incinerator location undefined.

Mass parking adjoining apartment high rise and commercial strip detracts from apartment house view. Lack of adequate number of auto parking.

Row house studio roof resolution resulted in effect of single story building and an extreme scale contrast with high rise which was disturbing.

High rise apartment planning: No dining space in one bedroom apartment plan. Bedroom storage wastefully defined in high rise duplex.

Town house planning: Room sizes excessively small with space relationship unnecessarily complicated. Question partial partition and skylights in bedroom.

Unfortunate that private outdoor living terraces were not provided in townhouse groups.

Advisory review panels operated in about 15 projects. They then faded out as massive clearance gave way to other programs.

If the advantage of a different commission for each proposal is that it will not fix forever one set of amaranthine predilections, this is not to say it should or can be without some guidance from the legislature. We suggested above that the commission would "recommend" bonuses to the final decisionmakers. This was from an abundance of concern that, in such an inchoate field, the absence of standards would subject a final decision by an appointed body to legal challenge. It would be a better system if the legislature set broad policy guidelines and left the particular applications to the commission. A growing number of recent decisions demand that, even when the legislature is making the final decision in zoning cases, it do so in accordance with pre-ordained policies and standards.[7] We suspect that trend will continue. But whatever the dictates of the law, fairness compels the legislature to speak out on design policy. What are the city's basic objectives? Does it want pedestrian-oriented retail or commuter-oriented offices or entertainment centers or parks or whatever? Does it want to discourage or accommodate auto use? Does it want to attract shoppers or conventions or tourists or locals after 6:00 P.M.? What about specific design components? Is similarity in appearance a virtue or vice? Will diversity be encouraged? Are plazas or arcades or pedestrian passages or whatever to be encouraged and, if so, under what circumstances? Is the site to be evaluated independently of its surroundings, or may even an innovative scheme be penalized because it does not take into account neighboring development? Is the use and design of interior public space as important as the exteriors? Is color or texture significant and, if so, in what degree and respects? Does the relation to existing or planned public facilities merit consideration?

Such issues should be faced and policies articulated, not, above all, in precise regulations but with sufficient clarity that the developer will know the areas in which bonus consideration will be given and that the commission will understand the goals of the community while still retaining substantial discretion to decide whether those goals have been accomplished. Perhaps the analogy to a judge and jury in a trial is not inapt. The jury makes the final decision, but the judge through instructions provides the framework within which that decision shall be made.

For those who think this is just too much for the system to swallow, we return to an earlier theme: the necessity of building on what you have and packaging new ideas to blend easily into the existing pattern of regulation. We suggest that what we have outlined here could be accomplished by taking a typical incentive shopping list ordinance with specific bonuses tied to specific amenities and amending it to say something like this:

> *provided, however,* that no such bonus shall be given for any such amenity unless the commission [as we've defined it] shall determine that the specific amenity as proposed will implement the general policies [stated elsewhere] which such bonuses are established to promote; and *provided further, however,* that any such bonus may be increased by up to 20 percent based on the recommendation of the commission that a specific percentage increase is warranted based upon the excellence of design and implementation of the amenity in question; and *provided, further,* that the City Council may, in lieu of granting the aforesaid bonuses for the specific amenities hereinabove set forth, grant a bonus of not more than the maximum bonus achievable by the provision of such specific amenities based upon the recommendation of the commission that a specific percentage bonus is warranted based upon excellence and innovation in design which, while not providing the particular amenities hereinabove specified, implements the general policies which the specific bonus and amenity provisions of this section are intended to promote.

That ought to sneak it by without anyone noticing. The first "provided, however..." is to be sure we quit giving bonuses for schlock; the "provided, further, however..." is where we'll get the good, but predictable, urban design; the final "provided, further..." is where the history will be made.

At this point, we cannot resist an extended quote from Richard Cornuelle's *Demanaging America*, which says it all—and is a good story to boot:

The economic process thus creates a unique psychological atmosphere. It does much more than simply motivate people to act. It invites them to act imaginatively. It invites them to innovate, to discover new, promising ways to get things done.

B. F. Skinner has developed psychological atmospheres which cause people to behave in "desired" ways. His method, popularly known as positive reinforcement, has been widely adopted by teachers and managers, and to teach pigeons to play ping-pong. The economic process is slightly Skinnerian. It reinforces success and is comparatively gentle with failure. It doesn't rebuke or punish those who fail. It just doesn't reward them.

But the economic process really goes beyond Skinner. Its workings were greatly illuminated for me when I read about some remarkable experiments with porpoises conceived by Karen Pryor at Sea Life Park in Hawaii. She had been training sea animals for some time using conventional Skinnerian methods, which she described in *Psychology Today* with a fine clarity:

"Suppose you want to train a pilot or killer whale. You must first teach the whale that when he hears a whistle he will be given a fish. Then you decide exactly what you want the whale to do and teach him to perform by rewarding actions that come closer and closer to your goal, marking each action with a whistle blast and then a fish. If you want your whale to jump 20 feet straight up out of the water, you hold a padded stick in the water. When the whale, out of curiosity, touches the stick, you blow the whistle and feed the whale. Soon the whale will touch the stick eagerly each time he sees it. Now you hold the stick just out of the water; the whale touches it and gets his fish. Gradually you raise the stick higher and higher. In a few days the whale will jump 20 feet to earn his fish—and will jump at the sight of the stick held in the air. This process is called shaping."

And this is, at least in part, the psychological atmosphere the economic process creates. It is possible to imagine Adam Smith writing: "Suppose you want to train a businessman. You must first teach the businessman that. . . ." And so forth.

But then came Karen Pryor's delicious post-Skinnerian discovery. She and her crew give daily public demonstrations of their teaching methods. One of the things they demonstrate at these shows is the process described above, the "shaping" of new "behavior." But of course they can't show how porpoises learn by putting them through paces they already know. It has to be something new. So, Ms. Pryor writes, "We adopted a new rule: we would only reward those actions that had not been rewarded before." The results were astonishing. "Within a few days we had used up all the normal casual actions of a porpoise. Then Malia [the female porpoise they had used in these demonstrations] began doing serial flips, gliding with her tail out of water and skidding on the tank floor. . . . *Some of Malia's spontaneous stunts were so unusual that the trainers couldn't imagine achieving them with the shaping system.*

And that is what the economic process does. It invites and rewards behavior that can exceed the imagination. It is open-ended. No shaping system could have produced Henry Ford. No shaping system could produce another Henry Ford. The economic process is *not* a shaping system. It is the opposite. That is why the free economy process is superproductive. It has much less to do with the nature of the incentives it provides—money or makerel or medals—than with the *kind* of behavior it "chooses" to reward.[8]

In development of a major city's CBD, indeed in the redevelopment of a major city, what we need and want is creative excellence. A system that tries to define it won't get it. A system that invites and rewards it just might—which is not a bad note on which to conclude.

FOOTNOTES

1. *Penn Central Transportation Co.* v. *City of New York,* 42 N.Y.2d 324, 397 N.Y.S.2d 914, 366 N.E.2d 1271 (1977) *aff'd,* 438 U.S. 104, 98 S. Ct. 2646 (1978).

2. Norman Marcus, "Villard Preserv'd: Or, Zoning for Landmarks in the Central Business District," 44 *Brook. L. Rev.* 1 (1977).

3. Stephen A. Williams, "Subjectivity, Expression, and Privacy: Problems of Aesthetic Regulation," 62 *Minn. L. Rev.* 1 (1977); footnotes omitted.

4. *New York Times,* January 26, 1978, p. 19.

5. Personal letter, March 28, 1978

6. *United Airliner Mainliner,* May 1978, p. 63.

7. See, for example, *Fasano* v. *Board of Washington Co. Comm.,* 264 Or. 574, 507 P.2d 23 (1973).

8. Richard Cornuelle, *Demanaging America: The Final Revolution* (New York City: Vintage Books, 1976), pp. 88-90.

Index